"I've been watching Natasha in her kitchen on social media for years, and it's amazing to see her delicious and nutritious recipes come to life in this cookbook. It will be a great mealtime resource!"

—Yumna Jawad, founder of *Feel Good Foodie*

"Natasha's passion for cooking shines through in this amazing cookbook. With delicious recipes and fun entertaining ideas (the party-size fish taco bar is a must-try!), you'll find inspiration and joy on every page."

—Jennifer Segal, author and creator of *Once Upon a Chef*

"This collection of heartfelt, mouthwatering recipes makes me want to storm into my kitchen and cook up a fresh, comforting meal for the people I love most. This book has just the right recipe for any occasion."

—Erin Clarke, author of *The Well Plated Cookbook*

"Natasha has a knack for transforming everyday ingredients into delicious meals that your whole family will love. You'll find yourself reaching for this cookbook again and again."

—Holly Nilsson, creator of *Spend with Pennies*

"Natasha not only serves up a variety of approachable recipes the whole family will love but she also magically serves up a welcome dose of warmth and inspiration with every meal!"

—Lisa Bryan, author of *Downshiftology Healthy Meal Prep*

"Natasha's recipes are loaded with comfort and a variety of flavors, from Cucumber Pico de Gallo to Lasagna, Zuppa Toscana, Chicken Pot Pie, and the iconic Ukrainian borscht, a homage to her homeland. And along with the recipes, Natasha gives us her inspiring immigrant story, told with a good dose of joy and gratitude."

—Suzy Karadsheh, *New York Times*–bestselling author of *The Mediterranean Dish*

"*Natasha's Kitchen* is filled with foolproof recipes that the entire family will love. Whether you want a quick and easy weeknight dinner, an indulgent weekend breakfast, or a decadent dessert for a special occasion, Natasha has you covered! The recipes are approachable and perfect for sharing with loved ones."

—Maria Lichty, author of *Two Peas & Their Pod Cookbook*

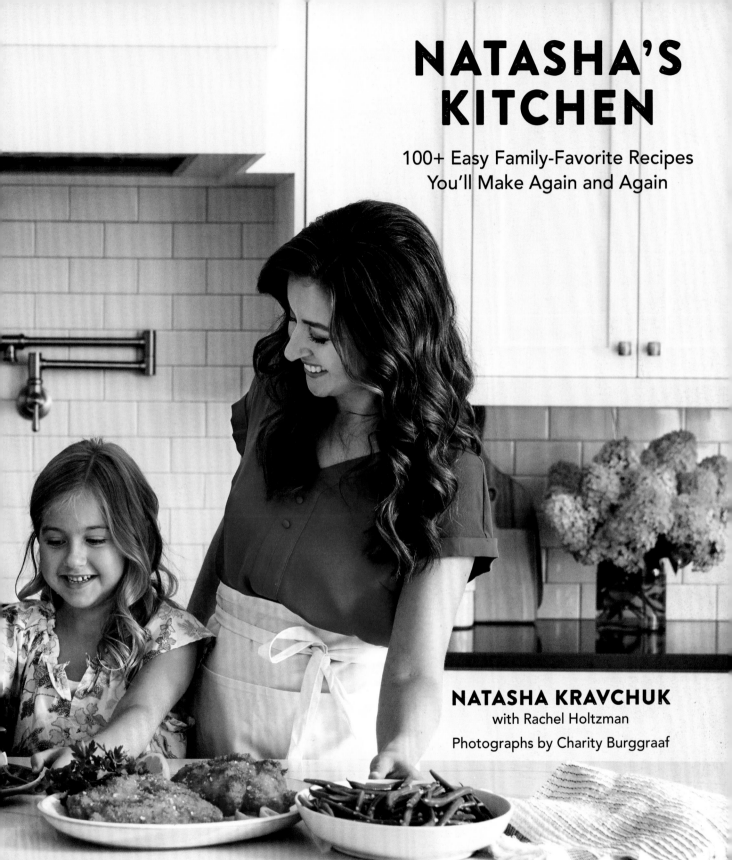

NATASHA'S KITCHEN

100+ Easy Family-Favorite Recipes
You'll Make Again and Again

NATASHA KRAVCHUK

with Rachel Holtzman

Photographs by Charity Burggraaf

Clarkson Potter/Publishers | *New York*

Library of Congress Cataloging-in-
Publication Data
Names: Kravchuk, Natasha, author. |
  Holtzman, Rachel, other. | Burggraaf,
  Charity, other.
Title: Natasha's kitchen : 100+ easy
  family-favorite recipes you'll make
  again and again / Natasha Kravchuk
  with Rachel Holtzman ; [photography
  by Charity Burggraaf].
Description: New York : Clarkson Potter,
  [2023] | Includes index.
Identifiers: LCCN 2022055862 (print) |
  LCCN 2022055863 (ebook) | ISBN
  9780593579213 (hardcover) | ISBN
  9780593579220 (ebook)
Subjects: LCSH: Cooking. | Cooking,
  Ukrainian. | LCGFT: Cookbooks.
Classification: LCC TX714 .K733 2023
  (print) | LCC TX714 (ebook) | DDC
  641.5--dc23/eng/20221128
LC record available at https://lccn.loc.
  gov/2022055862
LC ebook record available at https://lccn.
  loc.gov/2022055863

ISBN 978-0-593-57921-3
eBook ISBN 978-0-593-57922-0

Printed in China

Photographer: Charity Burggraaf
Food Stylist: Nathan Carrabba
Food Styling Assistants: Tyler Hill,
  Julie Bishop, Michelle Weller, and
  Devan Dror
Editor: Susan Roxborough
Editorial Assistant: Bianca Cruz
Designer: Marysarah Quinn
Production Editor: Bridget Sweet
Production Manager: Heather Williamson
Compositor: Merri Ann Morrell
Copy Editor: Michelle Gale
Indexer: Jean Mooney
Marketer: Stephanie Davis
Publicist: Kristin Casemore

10 9 8 7 6 5 4 3 2 1

First Edition

This book is for my husband, Vadim, whose love and support have lifted me up since the day we met.

It is also for our parents, whose courage and sacrifices changed my and Vadim's lives forever.

And it is for Jesus, for the opportunity to write this book and share my recipes—what a gift!

Contents

Recipe Contents

Natasha with her parents and older sisters in 1985

Natasha's family sleeping on suitcases in a New York City airport on their way to Seattle

Family photo in their first rental home circa 1991

My Story

I learned to cook under very *real* circumstances. My parents were from Ukraine, where they made a living growing and selling chrysanthemums. In 1988, they arrived home to find the little white envelope that would change their lives and mine. You see, at the time, Christians in Communist U.S.S.R. faced religious persecution, and it was difficult to make a good life there. The U.S.S.R. wasn't releasing refugees to the U.S., but thanks to a backdoor visa agreement between Israel and America, one unassuming slip of paper meant that we would be able to leave for the Land of the Free.

But the early days of our new lives were not easy. My parents had to pack all the worldly possessions of five tiny girls ranging in age from two to seven (I was four) into two suitcases each, schlep through airports across the world (Austria, Italy, New York), and find a safe place to sleep. At one point, we were among fifteen people crammed into one hotel room in a refugee shelter in Austria. Once we were in the U.S., my parents had to navigate a new country and a completely new culture, learn a second language, and figure out how to support our seven-person family with jobs that paid very little.

My father chose to forgo being on welfare so he could work eighty hours a week as a toolmaker, earning just seven dollars an hour with the hope that he would eventually climb the corporate ladder (and he did—I'm so proud of you, Dad!). Mom, on the other hand, dreamed of becoming a restaurant chef and went to culinary school to learn the ins and outs of working in a commercial kitchen. One month before she was set to graduate, she had to undergo emergency back surgery, and although she never returned to a professional kitchen, she raised us girls in our very own "restaurant" at home. Some of my favorite childhood memories are of watching her create—stirring seemingly random ingredients into delicious and fragrant soups, whipping up the fluffiest Oladi Pancakes (page 45), and, of course, making her now-famous Potato

Mom in her chef's uniform at culinary school

Natasha with an early food bank haul

Pierogi (page 145). (You should have seen her face when I told her that, between my Facebook and YouTube followers, almost eleven million people have watched that video!) As a child, I remember loving those little potato parcels so much that I would bite off the corner of each one on my plate just in case my dad—who loved them as much as I did—was tempted to nab one when I wasn't looking. You can imagine how hard I laughed when my six-year-old daughter did the same thing at dinner one night!

For my mom, cooking was a magical combination of necessity and pleasure, something I've carried with me since starting my own family and the Natasha's Kitchen platforms. She never measured anything; she just cooked from the heart. And somehow, she managed to keep us girls from getting underfoot—we were more taste testers than sous chefs. In fact, she never wanted to let us cook because she saw it as a way to spoil us in one of the small ways that she could—though, it's also why I eventually had to teach myself how to cook, but more on that in a bit. What was most impactful for me, though, was watching how she turned the humblest of ingredients into purposeful, inventive, and incredibly delicious dishes. It wasn't because she prided herself on being frugal—although she did—it was because she had to, or else we wouldn't have anything to eat.

You see, when we first came to the United States as refugees, we started with nothing. There were nights when we were cold and days when there wasn't enough food. It wasn't easy for my parents who had left everything they had and everyone they'd known to come to a new world where their five children would cry at bedtime because they were so hungry. The breakthrough came when they discovered that in America there were food banks that could provide families like ours with the groceries we would never be able to buy ourselves. Since I was too young to start kindergarten, I would tag along with my mom. I remember standing in line in the freezing-cold Seattle mornings, waiting to go in, as volunteers handed us steaming-hot cups of hot chocolate. Then we'd come home and triumphantly stack our haul on the dining room table, always grateful for the abundance.

My mom would combine the skills and confidence she had gained in culinary school with her experience cooking traditional Ukrainian food to transform staple ingredients like rice, cabbage, and potatoes. She always made sure we ate well, and as a result we felt nourished in body and soul. Because of that food, we never felt poor. We were grateful that God had provided and carried us through. And now I run one of the top online cooking platforms in the world—if that's not the American Dream, I don't know what is!

Welcome to My Kitchen

I think what has made my website, Natasha's Kitchen, so successful is that I've taken my story, less happy bits and all, and used it as inspiration. My food isn't complicated because that's not what food needs to be in order to taste good. Because I was never formally taught to cook (unless you count my first job "cooking" at McDonald's, which only lasted three months because I was fourteen and my coworker sister suddenly quit, so I lost my ride), I remember what it feels like to twist into a pretzel trying to make a recipe, wishing I had four more hands. I know what it's like to learn from scratch. When I first started Natasha's Kitchen in 2009, my newlywed husband, Vadim, and I couldn't do much more in the kitchen than add toppings to a frozen pizza. So, we set out to share with our readers—the very, very few we had at the time—our experiences and discoveries as we taught ourselves how to cook.

After two years of running the blog as a hobby, we had a steady following and decided to place a Google ad on our home page. In one month, we made enough money for . . . um . . . one cup of coffee? Woohoo! But over time, as I curated recipes that I was learning from cookbooks at the library as well as from my Ukrainian mother and mother-in-law, our following grew. My readers loved that I had exactly what they needed to feel confident in the kitchen because I, too, had once needed those same tools and tricks. They felt comforted by classic, recognizable dishes. Plus, they trusted that if I was sharing a recipe, whether it was classic Cheeseburger Sliders (page 178), Famous Fish Tacos (page 263), or Loaded Corn Chowder (page 116), or my mother's rugelach cookies (page 245), it was going to deliver because I myself was bringing those dishes to my family's Sunday after-church lunches and church potlucks or special occasions like birthday parties, baby showers, and holidays.

The recipes in this book—like those on my site—will rarely take more than thirty minutes to make because most busy families don't have more time than that unless it's a special occasion. By giving you lots of my "Pro Tips & Tricks," I'll make sure you feel like you can tackle any recipe in this book.

The dishes I remember so fondly from childhood are also why my recipes only call for ingredients that you already have in your fridge or pantry or that you can easily find at your local grocery store. You might need to travel to a different aisle than you're used to, but your groceries are always going to be a one-stop shop. And I guarantee that they're not going to cost you more than your normal trips—even if you're feeding an entire family, including a ravenous fourteen-year-old boy!—because you won't be buying any more pre-prepared or frozen meals. That also makes these recipes more nutritious than anything you could order in or pop into the microwave. (When Vadim and I started cooking more at home, we each lost five pounds during the first six months!) Not to mention the fact that when you're "shopping" out of your well-stocked pantry—something I'll help you get started with—you're going to see the savings in your grocery bill.

Natasha's Kitchen is also inspired by how food brings my family together—and probably yours, too. When I was fourteen, my parents moved all of us to Meridian, Idaho. Unlike big metropolitan Seattle, Meridian was exactly what my parents wanted for us: a place with a slow, sweet pace of life, where the kids safely go on bike adventures around the neighborhood, and pretty much everyone is on a first-name basis. Even now, my sisters and I live within ten minutes of each other and our parents, and we get together every Sunday to share news of our week, let the twelve grandkids visit with their grandparents, and, of course, eat! We each bring our own dishes with enough food to feed a small army—something we Ukrainian Americans know how to do. For real, if you've ever been lucky enough to go to a Ukrainian community potluck, you'll see that there are at least thirty different kinds of side dishes and desserts. This is why all my recipes can be scaled way up or down—I believe you should always be prepared to feed the entire neighborhood! Plus, I always encourage my followers to make extra to stash in the freezer, so they'll never run out of home-cooked meals and can resist the urge to get fast food. Anyway, at our Sunday gatherings my mom will usually make something in the slow cooker, plus a salad with fresh vegetables from her massive garden. My sisters bring sides and salads, the husbands take charge of the grill, and I'm usually tasked with the desserts since I've learned my way around a pastry recipe—and I'll usually bring something else I'm still testing to get just right, since my family makes the best guinea pigs. They know how to tell it to me straight!

True to our reputation at Natasha's Kitchen, in this cookbook you'll find recipes that are approachable, loved by the whole family, and that impress company, even in-laws. I've even been told that our recipes have garnered wedding proposals (though, I can't guarantee that). I like to think of each recipe as a piece of gold, honed by me, my own family's picky palates, and literally hundreds of recipe testers. When I announced that I was writing this cookbook, I asked my readers if they would be interested in testing the recipes. Within twenty-four hours, exactly 2,761 people had volunteered and we had to close the survey because the responses kept pouring in. I think it's safe to say that by the time you're reading this book, the recipes will *work*, no matter what kind of kitchen you're in.

Ultimately, I'm so excited to share this book with anyone who wants to learn how to cook simple, nourishing recipes for themselves, their families, and their communities. Our fans have blessed us with their enthusiasm, and now it's time to give back with even more great recipes with new flavors, new techniques, and new stories from the Kravchuk kitchen. So, as I like to say in the introductions to all my videos: drumroll . . . "Let's get started!"

Natasha

1

TIPS, TRICKS,
AND GETTING PREPARED

When I share a recipe with my followers, my number-one goal is to set them up for success. I want them to have the confidence and know-how to step into their kitchens and feel prepared for whatever questions or challenges come their way. The recipes in this book are no exception. That's why I've included my Pro Tips & Tricks throughout the book. In addition, there are some universal guidelines, nuggets of wisdom, and shortcuts that will be helpful across the board. I've also included a list of my favorite pantry staples and kitchen tools. With these in hand, you can make any dish in this book with minimal additional grocery shopping.

Room-Temperature Ingredients
(aka Shortcuts)

Properly softened or room-temperature ingredients will make all the difference in the quality of your baked goods (sweet and savory). Cold ingredients don't like to blend together, but room-temperature ingredients will incorporate nicely so that your cakes will bake up evenly and you won't end up with lumps in your frosting. That said, people will often write to me and say their cream cheese frosting is too soft, and 99 percent of the time, it's due to ingredients that were *over* softened. Aim for a temperature of 65°F to 70°F. It should feel a little cool to the touch unless the recipe specifically asks for a warm or hot ingredient.

Butter

- Soften refrigerated butter at room temperature (70°F) for about 1 to 1½ hours. You should be able to indent the butter with your fingertip, but it should not be overly soft and should never be partially melted.

- **The 15-minute method:** Dice butter into ½-inch cubes and let sit at room temperature for 15 minutes. Butter should reach 65°F to 70°F when ready.

- **The 5-minute method/speed soften:** Fill a tall glass with boiling hot water, let it sit for a minute to heat up, then drain. Place a wrapped stick of butter standing vertically on a paper towel and cover with the hot empty glass. Let rest for 5 to 7 minutes, depending on the thickness of your butter stick, for perfectly softened butter.

- Avoid microwaving butter since there is high risk of melting or uneven softening.

Cream Cheese

- Soften refrigerated cream cheese at room temperature (70°F) for 1 to 1½ hours. Cream cheese should be softened but feel slightly cool to the touch (not smooshy or overly soft).

- **The 30-minute method:** Cut the cream cheese into ½-inch cubes and let sit on a plate, uncovered, for 30 minutes. Increasing the surface area will help it soften more quickly.

- **The 15-second method/speed soften:** Remove the cream cheese from the wrapper, place it on a microwave-safe plate, and microwave for 15 seconds for an 8-ounce block. Add 10 seconds for every additional block of cream cheese.

- For dairy food safety, do not soften cream cheese longer than 2 hours at room temperature.

Eggs

- Fill a medium bowl with warm water (100°F) and place the eggs in the water for 5 to 7 minutes.

How to Measure Flour Properly

Whether you're making a sweet or savory recipe, you will get the most accurate flour measure if you first "fluff" the flour before spooning it into a dry-measure measuring cup, then use a knife to level off the top.

Tips for Working with Yeast

- Be sure to use the "right" yeast. Different types of yeast require different processes for activation, which is why it's important to use what is called for in a recipe. "Rapid-rise yeast" and "instant yeast" are used interchangeably, but they are not the same as "active dry yeast," which requires additional activating and longer rising times.

- 1 (0.25-ounce) packet = 2¼ teaspoons = 7 grams

- Heat kills yeast, so overheating a yeasted mixture will stop the rising process. Keep any mixture containing yeast between 110°F and 115°F, and keep the oven temperature under 110°F if using it to proof dough. You can double-check temperatures with an instant-read thermometer.

- Cold temperature slows rising. For optimal rising and proofing, your room temperature should be between 70°F and 80°F. If it's cooler or you add cold liquids to your yeasted mixture, you'll dramatically slow the rising process.

- Check the expiration date. Expired yeast will not work properly and can ruin your baking project. Once the package is opened, yeast must be stored in an airtight container and refrigerated (up to 4 months) or frozen (up to 6 months). Label your jars so you can keep track, though I've found that with proper airtight storage, yeast can last even longer.

- Test your yeast. In order to make sure that your yeast is still alive and active, I begin all my recipes containing yeast with a test. That's why I have you mix the yeast with warm water and a bit of sugar before adding the other ingredients. The yeast should form a creamy layer at the top and create small bubbles within 5 to 10 minutes. If it doesn't bubble, buy fresh yeast before proceeding with your recipe.

- Use room-temperature yeast. If your yeast has been refrigerated or frozen, bring it to room temperature for 1 hour before using it.

- Measure your ingredients correctly. Sugar feeds yeast and flour stimulates its rise, so if you add too much or too little of either, it can affect the success of the recipe. (See How to Measure Flour Properly above.)

Kitchen Staples

While my husband and I were house hunting and eventually building our dream home a few years ago, we ended up unexpectedly living with my parents for two and a half years. (I guess we were pickier about our "forever home" than I realized we would be!) This meant that we shared a kitchen and pantry, so I had to be mindful of what I was keeping in our limited space for testing recipes and filming videos. Because I had to keep things to a bare minimum, I quickly learned which tools and pantry items were true staples for me. It reinforced my philosophy that it's not necessary to spend tons of money on a million and one spices and gadgets.

Dried Spices

Bay leaves

Black pepper (preferably freshly ground)

Crushed red pepper flakes

Garlic powder

Ground cinnamon

Ground cumin

Ground nutmeg

Onion powder

Oregano

Paprika

Salt (fine sea salt and kosher salt)

Oils and Vinegars

Apple cider vinegar

Balsamic vinegar

Extra-light olive oil

Extra-virgin olive oil

Red wine vinegar

Sesame oil

Vegetable oil, for deep-frying

From a Jar, Can, or Carton

Artichoke hearts

Canned black beans

Canned corn

Chicken stock (low sodium if store-bought, but homemade is even better; see my recipe on page 126)

Croutons

Crushed tomatoes (I prefer the 15-ounce cans)

Kalamata olives

Whole peeled tomatoes (I prefer the 15-ounce cans)

Condiments

Dijon mustard

Hot sauce

Ketchup

Mayonnaise

Yellow mustard

Dry Goods and Baking

All-purpose flour

Aluminum-free baking powder

Baking soda

Bread flour

Cocoa powder

Cornstarch

Granulated sugar

Honey

Instant yeast and active dry yeast

Light brown sugar

Maple syrup

Old-fashioned rolled oats

Panko breadcrumbs

Pure vanilla extract

Shredded coconut flakes

Nuts and Seeds

Chia seeds

Raw, unsalted pecans

Sesame seeds

Slivered almonds

Noodles and Rice

Elbow macaroni

Fettuccine noodles

Fusilli

Lasagna noodles

Medium-grain white rice

Small-cut pasta for soups (such as orzo, ditalini, or fideo)

Spaghetti noodles

Wine and Spirits

Dry white wine (such as sauvignon blanc)

Grand Marnier

Tools

I think of kitchen tools as an investment and buy the best quality that I can afford. With proper care, good kitchen tools can last a lifetime. I'm not exaggerating when I say that many of these tools have the power to make you a better cook. For example, an instant-read thermometer has been a game changer for me. Because I can just check the internal temperature (which I've provided for you in each of my recipes) of whatever meat I'm cooking, I know that I'm going to get a juicy, tender, perfectly done end result every single time. (People often ask me how I make such tasty chicken, steaks, burgers, or pork chops, and I just tell them, "I didn't overcook it!") Quality kitchen tools also make your prep work and cooking more enjoyable. One year I forgot to take my good knives on our family camping trip, and the dull knife that I had to borrow made our dinner the most torturous pot of soup I'd ever experienced. All to say, a few good things make a big difference. Here's what I recommend having:

Thermometers (instant read, in oven, and clip on)

Thin-edge spatula

Chef's knife

Paring knife

Bread knife

Whisk

Tongs

Ladle

Pastry brush

Citrus squeezer

Cutting boards (one for fruit, one for vegetables, and a dishwasher-safe one for meats)

Wooden spatula

Flexible spatula

Rolling pin

Fine-mesh sieve

Mixing bowls (various sizes)

Measuring cups, for liquid and dry ingredients

Measuring spoons

Potato masher

Box grater

Bench scraper

Ice cream scoop

Potato peeler

Zester

Can opener

Salad spinner

Cookware

10-inch cast-iron skillet

5½-quart Dutch oven with lid or a large heavy-bottomed pot

Nonstick pan, for crepes

Large sauté pan

Large saucepan

Appliances

Stand mixer or hand mixer

Food processor

Blender

Bakeware

Standard 12-cup muffin tin (plus cupcake liners)

Rimmed baking sheet (preferably nonstick)

Parchment paper

Two 9-inch cake pans

9-inch springform pan

9 × 9-inch metal baking pan

9 × 13-inch nonstick metal baking dish

18 × 13-inch rimmed baking sheet

9 × 13-inch casserole dish

Cooling racks (ideally 2)

2

BREAKFAST

All the recipes in this book are rooted in love and the delicious traditions that I regularly enjoy with my family. But breakfast is particularly close to the heart for me. During the week, I'm all about grab-and-go options that can be prepped ahead, like Overnight Oats (page 46) and Homemade Granola–Berry Parfaits (page 50). Then there's the weekend, when we can slow down and enjoy a little more time together while I make something from scratch, like Sweet Potato and Bacon Hash (page 27), Ricotta Waffles (page 37), or Special-Occasion Croissant French Toast (page 49) with everyone's favorite toppings. And the holidays, when the morning's spread of Sweet Cheese Crepes with Raspberry Sauce (page 31) or Cinnamon Rolls with Cream Cheese Frosting (page 33) sets the tone for an extra-special special day. These are the moments that make me think about my mom (or Baba, as my kids call her) and her Fluffy Oladi Pancakes (page 45). I can still feel the warmth and comfort of smelling them cooking in the pan when I was a little girl, and I want to create the same experiences for my family. That's a big reason why I feel fortunate to live so close to my parents and sisters, whom I get to see for brunch every Sunday (and where you can often find a platter full of piping hot oladi). While it is the company that sets these meals apart, it's the food that makes them really magical.

Sweet Potato and Bacon Hash

We often buy sweet potatoes in bulk at Costco and then find creative ways to use them up, from sweet potato soup to casseroles. Here we're using them for breakfast in a fresh take on a classic hash. The combination of maple-sweetened potatoes plus crispy, salty bacon makes for a hearty breakfast when served with fried eggs and avocado slices. It's quick to come together and to scale up, which is perfect for when you're expecting breakfast, brunch, or even dinner company, or if you're meal planning for the week (it reheats beautifully in a skillet or toaster oven).

SERVES 4

3 medium sweet potatoes (about 2 pounds), peeled and cut into ½-inch cubes (see Pro Tips & Tricks)

2 tablespoons real maple syrup

1 tablespoon extra-light olive oil or vegetable oil

¾ teaspoon fine sea salt

½ teaspoon ground paprika

¼ teaspoon freshly ground black pepper

6 slices regular-cut bacon, chopped (see Pro Tips & Tricks)

1. Preheat the oven to 425°F. Line a rimmed baking sheet with parchment paper and set aside.

2. In a large bowl, combine the sweet potatoes, maple syrup, oil, salt, paprika, and pepper and toss to coat. Spread the sweet potatoes over the prepared baking sheet in a single layer. Scatter the bacon over the top and bake for 20 minutes. Flip the sweet potatoes and bake for another 10 to 12 minutes, until the bacon is crisp and the sweet potatoes are tender.

3. Transfer the hash to a platter and serve immediately.

Pro Tips & Tricks

- To cut sweet potatoes, you'll want to use a heavy and sharp knife. Start by peeling the potatoes, then cut them in half widthwise so you have a flat base for each half to stand on. Cut the potatoes into ½-inch-thick slices, then into ½-inch-thick spears, then finally into ½-inch-thick cubes.

- Don't use thick-cut bacon for this recipe; it takes longer to crisp and your cook times will be off.

Maple-Bacon Oatmeal

Most of the oatmeal recipes floating around the internet have two things in common: they're bland and they're boring. I had heard through the grapevine that my friend Adrienne makes the best oatmeal (good recipes travel fast!), and she gladly shared what she refers to as Grandma's Oatmeal, because it reminds her of her grandma's house. I instantly fell in love with her version because of the rich, creamy texture from cooking the oats low and slow, then I added lots of sweet-salty flavor by swirling in maple, cinnamon, and bits of crispy bacon.

SERVES 4 TO 6

6 slices regular-cut bacon

6 tablespoons (¾ stick) unsalted butter, divided

2 cups water

2 cups milk of any kind

2 cups old-fashioned rolled oats

¼ teaspoon fine sea salt, plus more to taste

6 tablespoons real maple syrup, plus more for serving

2 teaspoons pure vanilla extract

1½ teaspoons ground cinnamon, plus more to taste

½ teaspoon ground nutmeg

Your favorite fresh fruit or nuts, for serving (I love a mix of berries or using seasonal fruit with toasted nuts)

1. In a large skillet over medium heat, cook the bacon about 3 minutes per side, until crisp and browned. Transfer the bacon to a paper towel–lined plate to cool. Chop the bacon into small bits and set aside.

2. In a 5½-quart Dutch oven or large soup pot over medium-high heat, melt 4 tablespoons of the butter. Add 2 cups water, the milk, oats, and salt and bring to a boil, stirring occasionally. Reduce the heat to a simmer and cook, uncovered, for 8 minutes. Stir in the maple syrup, vanilla, cinnamon, and nutmeg. Simmer the oats for another 3 minutes, then remove the pot from the heat.

3. Cut the remaining 2 tablespoons of butter into pieces and stir into the oatmeal. Cover and let the oatmeal rest for 5 minutes. Season with more salt or cinnamon, if needed. (You want just enough to balance the sweetness of the maple syrup.)

4. Divide the oatmeal between bowls and top with the bacon. Finish as desired with extra maple syrup and your toppings of choice.

Sweet Cheese Crepes
with Raspberry Sauce

Growing up, this was the special Sunday-morning breakfast that my mom made for us. Every weekend we'd get so excited to have warm-from-the-pan crepes rolled with sweet, tangy cheese filling and topped with a generous dollop of sour cream. Now I make them for my own family with the addition of a homemade raspberry sauce. While traditional Ukrainian cheese crepes call for farmer's cheese, my family prefers the taste and texture of a cottage cheese–cream cheese blend, which also happens to be easier to find at the grocery store. You can easily make a batch the night before and heat them before serving, which I especially love to do around the holidays.

MAKES TWELVE 9-INCH CREPES

FOR THE RASPBERRY SAUCE

1 lemon

1 tablespoon cold water

1 teaspoon cornstarch

1 (12-ounce) bag frozen raspberries

¼ cup sugar

FOR THE BATTER

1 cup milk of any kind, warmed

1 cup all-purpose flour (see How to Measure Flour Properly on page 20)

4 large eggs

½ cup warm water

¼ cup (½ stick) unsalted butter, melted, plus more for the pan

2 tablespoons sugar

1 teaspoon pure vanilla extract

Pinch of fine sea salt

1. MAKE THE RASPBERRY SAUCE: Zest the entire lemon and set aside for the filling. Squeeze 2 teaspoons of lemon juice and set aside for the sauce.

2. In a small bowl, combine 1 tablespoon cold water and the cornstarch to create a slurry. Set aside.

3. In a medium saucepan over medium heat, combine the raspberries, sugar, and 2 teaspoons lemon juice. Bring to a boil, stirring often. Add the slurry and continue boiling for another minute. Remove the pan from the heat and set aside to cool completely. If not serving right away, store the sauce in an airtight container in the refrigerator for up to 1 week.

4. MAKE THE CREPES: In a blender, combine the milk, flour, eggs, water, butter, sugar, vanilla, and salt. Blend until smooth.

5. Brush a medium nonstick pan with butter and set it over medium heat. When the pan is hot, pour in ¼ to ⅓ cup of the batter and immediately swirl the pan so the batter coats the bottom. Cook the crepe until golden brown at the edges, less than 1 minute. Flip and cook for another 30 seconds, until the crepe is golden in some spots on the second side. Transfer the crepe to a cutting board or platter and repeat with the remaining batter. It is not usually necessary to keep buttering the pan after the first crepe. Once the crepes are at room temperature, they can be stacked.

6. MAKE THE FILLING: Place the cottage cheese in a fine-mesh strainer over the sink and rinse under cold water until the water runs clear, then drain thoroughly.

INGREDIENTS CONTINUE

RECIPE CONTINUES

Sweet Cheese Crepes with Raspberry Sauce *continued*

FOR THE FILLING

1 (16-ounce) container cottage cheese

8 ounces plain cream cheese, softened

¼ cup sweetened condensed milk or sugar

Sour cream, for serving

7. In a large bowl, combine the cottage cheese, cream cheese, sweetened condensed milk, and 1 teaspoon of the reserved lemon zest. Using a potato masher, mash the mixture together until creamy.

8. ASSEMBLE: Spread 2 to 3 tablespoons of the filling mixture over the center of one crepe, leaving a 1-inch border around the edges. Roll the crepe tightly into a log. Repeat with the remaining crepes and filling.

9. In a large nonstick pan over medium-low heat, melt 1 tablespoon of butter. When the butter is done sizzling, arrange the crepes in a single layer seam side down. Cook for 1½ to 2 minutes per side, until golden brown on both sides.

10. To serve, transfer the finished crepes to a plate, drizzle with the raspberry sauce, and top with a dollop of sour cream.

Pro Tips & Tricks

- **Make ahead:** You can make the crepe batter 2 days ahead, cover, and refrigerate. You can also assemble the crepes ahead, stack them in a casserole dish, then cover and refrigerate them for 3 to 5 days. Sauté the crepes in butter before serving.

Cinnamon Rolls
with Cream Cheese Frosting

Nothing comes close to the excitement of pulling out a batch of sweet-and-sticky homemade buns for breakfast. These, in particular, somehow manage to be soft, fluffy, and gooey all at once with layers of buttery cinnamon and brown sugar topped with cream cheese frosting that melts into the grooves of the rolls. But the best part is that you don't have to wake up at 3 a.m. to make these. The rolls are perfect for prepping the evening before and baking off when you're ready to serve them, which is what we do for Christmas morning.

MAKES 12 ROLLS

FOR THE ROLLS

1 cup milk of any kind, warmed to 110°F to 115°F

2¼ teaspoons instant or rapid-rise yeast (0.25 ounces)

1 large egg, room temperature

¼ cup granulated sugar

5 tablespoons unsalted butter, melted

½ teaspoon fine sea salt

3 cups bread flour, plus more as needed (see How to Measure Flour Properly on page 20)

Vegetable or extra-light olive oil, for greasing

6 tablespoons (¾ stick) unsalted butter, softened, plus more for greasing

⅔ cup (packed) light brown sugar

1½ tablespoons ground cinnamon

1. MAKE THE ROLLS: In a large bowl, add the milk and sprinkle with the yeast. Whisk in the egg, granulated sugar, 3 tablespoons of the melted butter, and the salt. Add the flour and stir with a wooden spoon or spatula to incorporate. Add more flour, 1 tablespoon at a time, until the dough is still tacky but no longer sticks to the sides of the bowl or your fingertips.

2. Turn out the dough onto a well-floured surface and knead for 3 minutes, or until the dough forms a fairly smooth ball. (It will still feel slightly sticky.) Lightly grease the bowl with the oil and return the dough to the bowl. Cover with plastic wrap and let the dough rise in a warm place (about 100°F) for 30 to 45 minutes or at room temperature for 1 to 1½ hours, until doubled in size.

3. Turn out the dough onto a well-floured surface and sprinkle it lightly with flour. Roll the dough into a 17 × 10-inch rectangle, squaring off the sides. Dot the dough with the softened butter and spread it evenly all the way out to the edges.

4. In a small bowl, stir together the brown sugar and cinnamon. Sprinkle the mixture evenly over the dough and gently press it into the butter. Starting with the long end and moving to the other end like a typewriter, roll up the dough, keeping it tight and even as you work. Push the ends in slightly to keep a uniform width and cut the roll into 12 equal pieces.

5. Generously butter the sides and bottom of a 9 × 13-inch nonstick metal baking pan and arrange the rolls so they're evenly spaced and cut side down. Cover the pan with plastic wrap and let the rolls rise in a warm place (about 100°F) for 20 to 30 minutes or at room temperature for 45 to 60 minutes, until visibly puffed.

INGREDIENTS CONTINUE

RECIPE CONTINUES

Cinnamon Rolls with Cream Cheese Frosting *continued*

¼ cup (½ stick) unsalted butter, softened

4 ounces plain cream cheese, softened

1½ teaspoons pure vanilla extract

1 cup confectioners' sugar, plus more to taste

Pinch of fine sea salt

6. Preheat the oven to 350°F.

7. Brush the tops of the rolls with the remaining 2 tablespoons of melted butter. (You may need to melt the butter again if it's resolidified.) Bake for 20 to 22 minutes, or until the edges are lightly golden and the center registers 200°F on an in-oven or instant-read thermometer. Let the rolls cool in the pan for 10 minutes before frosting them. (Don't wait longer than 10 minutes or you won't get that nice melting effect.)

8. WHILE THE ROLLS BAKE, MAKE THE FROSTING: In the bowl of a stand mixer fitted with the paddle attachment or in a large bowl with a hand mixer, beat together the butter and cream cheese. Add the vanilla and beat until incorporated. With the mixer on low speed, add the confectioners' sugar and a pinch of salt and beat until smooth. Taste and add more sugar, if desired. Increase the speed to high and beat 2 to 3 minutes, until the mixture is fluffy, scraping down the bowl as needed.

9. Generously frost the warm cinnamon rolls and serve immediately.

Pro Tips & Tricks

- For best results, use a nonstick metal baking pan and not ceramic. It browns the edges more quickly, so you're less likely to overbake the cinnamon rolls and dry them out in the center.

- **Make ahead:** To make the cinnamon rolls in advance, skip the second rise, cover the tray with plastic wrap, and refrigerate for 8 to 12 hours (but no longer). Before baking, let the rolls rise at room temperature for 2 hours (or 1 hour in a warm environment), then bake as usual.

Ricotta Waffles

I love the taste and texture of ricotta cheese and have experimented with using it in everything from pancakes to cake. These ricotta waffles were a happy accident when I'd originally planned to make ricotta pancakes for breakfast but my daughter requested waffles instead. Turns out, the only thing better than sweet, toasty waffles fresh out of the waffle iron are waffles made with rich, creamy ricotta! It gives the waffles a moist yet pillowy texture, not to mention more protein, which will keep you feeling satisfied for longer.

MAKES 8 STANDARD SQUARE WAFFLES (FEWER IF YOU'RE USING A BELGIAN WAFFLE MAKER)

Nonstick cooking spray, for greasing

2 large eggs

3 tablespoons sugar

1 cup ricotta cheese (8 ounces)

¾ cup whole milk

Zest of 1 lemon

1 teaspoon pure vanilla extract

1½ cups all-purpose flour (see How to Measure Flour Properly on page 20)

1 tablespoon aluminum-free baking powder

¼ teaspoon fine sea salt

6 tablespoons (¾ stick) unsalted butter, melted

Real maple syrup, for serving

Fresh fruit or your favorite waffle toppings, for serving (optional)

1. Heat your waffle iron according to the manufacturer's instructions and grease the grates with the cooking spray.

2. In a large bowl, whisk together the eggs and sugar until well blended. Add the ricotta, milk, lemon zest, and vanilla and whisk until smooth.

3. In a medium bowl, whisk together the flour, baking powder, and salt. Add the dry ingredients to the wet ingredients, whisking just until the mixture is moistened. Add the butter and whisk again until just incorporated. The batter will be lumpy, but don't be tempted to overmix or your waffles will get tough.

4. Ladle about ⅓ cup of the batter onto the center of the waffle maker (your waffle maker may require more or less batter, depending on its size). Cook the waffles 3 to 4 minutes, until golden and crisp, and repeat with the remaining batter. Serve with the maple syrup and fruit (if using).

Pro Tips & Tricks

- Preheating your waffle iron is the key to getting waffles with a crisp outside and fluffy center. Only add your batter when the iron is fully preheated, and let the iron reheat for a minute between batches.

- To keep your waffles warm until you're ready to serve, add them to a baking sheet in a 200°F oven.

- **Make ahead:** These waffles freeze really well and are perfect for busy mornings! Put the cooled waffles into a freezer-safe zip-top bag, squeeze out any excess air, and freeze for up to 2 months. Reheat the waffles in the toaster or air fryer.

Blueberry Crumb Muffins

When I was little and living in Seattle, my parents took us blueberry picking at an abandoned fruit orchard in town. We collected two big buckets full and feasted on berries for days. Mom made jam and blueberry-stuffed pierogi and piroshki. As delicious as the fruit was when freshly picked, something magical happened when it was cooked, turning deeply sweet and jammy. I wanted to capture that same magic in a muffin, which will also fill your kitchen with the aroma of a fancy bakery.

MAKES 12 MUFFINS

FOR THE CRUMB TOPPING

½ cup all-purpose flour

¼ cup sugar

¼ teaspoon fine sea salt

¼ teaspoon ground cinnamon

¼ cup (½ stick) unsalted butter, softened at room temperature

FOR THE BATTER

2 cups all-purpose flour (see How to Measure Flour Properly on page 20)

2 teaspoons aluminum-free baking powder

½ teaspoon fine sea salt

¼ teaspoon ground cinnamon

1 cup sugar

½ cup (1 stick) unsalted butter, room temperature

2 large eggs

1 teaspoon pure vanilla extract

½ cup whole milk, at room temperature

2 cups blueberries, rinsed and dried

1. Preheat the oven to 400°F. Line a standard 12-cup muffin tin with liners and set aside.

2. MAKE THE CRUMB TOPPING: In a small bowl, whisk together the flour, sugar, salt, and cinnamon. Add the butter and use your fingertips to rub the mixture together until pea-size crumbs form and the mixture is no longer sandy. Set aside while you make the batter.

3. MAKE THE BATTER: In a medium bowl, whisk together the flour, baking powder, salt, and cinnamon. Set aside.

4. In the bowl of a stand mixer fitted with the whisk attachment or in a large bowl with a hand mixer, beat together the sugar and butter on high speed for 2 minutes, until lightened. Add the eggs one at a time, beating to incorporate between each addition. Beat in the vanilla extract.

5. Add half of the dry ingredients to the butter mixture and beat on medium speed until blended. Add ¼ cup of the milk and mix until blended. Repeat with the remaining dry ingredients, followed by the remaining ¼ cup of milk. Beat until well blended; the batter will be thick.

6. Use a spatula to gently fold the blueberries into the batter until just combined. Divide the batter evenly between the lined muffin cups. It will seem like too much batter, but it works.

7. Top each muffin with about 1 tablespoon of the crumb topping, keeping it toward the center of the muffins since the muffins spread and grow (and so will the crumbs). Bake for about 25 minutes, or until the tops of the muffins are golden and a toothpick inserted into the center comes out clean. Let the muffins cool in the muffin tin for 10 minutes, then transfer to a wire rack and enjoy.

Fudgy Banana Bread

Once when I was in kindergarten, I was given a chocolate bar at school—a rare treat at the time. To the surprise of just about everyone, instead of stuffing it into my little five-year-old face, I took it home and split it with my sisters. That's how it's always been for me—when I have something good, I need to share it. The same goes for recipes! And this banana bread is just too good to keep to myself. It has to be the richest, most chocolatey (and yet perfectly acceptable for breakfast) loaf I've baked. An added bonus is that it will stay nice and moist for a few days, but we both know it won't last that long!

MAKES ONE 9-INCH LOAF

½ cup (1 stick) unsalted butter, softened, plus more for greasing

⅔ cup sugar

2 large eggs, lightly beaten, room temperature

3 medium very ripe bananas, mashed (about 1¾ cups; see Pro Tips & Tricks)

½ teaspoon pure vanilla extract

1 cup all-purpose flour (see How to Measure Flour Properly on page 20)

⅓ cup natural unsweetened cocoa powder

1 teaspoon baking soda

½ teaspoon fine sea salt

1 cup semisweet chocolate chips, divided

1. Preheat the oven to 350°F. Grease a 9-inch loaf pan with butter and line it with a sheet of parchment paper, letting about 2 inches hang over either side. (This will help you more easily lift the bread out of the pan.) Set aside.

2. In the bowl of a stand mixer fitted with the paddle attachment or in a large bowl with a hand mixer, cream together the butter and sugar at medium speed. Add the lightly beaten eggs and continue beating at medium speed until just combined. Add the mashed bananas and vanilla and beat until just combined.

3. In a large bowl, sift together the flour, cocoa powder, baking soda, and salt. Add the dry ingredients to the wet ingredients and mix on medium-low speed until just incorporated. The batter will be a little lumpy, and that's OK. Do not overmix or your loaf will be tough. Use a spatula to fold in ¾ cup of the chocolate chips.

4. Transfer the batter to the prepared loaf pan and top the batter with the remaining ¼ cup of chocolate chips. Bake for 55 to 65 minutes, or until a knife or toothpick inserted into the center comes out clean.

5. Let the banana bread rest in the pan for 10 minutes. Gently pull up on the parchment-paper handles and transfer the loaf to a cooling rack. Serve the banana bread at room temperature or when it is slightly warm to the touch.

Pro Tips & Tricks

- The key to great flavor is to use bananas that are very ripe or even overripe; the peels should be browning. If you have some that are overripe but you aren't ready to use them, peel and store them in a freezer-safe bag in the freezer, then thaw them at room temperature before baking. If your bananas are already yellow but not browned, you can help the process along: place the bananas on a foil-lined baking sheet and bake at 300°F for 30 minutes, or until softened and blackened on the outside.

Scrambled-Egg Breakfast of Champions

The name pretty much says it all! This recipe has you covered for perfectly fluffy scrambled eggs every time, and it's a complete meal, so you don't have to figure out what else to make. I've also worked it out so that all the components are ready at the same time and can be served fresh and hot with crispy bacon sprinkled over the top. Because it takes less than 30 minutes from start to finish, this is a great dish for busy weekdays, but it's also one of my favorite lazy Saturday breakfasts.

SERVES 4

6 slices regular-cut bacon, chopped (see Pro Tips & Tricks)

½ pound asparagus, ends trimmed (see Pro Tips & Tricks)

1 teaspoon extra-light olive oil or vegetable oil

Salt and freshly ground black pepper to taste

8 large eggs

¼ cup skim or whole milk

¼ teaspoon fine sea salt

2 tablespoons (¼ stick) unsalted butter

1. Preheat the oven to 400°F. Line a rimmed baking sheet with parchment paper.

2. On half of the baking sheet, arrange the bacon pieces in a single layer. On the other half, arrange the asparagus spears in a single layer. Lightly brush the asparagus with the oil and season with a sprinkle of salt and pepper. Bake for 16 to 18 minutes, until the bacon is browned and the asparagus is tender.

3. When the asparagus and bacon are about halfway done, start the eggs.

4. In a medium bowl, combine the eggs, milk, and salt. Use a fork to beat the mixture until the eggs are well blended.

5. In a large nonstick skillet over medium-low heat, melt the butter. Once the butter is foaming, slowly add the egg mixture and let sit undisturbed for about 30 seconds, until you see the edges start to solidify and cook. Use a silicone spatula to scrape the bottom of the pan and push the cooked eggs toward the middle, letting the uncooked eggs fill in the space underneath. Repeat, working around the skillet as you go. When the eggs are nearly cooked, fold them onto themselves to bring them together and keep them fluffy. Remove the pan from the heat and season with salt and pepper.

6. Divide the asparagus between four plates and top with the scrambled eggs. Sprinkle the bacon over the eggs and serve immediately.

Pro Tips & Tricks

- Don't use thick-cut bacon for this recipe; it takes longer to crisp and your cook times will be off.

- The keys to making perfectly scrambled eggs are (1) beating the eggs well before adding them to the skillet, (2) keeping the heat on medium-low, (3) patiently scraping the bottom of the pan and moving around in circles so you don't over-stir your scrambled eggs, which will make them flat and choppy, and (4) most importantly, not overcooking the eggs!

- If you like your asparagus more al dente (or are using very thin asparagus spears), you may want to pull them out of the oven a minute or two earlier.

Baba's Fluffy Oladi Pancakes

My mom (or Baba, as my kids call her) makes these Ukrainian pancakes every Sunday, and every Sunday we gobble them all up. Like American pancakes, they're light and fluffy, but otherwise they're in a class all their own. The yeasted batter gives them even more flavor, rise, and substantial texture, and they puff up like donuts when they hit the hot oil in the pan. I also love that the batter is make-ahead friendly and tastes even better as it sits and ferments in the fridge, which gives the oladi a subtle sourdough-like flavor.

SERVES 6 TO 8

1 cup water, warmed to 115°F

1 cup buttermilk

1 large egg, room temperature

2 tablespoons extra-light olive oil or vegetable oil, plus more for the pan

2 tablespoons sugar

1½ teaspoons instant yeast

1¼ teaspoons fine sea salt

2¾ cups all-purpose flour (see How to Measure Flour Properly on page 20)

FOR SERVING

Honey or real maple syrup

Raspberry Sauce (page 31) or jam of your choice

Sour cream

1. In a large bowl, whisk together the water, buttermilk, egg, oil, sugar, yeast, and salt. Add the flour, 1 cup at a time, whisking to incorporate each addition before adding more. Continue whisking until the batter is smooth with a thin cake-batter consistency.

2. Cover the bowl with plastic wrap and let the batter rise at room temperature for 1½ to 2 hours or in a warm place (about 100°F) for 1 hour. The mixture should become very bubbly and almost double in size.

3. In a large nonstick or cast-iron skillet over medium heat, add enough oil to coat the bottom of the pan. Working in batches, add heaping tablespoons of the batter to the hot skillet, spacing them just far enough apart that they aren't touching and can still be flipped easily. Cook the pancakes for about 1½ minutes per side, until golden brown, adding more oil as needed after flipping. Feel free to reduce the heat if you find they're browning too quickly. Continue with the remaining batter, keeping the skillet well-oiled between batches to ensure crisp, tasty, and beautifully golden edges on the pancakes.

4. Transfer the pancakes to a platter and serve warm with honey, raspberry sauce, and sour cream.

Pro Tips & Tricks

- This recipe yields a big batch, but you could halve the ingredients for a smaller number of servings. These also reheat very well, so you could make the entire batch and reheat them in the toaster.

Overnight Oats

Overnight oats are not only healthier than cooked oats (they have more fiber and are easier to digest!), but they're also the easiest breakfast ever. They're perfect for prepping ahead and keep well for several days in the fridge, so my husband makes six of these on Sunday nights for us to grab throughout the week—which we've been enjoying regularly for more than a year and are still going strong! To keep this breakfast staple exciting, you can change up the toppings.

SERVES 1

5 ounces almond milk or your milk of choice (just shy of ⅔ cup)

½ cup rolled or old-fashioned oats

¼ cup Greek yogurt (fat-free or whole; see Pro Tips & Tricks)

1 tablespoon real maple syrup

1 tablespoon chia seeds

Toppings of your choice (see My Favorite Variations)

1. In a resealable jar or container with a fitted lid, combine the milk, oats, yogurt, maple syrup, and chia seeds. Stir well, cover, and refrigerate overnight or up to 5 days.

2. To serve, add your favorite toppings and enjoy straight from the jar, or transfer the oats to a bowl, top as desired, and enjoy.

MY FAVORITE VARIATIONS

Here are some of my favorite topping combinations:

Sliced strawberries and shaved chocolate

Blueberries and lemon zest

Chopped apple, dried cranberries, and ground cinnamon

Mango and coconut flakes

Banana, mini chocolate chips, and drizzled peanut butter

Mixed berries (raspberries, blueberries, blackberries, or strawberries)

Sliced stone fruit (peach, nectarine, apricot, or plum)

Pro Tips & Tricks

- This recipe makes one serving, which is because I love being able to make a smaller batch as needed, but you can easily scale this up to make more servings.

- If using a sweetened or flavored yogurt, you can omit the maple syrup or add it to taste.

Special-Occasion Croissant French Toast

I came up with this recipe when I found myself with a big package of croissants that were starting to dry out, but I couldn't throw away a perfectly delicious baked good. Since one of my favorite ways to use up dried-out bread is French toast, I figured using flaky, buttery day-old croissants was definitely worth a try. Well, it's now officially my favorite way to repurpose any leftover croissants! To make this dish even more decadent, I add a splash of Grand Marnier, though you could easily substitute it with vanilla extract.

SERVES 6

6 large or 10 small croissants

6 large eggs

2 large egg yolks

¾ cup whole milk

2 tablespoons Grand Marnier or bourbon, or 2 teaspoons pure vanilla extract

1 tablespoon honey, warmed, or real maple syrup

1 teaspoon ground cinnamon

¼ teaspoon fine sea salt

¼ cup (½ stick) unsalted butter, or as needed

FOR SERVING (OPTIONAL)

Fresh berries

Confectioners' sugar

Real maple syrup

Whipped cream

1. Preheat the oven to 200°F.

2. Slice the croissants in half, as though you were making a sandwich. Set aside.

3. In a large bowl, add the eggs, egg yolks, milk, Grand Marnier, honey, cinnamon, and salt. Whisk until well combined, making sure the honey is dissolved. Transfer the mixture to a 9 × 13-inch casserole dish.

4. Heat a large cast-iron or nonstick sauté pan over medium-low heat. Add 2 tablespoons of the butter.

5. Meanwhile, working in batches, submerge the croissant halves in the egg mixture until they are fully soaked on both sides. Allow excess egg mixture to drip back into the dish and transfer the soaked croissants directly into the hot skillet cut side down. Only add as many croissant slices as will fit in a single layer in the pan.

6. Cook for 3 to 4 minutes, or until the first side is golden brown. If your croissants brown too quickly, reduce the heat. Flip the croissants over and cook for another 2 to 3 minutes, until the second side is golden brown. Transfer the finished croissants to a baking sheet and keep them warm in the oven while you repeat with the remaining croissant slices.

7. Arrange the croissants on a platter and sprinkle them with fresh fruit and a dusting of sugar. Serve with the maple syrup and whipped cream (if using).

Pro Tips & Tricks

- Day-old or slightly dried-out croissants are preferable here because they'll soak up the custard much better than fresh.

- The key to perfect French toast is to patiently let it sauté over medium-low heat, allowing the custard to fully cook through.

Homemade Granola–Berry Parfaits

Our family has about five breakfasts that we enjoy on a regular basis, and this is one of them. I can't stress enough how easy it is to make a big batch of homemade granola for the week, which not only keeps well but will also taste ten times better than anything you can buy at the store. (Not to mention the fact that it won't have tons of sugar or cheap fillers.) I love knowing that with every scoop, we're getting lots of whole grains and seeds, plus there's not much more to do for breakfast prep than sprinkle the granola over yogurt with some honey and fresh berries.

MAKES 1 PARFAIT AND 6 CUPS GRANOLA

FOR THE GRANOLA

3 cups rolled oats or old-fashioned oats (see Pro Tips & Tricks)

1 cup shaved or slivered almonds

½ cup unsweetened coconut flakes

¼ cup coconut oil

¼ cup honey

¼ cup real maple syrup

½ teaspoon fine sea salt

FOR THE PARFAIT

¾ cup plain Greek yogurt (fat-free or whole)

½ tablespoon chia seeds

1 teaspoon honey, or to taste

¼ cup Homemade Granola

½ cup fresh berries, such as sliced strawberries, blueberries, or raspberries

1. MAKE THE GRANOLA: Preheat the oven to 325°F. Line an 18 × 13-inch rimmed baking sheet with parchment paper and set aside.

2. In a large bowl, combine the oats, almonds, and coconut flakes. Set aside.

3. In a large microwave-safe measuring cup, add the oil and honey and microwave on high for 15 to 30 seconds, or until just melted. In the same measuring cup, add the maple syrup and salt and stir to combine. If they aren't blending easily, you can microwave the mixture for 15 seconds.

4. Drizzle the coconut oil mixture over the dry ingredients and use a spatula to stir until everything is evenly coated. Spread the granola in an even layer over the prepared baking sheet and bake for 18 to 20 minutes, stirring about halfway through for even toasting. The granola should be golden.

5. Allow the granola to cool completely on the baking sheet, then use your hands to break it into crumbles. Transfer the granola to an airtight container and store at room temperature for up to 1 week.

6. MAKE THE PARFAIT: In a medium bowl, 16-ounce mason jar, or other glass container, add the yogurt. Top the yogurt with the chia seeds and honey and stir to combine. Drizzle with more honey, if desired, then top with the granola and berries.

Pro Tips & Tricks

- You can use classic rolled oats, thick-cut rolled oats, or even instant rolled oats for the granola. We have even tried sprouted rolled oats (although those didn't crisp up as nicely and ended up just slightly chewier in the granola). We use whichever one we have on hand.

Avocado Toast

By now you've probably heard that avocado toast is one of the easiest and most satisfying breakfast options there are. What I love about it is that you're getting a hearty, substantial meal in minutes, and you can change it up about one hundred different ways to keep things interesting. Here are the guidelines I use when building my toast, along with some of my favorite variations.

SERVES 4

FOR THE AVOCADO TOAST

1 tablespoon unsalted butter, softened

4 slices of your favorite bread (we love sourdough)

1 large ripe avocado

½ teaspoon freshly squeezed lemon juice

⅛ teaspoon fine sea salt, or to taste

⅛ teaspoon freshly ground black pepper, or to taste

GARNISHES (OPTIONAL)

Flaky sea salt

Crushed red pepper flakes

Everything-but-the-bagel seasoning

Fresh dill

Fresh chives

Fresh cilantro

Extra-virgin olive oil

1. MAKE THE AVOCADO TOAST: Spread the butter over both sides of each slice of bread. In a large skillet over medium heat, toast the bread 1 to 2 minutes per side, or until golden brown and crisp on both sides.

2. Slice the avocado in half lengthwise, remove the pit, and use a spoon to scoop the flesh into a medium bowl. Add the lemon juice, salt, and pepper and use a fork to mash the mixture until chunky or to your desired consistency. Spread the avocado over the toasted bread.

3. GARNISH THE TOAST: Top the toast with your seasonings or herbs of choice and finish with a drizzle of the oil (if using).

MY FAVORITE VARIATIONS

The Classic: Top with flaky sea salt, crushed red pepper flakes, and extra-virgin olive oil.

The Fancy: Rather than mashing the avocado, slice it into thin strips, "fan" them over your toast, then sprinkle flaky sea salt and everything-but-the-bagel seasoning, and drizzle with extra-virgin olive oil.

The Pico de Gallo: Add halved cherry tomatoes or sliced tomatoes, season with flaky sea salt and black pepper, sprinkle with fresh cilantro leaves, and drizzle with extra-virgin olive oil.

The Garden Special: Add sliced cucumber, dill sprigs, and flaky sea salt.

The Works: Season the avocado toast to your liking and top with bacon and scrambled eggs. (See page 42 for how to make my favorite scrambled eggs.)

Pro Tips & Tricks

- To make a bigger batch of avocado toast, use the baking instructions for toasting bread from Caprese Bruschetta on page 74.

3

APPETIZERS AND SNACKS

Let me count the ways I love the recipes in this chapter. First of all, you can't go wrong with a single one of them when it comes to easy entertaining or bringing a dish to a party. I'm not exaggerating when I tell you that my Smoked Salmon Crostini (page 58) has been showing up at major life events in our family for years—and it quickly disappears every time! You could whip up just one dish to hold guests over until dinner is ready or put together a few of them to make fun bites before the main event. You'd also be amazed what a quick batch of Baked Spinach-Artichoke Dip (page 62) or Crispy Coconut Chicken Strips with Two-Ingredient Sauce (page 70) can do to take the edge off hungry kiddos (or grown-ups) in the afternoon. But I think my favorite time to reach for these recipes is when Vadim and I skip family dinner, get the kids in bed, and throw together a big bowl of Chunky Guacamole (page 61) or Cowboy Caviar Salsa (page 66) to devour with chips while we watch a movie. It just goes to show—there's no right or wrong way to enjoy these recipes.

Secret-Ingredient Deviled Eggs

Rather than adding the usual white vinegar to this potluck and cookout staple, I go for something a little less traditional . . . dill pickle brine! It adds that brightness and acidity you'd normally get from the vinegar, plus an extra zip that you can't quite place—and definitely can't resist. Plus, I toss in some chopped dill pickles for crunch. If the batches I always bring with me to gatherings, especially Easter dinner, are any indication, you'll have everyone asking you, "What's in them?" Which is code for, "Can I have the recipe?"

MAKES 24 DEVILED EGGS

12 large eggs

½ cup mayonnaise

2 teaspoons dill pickle juice

1 teaspoon yellow mustard

½ teaspoon garlic powder

2 baby dill pickles, finely chopped (about ¼ cup)

Fine sea salt and freshly ground black pepper

Paprika, for garnish

Small fresh dill fronds, for garnish (optional)

1. In a large pot, gently place the eggs and add enough cold water to cover by 1 inch. Set the pot over high heat and bring to a boil. Reduce the heat to medium and boil the eggs for 8 minutes. While the eggs cook, fill a large bowl with ice and water. Using a slotted spoon, quickly transfer the eggs to the ice bath and let them sit for 5 minutes to stop the cooking process.

2. Peel the eggs and cut each in half lengthwise. Pop the cooked yolks into a medium bowl and set the whites on a serving platter and set aside.

3. Mash the yolks with a fork to a fine-crumb consistency. Add the mayo, dill pickle juice, mustard, and garlic powder and mash until the mixture is smooth and creamy. Stir in the pickles and taste the mixture, seasoning with salt and pepper as needed.

4. Spoon the filling into each egg half or put the filling into a large zip-top bag, snip off a corner, and pipe it into the eggs. Dust with the paprika and garnish each egg with a sprig of dill (if using).

Pro Tips & Tricks

- When peeling the hardboiled eggs, keep in mind that fresh eggs can be more difficult to peel. If you're having trouble, peel the eggs under a stream of running water, which will help loosen the shells.

- When making the filling, the most important advice I have is to not oversalt. I've ruined a couple of batches this way because you can't un-salt something. To be safe, add the salt at the very end and start with just a pinch.

Smoked Salmon Crostini

I have been making these elegant but surprisingly simple crostini for years, and just when I thought they couldn't get any better, I made one final adjustment to the recipe. I was served a similar appetizer at a ladies' brunch, and the hostess had added little slices of lemon. I was blown away by how that balanced the saltiness of the smoked salmon and played up the fresh flavor of the herbs. So, I adjusted my recipe to include fresh lemon juice and zest, which fold seamlessly into the dish and make everything better and brighter.

MAKES 25 CROSTINI

FOR THE CROSTINI

1 (16-ounce) baguette

Extra-virgin olive oil, for brushing

FOR THE HERB CREAM CHEESE

1 medium lemon

6 ounces plain cream cheese, room temperature

2 tablespoons thinly sliced green onions (dark green parts) or chives

1 tablespoon finely chopped fresh dill, plus more for garnish

1 tablespoon mayonnaise

1 small garlic clove, pressed or grated

¼ teaspoon fine sea salt

FOR ASSEMBLING

½ English cucumber, cut into 25 thin slices

8 to 10 ounces thinly sliced cold-smoked salmon (see Pro Tips & Tricks)

1. MAKE THE CROSTINI: Preheat the oven to 350°F.

2. Slice the baguette diagonally into 25 slices and arrange them in an even layer on a rimmed baking sheet. Brush both sides lightly with the oil and bake for 5 minutes, until the edges are crisp and the centers are still soft. Set aside to cool to room temperature.

3. MAKE THE HERB CREAM CHEESE: Zest the entire lemon and set aside for assembling the crostini. Juice the lemon and reserve 1½ teaspoons. In a medium bowl, combine the cream cheese, green onions, dill, mayo, garlic, salt, and reserved lemon juice. Use a fork to mash the mixture until it's uniform.

4. ASSEMBLE: Spread a thin layer of the herb cream cheese on each of the toasts and top with a slice of cucumber and a slice of salmon. Transfer the crostini to a serving platter as you top them.

5. Sprinkle the finished crostini with more dill and the reserved lemon zest. Serve right away or cover with plastic wrap and refrigerate until ready to serve, up to 4 hours.

Pro Tips & Tricks

- Cold-smoked salmon is perfectly moist and tender, plus it's sold in thin slices, which makes assembling the crostini even easier.

Cucumber Pico de Gallo

This is the summer salsa we make on repeat to take advantage of all the glorious cucumbers and tomatoes we have coming up in our garden. Cucumbers add such great texture to a traditional pico de gallo and make the salsa feel even more substantial—plus, they just make sense in such a light, refreshing dish. It's wonderful as an appetizer served with tortilla chips, as a topping for chicken or fish, or as a condiment with tacos, burritos, or quesadillas. Feel free to customize the heat level to your preference; if you really want to crank it up, add both jalapeño and your favorite hot sauce.

SERVES 4 TO 6

4 medium Roma tomatoes, cored and diced

3 small garden cucumbers or 1 English cucumber, diced

2 medium avocados, pitted, peeled, and diced

1 medium yellow onion, finely diced

2 to 3 medium jalapeños, stemmed, seeded, and chopped, or to taste (optional)

½ bunch of fresh cilantro, chopped

Juice of 2 limes (about ¼ cup)

½ teaspoon fine sea salt, plus more to taste

¼ teaspoon freshly ground black pepper

Your favorite hot sauce (we love Cholula or Tabasco) to taste (optional)

1. In a large bowl, combine the tomatoes, cucumbers, avocados, onions, jalapeños (if using), and cilantro. Squeeze the lime juice over the top and season with the salt and pepper. Give everything a gentle toss and season with more salt, if needed. Add the hot sauce (if using).

2. Serve immediately or cover and refrigerate for up to 1 day.

Chunky Guacamole

If my husband and I had a list of the top ten recipes we make the most frequently, this would not only be on the list, it would be toward the very top. We love the texture from bits of avocado, onion, and diced tomato—it's a dip, not a spread!—but there's one ingredient that we finally discovered thanks to lots and lots of "testing" that adds instant depth of flavor: cumin. Just writing about it makes me look forward to our weekly ritual of whipping up a batch for date night and devouring the entire thing ourselves.

MAKES 5 CUPS

3 large ripe avocados, pitted and peeled

1 medium tomato, diced

½ medium white onion, diced

½ cup finely chopped fresh cilantro (about ½ bunch)

3 tablespoons freshly squeezed lime juice

½ teaspoon fine sea salt

¼ teaspoon freshly ground black pepper

¼ teaspoon ground cumin, or to taste

In a medium bowl, add the avocados. With a potato masher or fork, mash the avocado to a chunky consistency. Fold in the tomato, onion, cilantro, lime juice, salt, pepper, and cumin until just combined. Season with more salt, pepper, or cumin, if needed. Serve immediately.

Pro Tips & Tricks

- For a spicy guacamole, add ¼ cup seeded and diced jalapeños. Whether you use fresh peppers or canned, it adds a lovely kick of heat. (Which you can feel free to adjust to suit your preferences.)

- When storing leftover guacamole, place a sheet of plastic wrap directly over the dip to keep the air out and prevent discoloration. That said, I always recommend serving this the day it's made.

Baked Spinach-Artichoke Dip

This updated take on the classic appetizer is always a hit at parties and family movie nights. I've been serving it for years and have experimented with everything from making it in the slow cooker to on the stovetop, but nothing beats how the cheese gets caramelized in the oven. The best part is that it's served in the same pan it's cooked in (fewer dishes for me!) and is also perfect for making a day ahead and popping into the oven just before we're ready to enjoy it. Word to the wise: don't skip the green onions—the subtle flavor really makes the dip!

SERVES 8 TO 10

6 tablespoons (¾ stick) unsalted butter

½ cup chopped green onions (white and green parts, dark green parts reserved for garnish)

8 ounces plain cream cheese, quartered

1 cup sour cream

1 (14-ounce) can quartered artichoke hearts in water, well drained and coarsely chopped (see Pro Tips & Tricks)

1 (10-ounce) bag frozen chopped spinach, thawed, drained, and excess water squeezed out (see Pro Tips & Tricks)

1 cup shredded Parmesan cheese

1 cup shredded mozzarella cheese

1 tablespoon finely minced garlic (about 3 cloves)

1 teaspoon hot sauce, or to taste

Fine sea salt and freshly ground black pepper

Tortilla chips or pita chips, for serving

1. Preheat the oven to 375°F.

2. In a 10-inch cast-iron or other oven-safe skillet over medium-low heat, melt the butter. Add the green onions (making sure to reserve the dark green parts) and cook, stirring frequently, until softened and fragrant, about 5 minutes. Remove the skillet from the heat and add the cream cheese and sour cream, stirring until smooth. Add in the artichokes, spinach, Parmesan, ½ cup of the mozzarella, the garlic, and hot sauce and stir to combine. Season with salt and pepper. Spread the mixture evenly in the skillet and top with the remaining ½ cup of mozzarella.

3. Bake for 20 minutes, or until the dip is bubbling and the cheese has melted. Switch the oven to broil and broil for 2 minutes, until the cheese is beginning to brown.

4. Let the dip cool slightly and garnish with the reserved green onions. Serve warm with the chips.

Pro Tips & Tricks

- I use canned quartered artichokes in water—not "marinated" artichokes. If you do use marinated, be sure to completely drain off the marinade and taste the dip before seasoning with salt, as marinated artichokes are saltier and tangier.

- It's critical to remove as much water as possible from the spinach. It will retain liquid even after it's been drained, and too much will ruin the dip! Place the thawed spinach in a colander and tightly squeeze the spinach in fistfuls to remove all the excess water.

Cheesy Chicken Fritters

My aunt Tanya introduced me to this recipe over ten years ago when about fifty of my relatives came to town to visit us. We needed to figure out how to feed everyone, and quickly, so we chopped up a ton of chicken and cooked it into these cheesy, juicy fritters. This dish has been well-loved ever since and can be served as an appetizer, alongside a main for dinner, or eaten right out of the fridge as a snack—if you're lucky enough to have leftovers.

SERVES 8
(MAKES 16 TO 18 FRITTERS)

FOR THE CHICKEN FRITTERS

1½ pounds chicken breasts (about 3 large breasts), diced into ⅓-inch pieces (see Pro Tips & Tricks)

1⅓ cups shredded mozzarella cheese

2 large eggs, lightly beaten

⅓ cup mayonnaise

⅓ cup all-purpose flour (see Pro Tips & Tricks)

1½ tablespoons chopped fresh dill

½ teaspoon fine sea salt, plus more to taste

⅛ teaspoon freshly ground black pepper

2 tablespoons extra-light olive oil or vegetable oil, plus more as needed

FOR THE GARLIC AIOLI DIP

⅓ cup mayonnaise

1 garlic clove, pressed or grated

½ tablespoon freshly squeezed lemon juice

¼ teaspoon fine sea salt

⅛ teaspoon freshly ground black pepper

1. MAKE THE FRITTERS: In a large bowl, add the chicken, mozzarella, eggs, mayo, flour, dill, salt, and pepper and stir thoroughly to combine. If you have time, cover the bowl with plastic wrap and refrigerate for at least 2 hours, or up to overnight. Otherwise, proceed with cooking the fritters.

2. In a large nonstick pan over medium heat, heat the oil until it shimmers. Working in batches, scoop 1 heaping tablespoon of the chicken mixture for each fritter. Slightly flatten out the top of each fritter with the back of a spoon and fry for 3 to 4 minutes, or until the bottom turns golden brown. Flip and cook for another 3 minutes, until the bottom is golden brown and the chicken is fully cooked through. Transfer the fritters to a paper towel–lined plate. Repeat with the remaining chicken mixture, adding more oil to the pan as needed.

3. MAKE THE AIOLI: In a medium bowl, whisk together the mayo, garlic, lemon juice, salt, and pepper. Serve with the fritters or store in an airtight container in the refrigerator for up to 3 days.

Pro Tips & Tricks

- This is a great recipe for using up leftover cooked chicken or store-bought rotisserie chicken.

- To make this recipe gluten-free, use cornstarch or potato starch in place of the flour.

- **Make ahead:** You can make the chicken mixture a day ahead and cook when you're ready to serve, or even easier, you can cook these fritters ahead of time and reheat them. Allow them to cool before storing them in the refrigerator for up to 4 days. You can either enjoy them cold (which is delicious), or you can warm them on a skillet over medium-low heat until just heated through.

Cowboy Caviar Salsa

I first had this dish when my friend Annie, a classmate from when I was in nursing school, made it for a potluck for our class. Back then, I didn't realize that this fresh, hearty combination of raw veggies, avocados, and black beans had an official name—cowboy caviar—but I did know that it was really good. It's the perfect salsa for pool parties and warm-weather cookouts, but it's also great year-round for potlucks and game days. My husband and I like throwing together a batch for movie nights and enjoying it in lieu of dinner with plenty of tortilla chips.

SERVES 10

6 Roma tomatoes, diced

1 bell pepper (any color), stemmed, seeded, and diced

1 medium yellow onion, finely diced

1 large avocado, pitted, peeled, and diced

1 (15-ounce) can corn, drained (or kernels from 1 cooked cob of corn)

1 (15-ounce) can black beans, rinsed and drained

½ cup chopped fresh cilantro leaves

2 jalapeño peppers, stemmed, seeded, and finely diced

½ cup store-bought light Italian dressing (see Pro Tips & Tricks)

3 tablespoons freshly squeezed lime juice, plus more to taste

4 medium garlic cloves, pressed or grated

1 teaspoon fine sea salt, plus more to taste

Tortilla chips, for serving

In a large bowl, toss together the tomatoes, bell pepper, onion, avocado, corn, black beans, cilantro, and jalapeños. Add the Italian dressing, lime juice, garlic, and salt and toss again to combine. Season with more lime juice or salt, if needed. Serve with the tortilla chips.

Pro Tips & Tricks

- Don't substitute the Italian dressing! It adds a little somethin' somethin' that just can't be replaced. I like using light Italian dressing since it has less oil than regular dressings and won't make your salsa greasy. My favorites are Newman's Own and Olive Garden brand.

Honey-Roasted Pecans

These are just the thing for snacking, including in a charcuterie spread, giving as gifts during the holidays, or for sprinkling over salads. (You'll especially love them with the Arugula Stone-Fruit Salad with Balsamic Glaze on page 90.) No matter when or how you're serving these addictive salty-sweet nuts, they always disappear *fast*—good thing that they're so easy to make. To kick them up a notch, I add a bit of cayenne pepper. It adds a surprising sweet and spicy note, but you can leave it out if you want to make this kid-friendly or prefer less heat.

MAKES 3 CUPS

2 tablespoons coarse turbinado sugar

½ teaspoon kosher salt

¼ cup honey

½ teaspoon ground cayenne pepper (optional)

2½ cups pecan halves (10 ounces)

1. Place an oven rack in the center of the oven and preheat the oven to 350°F. Line an 18 × 13-inch rimmed baking sheet with parchment paper and set aside.

2. In a small bowl, combine the sugar and salt and set aside.

3. In a large nonstick skillet over medium heat, melt the honey for 30 to 60 seconds. Quickly stir in the cayenne (if using) and pecans until the nuts are evenly coated, then remove the pan from the heat.

4. Spread the nuts in an even layer over the prepared baking sheet. Bake for 10 minutes, until toasted.

5. Let the pecans cool on the baking sheet for exactly 4 minutes, then transfer them to a large bowl. Immediately sprinkle the nuts with the reserved sugar and salt mixture and use a spatula to mix well. I find that gently pressing the pecans down into the bottom of the bowl, where the sugar collects, can be effective.

Pro Tips & Tricks

- This recipe fills exactly one baking sheet. If you wish to double the recipe, spread the mixture over two baking sheets and bake at the same time for 12 minutes, rotating halfway through for even toasting.

Crispy Coconut Chicken Strips
with Two-Ingredient Sauce

These were inspired by our popular coconut shrimp recipe, and if I'm being honest, I think these juicy chicken strips somehow manage to be even better. That mostly has to do with the fact that chicken requires less prep than shrimp, and you could easily serve them as a main course or snack. Plus, the combination of sweet chili sauce and apricot preserves creates a sticky, spicy, sweet sauce that couldn't be easier to make and perfectly complements the crispy coconut crust.

SERVES 4 TO 5
(MAKES 8 TO 10 TENDERS)

FOR THE DIPPING SAUCE

¼ cup sweet chili sauce

¼ cup apricot preserves or apricot fruit spread

FOR THE COCONUT CHICKEN STRIPS

¼ cup all-purpose flour

½ teaspoon garlic powder

½ teaspoon fine sea salt

¼ teaspoon freshly ground black pepper

2 large eggs

1½ cups sweetened shredded coconut

½ cup panko breadcrumbs

1 to 1¼ pounds chicken tenders (8 to 10 tenders)

Extra-light olive oil or vegetable oil, for frying

1 lime, sliced into wedges, for serving

1. MAKE THE DIPPING SAUCE: In a medium bowl, combine the chili sauce and apricot preserves and mix well. Set aside.

2. MAKE THE CHICKEN: Set up three medium shallow bowls. In the first, add the flour, garlic powder, salt, and pepper and whisk to combine. In the second bowl, use a fork to thoroughly beat together the eggs. In the third bowl, stir together the coconut and breadcrumbs.

3. Dredge two chicken tenders (I find that this goes more quickly if I'm doing two tenders at a time) in the flour mixture, turning them to coat well, then tap off any excess. Coat the chicken in the egg, allowing any excess to drip back into the bowl. Finally, roll the tenders in the breadcrumb mixture, using your hands to gently press the crumbs into the chicken to help them adhere for a nice thick coating. Transfer the breaded chicken to a plate and repeat with the remaining tenders.

4. In a large cast-iron skillet or heavy pan over medium heat, add about ¼ inch of oil—enough to generously coat the bottom of the pan. Once the oil is hot (about 350°F), add half of the chicken tenders. (Don't be tempted to cook them all at once; crowding the pan will cool the oil and make it difficult for the chicken to crisp up— no one wants soggy breading!) Cook for 3 to 4 minutes per side, or until the chicken is golden brown and cooked through. An instant-read thermometer inserted in the thickest part of the tender should register 165°F. Transfer the tenders to a serving platter.

5. Add more oil as needed and allow it to come back up to temperature and strain out any larger pieces of breading so it doesn't burn. Repeat with the remaining chicken tenders. Serve warm with the dipping sauce and lime wedges.

Pro Tips & Tricks

- To reheat, you can crisp them up in an air fryer at 350°F for 3 to 5 minutes or in an oven at 400°F for 10 to 12 minutes or until heated through.

Crispy Bacon Jalapeño Poppers

If you thought it was hard to resist ordering spicy, creamy jalapeño poppers at a restaurant, wait until you make a batch of these. I add salty, crispy bacon to the crumb topping, which is pretty much insurance that there will be no leftovers after this dish hits the table. These are perfect for serving anytime, but I love including them on my party menus because they're great warm or at room temperature.

MAKES 28 POPPERS

5 slices regular-cut bacon

8 ounces plain cream cheese, softened (see Pro Tips & Tricks)

½ cup shredded medium cheddar cheese (2 ounces)

¼ cup chopped fresh chives, plus more for garnish

1 garlic clove, minced

¼ teaspoon fine sea salt

¼ teaspoon freshly ground black pepper

14 to 16 medium jalapeño peppers (about 1 pound)

⅓ cup panko breadcrumbs

2 teaspoons unsalted butter, melted

1. In a large skillet over medium heat, cook the bacon for about 3 minutes per side, until crisp and browned. Transfer the bacon to a paper towel–lined plate to cool. Reserve 2 teaspoons of the rendered bacon fat if you'd like to use it for the breadcrumb coating (in place of the butter) and set aside. Chop the bacon into small bits and set aside ⅓ cup for the recipe; feel free to snack on the rest.

2. Place an oven rack in the center of the oven and preheat the oven to 400°F.

3. In a medium bowl, combine the cream cheese, cheddar cheese, chives, garlic, salt, and pepper. Use a fork to mash the mixture until everything is well incorporated.

4. Slice the jalapeños in half lengthwise (I recommend wearing kitchen gloves for this) and use a spoon to scrape out the seeds and white membranes. Discard.

5. Stuff each jalapeño half with enough cream cheese mixture to sit level with the sides. Don't be tempted to overstuff them! Arrange the stuffed peppers in a single layer on a rimmed baking sheet.

6. In another medium bowl, combine the breadcrumbs with the butter (or the reserved bacon fat, if you've gone that route) and stir until the crumbs are moistened. Stir in the chopped bacon and top each popper with about 1 teaspoon of the crumb mixture.

7. Bake for 17 to 20 minutes, until the peppers are tender and the breadcrumb topping is golden brown in spots. Let the poppers cool for 10 minutes before serving. Garnish with more chives.

Pro Tips & Tricks

- You can use cold or softened cream cheese for the filling. Cold will be a little harder to mash with a fork, but not impossible.

Caprese Bruschetta

It's hard to imagine bruschetta getting any better than sweet, juicy tomatoes and fresh basil loaded up on good, toasty bread. But I can assure you that if you add mozzarella and a sweet-salty balsamic glaze, things get a whole lot tastier. But what you'll love most about this dish is how the flavors continue to meld as they sit, which means you can make the topping a couple hours in advance—in addition to the glaze and toasts—then set everything out when guests arrive so they can assemble their own bruschetta. (A great hack to ensure that the toasts won't get soggy as they sit!) I've also been known to save any leftover topping and serve it over toast for breakfast or lunch the next day.

MAKES 25 TOASTS

FOR THE TOASTS

1 baguette, cut diagonally into ½-inch slices (about 25 slices)

3 to 4 tablespoons extra-virgin olive oil

FOR THE CAPRESE BRUSCHETTA

6 Roma tomatoes (about 1½ pounds), cored and diced

½ teaspoon fine sea salt, plus more to taste

8 ounces fresh mozzarella cheese, diced

⅓ cup fresh basil leaves, chopped (see Pro Tips & Tricks)

5 garlic cloves, minced

2 tablespoons extra-virgin olive oil

1 tablespoon balsamic vinegar

¼ teaspoon freshly ground black pepper

Balsamic Glaze (page 91) or store-bought, for serving

1. MAKE THE TOASTS: Place an oven rack in the center of the oven and preheat the oven to 400°F.

2. Arrange the baguette slices on a rimmed baking sheet and brush both sides with the oil. Bake for 7 to 9 minutes, until lightly toasted. They will start to get crisp at the edges but should still have some softness in the center. To save time, make the glaze while the bread is toasting.

3. MAKE THE BRUSCHETTA: Set the tomatoes in a colander over the sink. Sprinkle them with a pinch of salt and let any excess juice drain off while you prep the remaining ingredients.

4. In a large bowl, combine the tomatoes with the mozzarella, basil, garlic, oil, vinegar, ½ teaspoon of the salt, and the pepper. If not serving the bruschetta with the balsamic glaze, add more salt if needed. (You won't need more if using the glaze.)

5. To serve, transfer the bruschetta and balsamic glaze to serving bowls and arrange with the toasts on a platter.

Pro Tips & Tricks

- Sprinkling the tomatoes with salt as they sit in the colander helps the tomatoes tenderize and release their excess juice, so the bruschetta doesn't end up mushy or watery.

- Basil is delicate and easily bruised, so take care when chopping it. Stack the basil leaves, then roll them up tightly into a log. Slice the log into thin strips.

Cheese-and-Bacon Stuffed Mushrooms

As quickly as this decadent appetizer comes together, I guarantee you that they'll disappear just as quickly. They not only look so enticing on a platter, but their gooey, bacon-studded stuffing really does sell itself. And no more wasting time scraping out the centers of the mushrooms before stuffing them—you just need to pop off the stems and they're good to go.

MAKES 24 STUFFED MUSHROOMS

Extra-light olive oil or vegetable oil, for greasing

6 strips regular-cut bacon

4 ounces plain cream cheese, softened

½ cup shredded or freshly grated Parmesan cheese

2 garlic cloves, minced or grated

2 tablespoons finely chopped fresh parsley leaves, plus more for garnish

¼ teaspoon fine sea salt

¼ teaspoon freshly ground black pepper

24 cremini mushrooms (about 1 pound), stemmed (see Pro Tips & Tricks)

1. Preheat the oven to 400°F. Lightly coat a rimmed baking sheet with the oil and set aside.

2. In a large skillet over medium heat, cook the bacon for about 3 minutes per side, until crisp and browned. Transfer the bacon to a paper towel–lined plate to cool. Chop into small bits and set aside.

3. In a medium bowl, combine the cream cheese, Parmesan, garlic, parsley, salt, and pepper. Use a fork to mash the mixture together, then add half of the bacon bits. Continue stirring until incorporated. Divide the filling evenly between the mushrooms (about 2 teaspoons of stuffing per mushroom). Sprinkle the remaining bacons bits over the top.

4. Arrange the mushrooms on the prepared baking sheet, evenly spaced, and bake for 15 minutes, until the mushrooms are softened and the tops have started to brown in spots. (See Pro Tips & Tricks.) Transfer the mushrooms to a serving platter, sprinkle with more parsley, and serve.

Pro Tips & Tricks

- You could also use white or button mushrooms here. If you use larger mushrooms, just know they'll take longer to bake.

- Avoid washing your mushrooms because they will absorb all that water, resulting in soggy mushrooms. Instead, wipe the mushrooms with a damp paper towel to remove any dirt.

- Overcooked stuffed mushrooms get watery and limp. The mushrooms are done when the tops have started to brown, the mushrooms have released some of their moisture (you may see a little water at the base of some mushrooms), and the mushrooms feel soft when gently squeezed.

4

SALADS

Salads might just be my favorite chapter in this entire book. Nothing against any of the other (very good, very highly recommended) recipes here, but salads are what put Natasha's Kitchen on the map. When a TV news anchor shared my recipe for Cucumber, Tomato, and Avocado Salad (page 80) on Facebook in 2015, it went viral. People raved about how simple yet flavorful it was, which is 100 percent the point (and, as you know by now, what I'm all about). There's nothing that compares to a big hearty salad that's jam-packed with different flavors, textures, and pops of freshness. The recipes in this chapter are not your skimpy side-dish salads—these are powerhouse dishes in their own right and are often on our menu for lunch or dinner as a complete meal. They also look so pretty on the table, which makes them perfect for entertaining or taking with you to wherever you need to bring a dish. No one needs to know that it took barely any time to toss together!

Cucumber, Tomato, and Avocado Salad

As a mashup between a classic tomato-and-cucumber salad and guacamole, it's no wonder why people flock to this recipe—and why it's always the first thing to disappear at potlucks. This is the perfect dish for using up all the tomatoes and cucumbers coming out of your garden in the summer, although it's flavorful enough to use store-bought veggies as well. I love serving this salad with grilled steak, shrimp, or chicken, as well as roasted potatoes.

SERVES 4

1 pound Roma tomatoes, cored and diced

2 large avocados, pitted, peeled, and diced (see Pro Tips & Tricks)

1 English cucumber, sliced into ¼-inch-thick rounds

½ medium red onion, thinly sliced

¼ cup chopped fresh cilantro leaves (see Pro Tips & Tricks)

2 tablespoons extra-virgin olive oil

2 tablespoons freshly squeezed lemon juice

1 teaspoon fine sea salt, or to taste

⅛ teaspoon freshly ground black pepper, or to taste

In a large bowl, add the tomatoes, avocado, cucumber, onion, cilantro, oil, and lemon juice and toss to combine. Just before serving (and not earlier or the cucumbers and tomatoes will get too soft), season with the salt and pepper and toss once more.

Pro Tips & Tricks

- Try finding avocados that aren't too ripe so that they hold their shape.

- Over the years, many people have asked about a good cilantro substitute. For this salad, I would suggest adding freshly chopped dill or chives to taste.

Mediterranean Grilled Chicken Salad

This salad is in our regular rotation for a few good reasons: First, it's delicious. Second, there's something for everyone with tons of mix-ins like cucumbers, tomatoes, olives, avocado, and feta. And third, it's versatile. We love the flavor of charred grilled chicken, but sometimes we swap it out for steak, crisped gyro meat, or shrimp. Or we keep it vegetarian. No matter which way you go, you have a great go-to for lunch or dinner, or you can serve it as a side.

SERVES 4 (OR 6 AS A SIDE)

FOR THE GRILLED-CHICKEN MARINADE

1 pound boneless, skinless chicken breasts, sliced lengthwise into 4 cutlets

2 tablespoons extra-light olive oil or vegetable oil

1½ teaspoons dried oregano leaves

½ teaspoon fine sea salt

½ teaspoon freshly ground black pepper

½ teaspoon garlic powder

FOR THE SALAD DRESSING

¼ cup red wine vinegar

2 garlic cloves, grated or finely minced

1 teaspoon dried oregano leaves

¾ teaspoon fine sea salt, plus more to taste

½ teaspoon freshly ground black pepper, plus more to taste

½ cup extra-virgin olive oil

1. MARINATE THE CHICKEN: In a large zip-top bag, combine the chicken with the extra-light olive oil, oregano, salt, pepper, and garlic powder. Marinate in the refrigerator for at least 20 minutes or up to 8 hours.

2. WHILE THE CHICKEN MARINATES, MAKE THE SALAD DRESSING: In a small bowl, whisk together the vinegar, garlic, oregano, salt, and pepper. Stream in the extra-virgin olive oil while whisking to combine. Season with more salt and pepper, if needed. Set aside at room temperature for the flavors to meld while you prepare the remaining salad components.

3. MAKE THE SALAD: Preheat a grill to medium heat.

4. Grill the chicken for 4 to 5 minutes per side, or until the internal temperature registers 165°F on an instant-read thermometer at the thickest part of the meat. Transfer the chicken to a cutting board and let it rest for 15 minutes. Slice the chicken into bite-size strips and set aside.

5. In a large bowl, combine the lettuce, tomatoes, cucumber, avocado, olives, feta, onion, chicken, and dressing. Toss well to coat. For an extra punch of flavor, add the kalamata juice and toss well. Serve immediately.

FOR THE SALAD

1 large head of romaine or green leaf lettuce, chopped (about 10 cups)

1 cup cherry tomatoes, halved

½ English cucumber, sliced into ¼-inch-thick half-moons

1 large avocado, pitted, peeled, and sliced

½ cup pitted kalamata olives, halved, plus 2 tablespoons of their brine

½ cup crumbled feta cheese

¼ cup thinly sliced red onion

Pro Tips & Tricks

- If you don't have a grill, no problem! You can use a grill pan or cast-iron skillet. Cook the chicken with 1 tablespoon of oil using the same temperature and timing instructions the recipe calls for.

- **Make ahead:** With the exception of the avocado (because it will turn brown), you can fully assemble the salad and dressing ahead, then cover and store them separately in the refrigerator for a few hours. Just before serving, whisk the dressing since it will separate as it sits, then toss the dressing and avocado with the salad.

Avocado Chicken Salad

This seems to be the internet's favorite salad (with over 200 million views!), and I can see why: this recipe was the answer to my craving for a decadently creamy yet mayo-free chicken salad. The result is light and fresh thanks to avocado and lemon dressing, plus irresistible bites of bacon and corn. I don't think I'll ever stop loving this salad, so it makes me happy that it's now one of my son's favorites, too.

SERVES 6 AS A SIDE

FOR THE LEMON DRESSING

3 tablespoons freshly squeezed lemon juice

3 tablespoons extra-virgin olive oil

1 teaspoon fine sea salt, plus more to taste

⅛ teaspoon freshly ground black pepper

FOR THE SALAD

6 slices regular-cut bacon

1 pound cooked chicken breast, shredded or chopped (about 3 cups; see Pro Tips & Tricks)

2 large avocados, pitted, peeled, and cut into bite-size pieces

1 cup cooked or canned corn

¼ cup chopped fresh chives or green onions

2 tablespoons chopped fresh dill

3 hard-boiled large eggs, peeled and quartered (optional)

1. MAKE THE DRESSING: In a medium bowl, whisk together the lemon juice, oil, salt, and pepper. Season with more salt, if needed. Set aside.

2. MAKE THE SALAD: In a medium nonstick pan or cast-iron skillet over medium heat, cook the bacon for about 3 minutes per side, until crisp and browned. Transfer the bacon to a paper towel–lined plate and let cool completely. Chop the bacon into bite-size pieces.

3. In a large bowl, toss together the chicken, avocado, bacon, corn, chives, and dill. Drizzle the dressing over the salad and toss to coat. Serve with the hard-boiled egg quarters (if using).

Pro Tips & Tricks

- For this recipe, you could use leftover cooked chicken, rotisserie chicken, or well-drained canned chicken. You could also make chicken specifically for this salad—season chicken breasts with salt and pepper and grill or sear them in a pan.

Salade Maison
(Our House Salad)

This French-inspired salad may sound fancy, but it really just means "house salad." Or as we have come to call it, *our* house salad, because we make it so frequently. Aside from the great combination of sweet, salty, and crunchy toppings, the best part is the lemon vinaigrette that's inspired by a similar version that our friends Clark and Sara first introduced us to. This recipe makes a big batch of salad, so it's perfect for picnics and potlucks, in addition to meal prepping (just keep the salad and dressing separate until ready to serve).

SERVES 8 TO 10

FOR THE LEMON VINAIGRETTE

¼ cup freshly squeezed lemon juice (from 1½ to 2 lemons)

2 small garlic cloves, pressed or grated

1 tablespoon Dijon mustard (I love Grey Poupon)

1 teaspoon honey

½ teaspoon fine sea salt, plus more to taste

¼ teaspoon freshly ground black pepper, plus more to taste

⅔ cup extra-virgin olive oil

FOR THE SALAD

6 slices regular-cut bacon

½ cup slivered almonds

2 medium heads of romaine lettuce, chopped (about 12 cups)

2 cups cherry tomatoes, halved

¾ cup shredded Swiss cheese

½ cup finely shredded Parmesan cheese

1 cup store-bought croutons of your choice

1. MAKE THE VINAIGRETTE: In a resealable jar, combine the lemon juice, garlic, Dijon, honey, salt, and pepper. Add the oil, cover, and shake well to combine. Season with more salt and pepper, if needed. Set aside.

2. MAKE THE SALAD: In a medium nonstick pan or cast-iron skillet over medium heat, cook the bacon for about 3 minutes per side, until crisp and browned. Transfer the bacon to a paper towel–lined plate and let cool completely. Chop the bacon into bite-size pieces.

3. In a small dry skillet over medium heat, toast the almonds, tossing frequently, until they're golden and fragrant, 3 to 5 minutes. Set aside to cool.

4. In a large bowl, combine the lettuce, tomatoes, Swiss cheese, Parmesan, bacon, almonds, and croutons. Just before serving, add the vinaigrette to taste and toss well to coat. Serve immediately.

5. Store any leftover vinaigrette in the resealable jar in the refrigerator for up to 1 week.

Pro Tips & Tricks

- You can easily halve the salad and vinaigrette ingredients if you'd like to make a smaller batch.

- If you love crunchy croutons, add them after tossing the salad with the vinaigrette.

- If you like the vinaigrette as much as we do, you can double the recipe and keep it in the fridge for quick-fix salads throughout the week. We find that we eat more salad when we do!

Classic Greek Salad

This recipe has everything the perfect salad needs: plenty of fresh ingredients, lots of texture, a variety of flavors, and a little something for everyone. That way, if your kids are like mine and want to pick out the bell peppers or olives, no big deal! They're still getting plenty of veggies. I particularly love this in the summertime served with pretty much anything off the grill, but the dressing is flavorful enough to transform even wintertime tomatoes and cucumbers.

SERVES 6

FOR THE DRESSING

¼ cup red wine vinegar

1 teaspoon dried oregano leaves

2 garlic cloves, minced or grated

¾ teaspoon fine sea salt

½ teaspoon freshly ground black pepper

½ cup extra-virgin olive oil

FOR THE SALAD

2 cups cherry tomatoes, halved (or 1 pound garden tomatoes, chopped)

1 English cucumber, sliced into ½-inch-thick half-moons

1 bell pepper, any color, stemmed, seeded, and chopped

6 ounces feta cheese, diced (about 1 cup)

½ cup pitted kalamata olives, halved or roughly chopped

¼ cup thinly sliced red onion

1. MAKE THE DRESSING: In a medium bowl or resealable jar, combine the vinegar, oregano, garlic, salt, and pepper. Add the oil and whisk or cover and shake vigorously to combine. Set aside.

2. MAKE THE SALAD: In a large bowl, combine the tomatoes, cucumber, bell pepper, feta, olives, and onion. Just before serving, add the dressing and toss gently to coat. Serve immediately.

Pro Tips & Tricks

- Some Greek salad recipes call for the cucumbers to be seeded first so that they don't make the salad soggy. But I've found that this salad gets eaten up so quickly and completely that there's no time for the cucumbers to break down. Plus, it always feels wasteful to me to throw away so much perfectly good cuke. Now I just chop them up and save myself a step—and no one has ever complained!

- Feel free to customize this recipe to your or your family's taste. Want more olives? Add 'em! Don't like bell pepper? Leave it out!

Arugula Stone-Fruit Salad
with Balsamic Glaze

As unconventional as it may sound, my husband and I love making a meal of this salad for dinner. It's the most satisfying combination of sweet and salty thanks to a homemade balsamic glaze (or store-bought—who doesn't need a shortcut sometimes?!), it has great texture from fresh stone fruit and toasted pecans, and then there's the irresistibly creamy goat cheese. Plus, because we can switch up the fruit depending on the season—juicy peaches, nectarines, apricots, or plums from our fruit trees in the summer; pears, apples, and clementines in the fall and winter—it never gets old, no matter how many hundreds of times we've made it. Now can you see why we'll never stop loving this salad?

SERVES 4 AS A SIDE

½ cup unsalted raw pecans

5 ounces baby arugula (about 5 cups)

1 peach, pitted and sliced

1 nectarine, pitted and sliced

1 plum, pitted and sliced

2 apricots, pitted and sliced

1 cup cherries, pitted and halved (optional)

½ cup crumbled goat cheese, or to taste (see Pro Tips & Tricks)

3 tablespoons Balsamic Glaze (recipe follows) or store-bought, plus more to taste

1. In a small dry skillet over medium heat, toast the nuts for 3 to 5 minutes, tossing frequently, until they are fragrant. Transfer the nuts to a plate and set aside to cool.

2. Add the arugula to a large bowl. Top with the peach, nectarine, plum, apricots, cherries (if using), goat cheese, and pecans. Drizzle the top of the salad with the balsamic glaze. There is no need to toss this salad as it serves beautifully as is.

Pro Tips & Tricks

- I use about 4 cups of fruit for this salad. You can use a single fruit variety (which is what we do when our peach trees are producing like crazy) or a combination of seasonal fruit.

- I make cherries optional here because they have a fairly narrow window of availability. But when you can get your hands on them, they are a very exciting addition to this salad!

- I've been known to be a little heavy-handed with the goat cheese (because it's so tangy and creamy!), but if you prefer less, use less! Or more—I won't judge!

Balsamic Glaze

Don't be fooled by this simple two-ingredient recipe—it packs some seriously deep, complex flavor. It's just a reduction of balsamic vinegar and honey, which becomes a perfectly balanced drizzle that you can add to both sweet and savory recipes, especially my Caprese Bruschetta on page 74 and fruit-based salads. It lasts in the refrigerator for up to four weeks, too, so you can keep a batch on hand for adding a little extra somethin' anytime the mood strikes.

MAKES ABOUT ½ CUP

1 cup balsamic vinegar

1½ teaspoons honey (optional; see Pro Tips & Tricks)

1. In a small saucepan over medium heat, combine the vinegar and honey (if using). Bring the mixture to a low boil, stirring occasionally to dissolve the honey. Reduce the heat to low and simmer, stirring occasionally, for 12 to 15 minutes, until the vinegar is reduced by half and lightly coats the back of a spoon. Remove the pan from the heat.

2. Transfer the glaze into a resealable jar or other airtight container and let cool, uncovered, to room temperature. Seal and refrigerate for up to 4 weeks.

Pro Tips & Tricks

- If you're using this glaze for a savory recipe, you can omit the honey altogether because the balsamic vinegar will have enough natural sweetness.

- The time it takes balsamic vinegar to reduce will vary depending on the quality and thickness of your vinegar (some can be a little syrupy right out of the bottle and will reduce more quickly).

- When deciding when to take the glaze off the heat, remember that it will thicken as it cools. You can always put it back on the heat if you want it thicker.

Heirloom Tomato and Burrata Salad

This salad is a true family favorite. My husband loves it because of how delicious the tomatoes get after soaking up a garlicky vinaigrette with lots of fresh herbs. My kids love it because of the burrata, which is a soft, mild cheese that's like mozzarella in flavor and texture but with a creamy center. And I love it because it comes together in minutes and is a great way to showcase (and use up) all those gorgeous summer tomatoes coming out of the garden by the ton. Serve it as a light lunch with lots of fresh, crusty bread, or as an elegant dinner starter with multicolored heirloom tomatoes.

SERVES 4

FOR THE DRESSING

3 tablespoons extra-virgin olive oil

1 tablespoon minced or grated garlic

1 tablespoon finely chopped dill or parsley leaves

½ teaspoon lemon zest

1 tablespoon freshly squeezed lemon juice

FOR THE TOMATO SALAD

3 large heirloom tomatoes, sliced into ¼-inch rings

3 balls of burrata cheese (8 ounces total; see Pro Tips & Tricks)

1 tablespoon chopped fresh chives

Extra-virgin olive oil, for finishing

Fine sea salt and freshly ground black pepper

1. MAKE THE DRESSING: In a small bowl, whisk together the oil, garlic, dill, lemon zest, and lemon juice. Set aside.

2. MAKE THE SALAD: Arrange the tomatoes on a serving platter so they're slightly overlapping. Chop the burrata into bite-size pieces and scatter it over the tomatoes. Drizzle the dressing over the cheese and tomatoes and top with the chives. Just before serving, drizzle more oil over everything and season generously with salt and pepper.

Pro Tips & Tricks

- Use heirloom garden tomatoes when they are in season. If you want to re-create this dish in the winter, use the best tomatoes you can get your hands on, and mix in some halved cherry tomatoes, which have a sweetness that is closer to summer tomatoes.

- If you aren't able to get burrata cheese, you can substitute it with fresh mozzarella torn into bite-size pieces or use fresh mozzarella pearls.

- Adding the salt and pepper right before serving ensures that the tomatoes stay firm and don't juice out or get mushy. That said, make sure to season generously to taste. Salt really brings out the best flavor of the tomatoes. I always feel like I've added too much salt and then end up adding more at the table.

Apple-Pomegranate Kale Salad

Kale salads are the ultimate blank canvas. Once you combine chopped kale, goat cheese, toasted pecans, and a great maple-Dijon dressing as your base, then you can really get creative with the other toppings. I look to the seasons for inspiration: strawberries or blueberries in the summer, roasted sweet potatoes or butternut squash in the winter (which could make this a main dish that serves four), or this combination of apples and pomegranate seeds in the fall.

SERVES 6 AS A SIDE

FOR THE MAPLE-DIJON DRESSING

3 tablespoons apple cider vinegar

1 tablespoon real maple syrup

1 tablespoon Dijon mustard

1 garlic clove, finely minced or grated

⅓ cup extra-virgin olive oil

½ teaspoon fine sea salt

⅛ teaspoon freshly ground black pepper

FOR THE SALAD

½ cup unsalted raw pecans or slivered almonds (see Pro Tips & Tricks)

1 large bunch of curly kale (about 1½ pounds)

2 apples (any crisp variety), cored, quartered, and thinly sliced

½ cup pomegranate seeds or dried cranberries

2 ounces soft goat cheese, crumbled (about ½ cup)

1. MAKE THE MAPLE-DIJON DRESSING: In a small bowl or resealable jar, combine the vinegar, maple syrup, Dijon, garlic, oil, salt, and pepper in that order. Whisk or cover the jar and shake well until emulsified and set aside for the flavors to meld. You may need to re-whisk or shake before dressing the salad as the dressing can separate as it sits.

2. MAKE THE SALAD: In a small dry skillet over medium heat, toast the pecans for 2 to 3 minutes, tossing frequently, until the nuts are golden and fragrant. Remove the pan from the heat and set aside to cool.

3. Strip the kale leaves from their stems and discard the stems. Rinse the leaves under cold running water and use a salad spinner or a clean kitchen towel to dry them well. On a cutting board, stack several leaves and finely chop them into thin strips. Repeat with the remaining kale leaves and add the chopped kale to a large bowl.

4. Drizzle the kale with three-quarters of the dressing. Use two forks to toss the kale for a few minutes, until it is slightly softened, evenly coated with dressing, and reduced by about a quarter in volume. Let the salad rest for 15 minutes.

5. Scatter the apple slices over the top of the salad, along with the pecans, pomegranate seeds, and goat cheese. Drizzle with the remaining quarter of the dressing, or to taste, and serve right away.

Pro Tips & Tricks

- If you are new to toasting nuts in a skillet, the most important thing is to not walk away from it. I've burned several batches when I got distracted trying to multitask. They toast quickly, so remove them from the heat as soon as they are fragrant and starting to turn golden.

Cabbage Avocado Salad

I came up with this recipe when I had to improvise for dinner one night. I hadn't gone grocery shopping in a few days, so I knew I had to use whatever was lying around in the veggie bin. I got the idea to pair crisp cabbage and cucumber with creamy avocado and bring everything together with fresh dill and a simple vinaigrette. It was such a success that now I reach for this recipe any time I need an easy yet very satisfying salad or if I happen to have extra cabbage in the fridge, especially after making a pot of Classic Ukrainian Borscht (page 122).

SERVES 6

½ medium head of green cabbage, cored and thinly sliced into 1- to 2-inch strips (see Pro Tips & Tricks)

½ English cucumber, cut into ¼-inch-thick half-moons

1 large avocado, pitted, peeled, and cut into small cubes

¼ cup chopped fresh chives

2 tablespoons chopped fresh dill

3 tablespoons extra-virgin olive oil

3 tablespoons freshly squeezed lemon juice

Fine sea salt and freshly ground black pepper

In a large bowl, add the cabbage, cucumber, avocado, chives, and dill and toss to combine. Drizzle in the oil and lemon juice and season with the salt and pepper to taste. Toss again to coat and once again taste for seasoning. Serve immediately.

Pro Tips & Tricks

- To slice a head of cabbage, start by removing and discarding any dry or browned outer leaves. Next, cut the cabbage in half from its stem to the top. Lay one half of the cabbage cut side down so you have a flat base. Then, using a mandolin or serrated knife, begin thinly slicing the cabbage around its edges, working your way in. Stop when you reach the thick white core, which you can discard—or eat! The core is sweet and delicious; we used to fight over it as kids after Mom trimmed it for us.

Strawberry Salad
with Honey Vinaigrette

One of the first things people notice about this salad is how stunningly Instagram-worthy it is. But as much as I love a pretty food pic, what matters most to me is how the dish *tastes*. And let me tell you, this one hits all the right notes with sweet, tangy, and savory bites that will have this salad on your summer menu all season long.

SERVES 6

FOR THE HONEY VINAIGRETTE

¼ cup extra-virgin olive oil

¼ cup red wine vinegar

2 tablespoons honey

2 teaspoons Dijon mustard

½ teaspoon fine sea salt, plus more to taste

¼ teaspoon freshly ground black pepper, plus more to taste

FOR THE STRAWBERRY SALAD

½ cup sliced almonds

5 ounces spring greens mix (about 5 cups)

8 ounces strawberries, hulled and sliced (about 2 cups)

½ cup crumbled feta cheese

¼ cup thinly sliced red onion

1. MAKE THE VINAIGRETTE: In a medium bowl or resealable jar, whisk or cover and shake together the oil, vinegar, honey, Dijon, salt, and pepper. Season with more salt and pepper, if needed.

2. MAKE THE SALAD: In a small dry skillet over medium heat, toast the almonds, tossing frequently, until they are golden and fragrant, 3 to 5 minutes. Set aside to cool.

3. In a large bowl, combine the spring greens, strawberries, feta, almonds, and onion. Just before serving, drizzle with the vinaigrette to taste (I usually use all of it) and toss to combine. Serve immediately.

California BLT Chopped Salad
with Creamy Ranch Dressing

I've given the iconic BLT a healthier makeover by taking the best parts of the sandwich (the bacon and tomato) and heaping them on top of fresh greens along with creamy avocado—which is what makes it a California style. Both the kids and adults in my house love having this as part of our side-salad rotation. Just be sure to not skip the homemade ranch—it only takes a couple of minutes and really elevates the salad.

SERVES 4 (OR 6 AS A SIDE)

FOR THE CREAMY RANCH DRESSING

4 tablespoons sour cream

3 tablespoons mayonnaise

2 tablespoons milk of any kind

¼ cup finely chopped fresh chives

1 garlic clove, pressed or grated

¼ teaspoon fine sea salt

⅛ teaspoon freshly ground black pepper

FOR THE SALAD

1 medium to large head of romaine lettuce, chopped, rinsed, and dried well (see Pro Tips & Tricks)

12 ounces bacon, cooked until crispy (see Pro Tips & Tricks)

1½ cups cherry or grape tomatoes, halved

1 large avocado, pitted, peeled, and sliced

1 cup store-bought croutons of your choice

¼ cup finely chopped fresh chives

1. MAKE THE DRESSING: In a small bowl, whisk together the sour cream, mayo, milk, chives, garlic, salt, and pepper. Set aside for the flavors to meld while you assemble the salad.

2. MAKE THE SALAD: Add the lettuce to a large bowl. Sprinkle with the bacon, tomatoes, avocado, croutons, and chives.

3. Just before serving, drizzle the salad with the dressing to taste. (I usually use all of it.) Toss until the lettuce is evenly coated and serve right away.

Pro Tips & Tricks

- The fastest way to prep a head of romaine lettuce is to first cut it in half lengthwise. Trim off the core end of the stem, slice the lettuce into strips lengthwise, then chop crosswise into bite-size pieces. Working in two batches, transfer the lettuce to a salad spinner to give it a quick wash and spin it completely dry. It's crucial to get the lettuce dry or you'll end up with a soggy salad.

- To cook a full 12-ounce package of bacon, my favorite (and least messy) method is in the oven. Preheat the oven to 400°F and line a rimmed baking sheet with parchment paper. Arrange the bacon in a single layer (the pieces can be touching, just not overlapping) and bake for 15 to 20 minutes for regular-cut bacon or 20 to 30 minutes for thick-cut bacon (or to your desired crispiness). Transfer the bacon to a paper towel–lined plate to drain.

Spring Greens Salad
with Goat Cheese, Cranberries, and Balsamic Vinaigrette

This is one of those very handy recipes that checks a lot of boxes: it's easy to whip up, calls for ingredients that are inexpensive and available year-round, and looks fancy and beautiful (even though, between you and me, it only takes fifteen minutes to make—including the homemade dressing). The creamy, tart, crunchy ingredients do all the hard work for you because of the way they complement one another, while the balsamic vinaigrette brings it all together and is so versatile that you'll love having it in your dressing playbook.

SERVES 6 AS A SIDE

FOR THE BALSAMIC VINAIGRETTE

⅓ cup extra-virgin olive oil

3 tablespoons balsamic vinegar

1 tablespoon Dijon mustard

1 garlic clove, pressed or grated

¼ teaspoon fine sea salt

⅛ teaspoon freshly ground black pepper

FOR THE SALAD

½ cup sliced or slivered almonds

5 ounces spring greens mix (see Pro Tips & Tricks)

2 cups cherry tomatoes, halved

1 cup dried cranberries

⅔ cup crumbled goat cheese

1. MAKE THE DRESSING: In a resealable jar, combine the oil, vinegar, Dijon, garlic, salt, and pepper. Cover and shake until the dressing has emulsified (see Pro Tips & Tricks).

2. MAKE THE SALAD: In a small skillet over medium heat, toast the almonds, tossing frequently, until they're golden and fragrant, 3 to 5 minutes. Set aside to cool.

3. Add the greens to a large shallow salad bowl. Sprinkle over the tomatoes, cranberries, nuts, and goat cheese.

4. Give the dressing a shake if it has separated, then drizzle it over the salad to taste. (I usually use all of it.) No need to toss the salad before serving; just scoop it up with tongs or salad servers.

Pro Tips & Tricks

- Some spring green mixes have cilantro in them, which is a nice addition to this salad. If yours doesn't, consider adding 2 tablespoons of chopped fresh cilantro for another layer of exciting flavor.

- **Make ahead:** The dressing can be refrigerated for up to 1 week; just bring it to room temperature before serving and give it a good shake when the olive oil re-liquifies.

Mexican Street Corn Salad

Esquites is a popular Mexican street food that combines smoky grilled corn with a creamy dressing and lots of cotija, a mild white cheese. Since I love just about anything with corn in the summer—not to mention creamy dressings and cheese—I wanted to put my spin on this dish and come up with a version that could be a light, refreshing side for any meal that can be served at room temperature or chilled.

SERVES 6 AS A SIDE

FOR THE CHARRED CORN

2 tablespoons extra-light olive oil

6 ears of corn, shucked, kernels removed (about 4½ cups; see Pro Tips & Tricks)

½ teaspoon fine sea salt

¼ teaspoon freshly ground black pepper

FOR THE DRESSING

¼ cup sour cream

¼ cup mayonnaise

2 tablespoons freshly squeezed lime juice

1 teaspoon finely minced garlic (1 to 2 cloves)

¼ teaspoon ground cayenne pepper

¼ teaspoon ground cumin

FOR THE SALAD

1 red bell pepper, stemmed, seeded, and finely diced (about 1 cup)

½ cup finely diced red onion

½ cup finely chopped fresh cilantro leaves, plus more for garnish

1 medium jalapeño, stemmed, seeded, and finely diced (optional)

½ cup crumbled cotija cheese, plus more for garnish

1. MAKE THE CORN: In a large nonstick skillet over medium-high heat, heat the oil. When the oil shimmers, evenly spread the corn over the bottom of the pan and season with the salt and pepper. Let the corn sit undisturbed to char for 2 minutes. Stir, then char for another 2 minutes. Continue stirring and cooking just like this for a total of 5 to 7 minutes, until the corn is tender and the starchy taste has cooked off. Transfer the corn to a large serving bowl and allow it to cool to room temperature while you assemble the rest of the salad.

2. MAKE THE DRESSING: In a small bowl, stir together the sour cream, mayo, lime juice, garlic, cayenne, and cumin. Set aside for the flavors to meld.

3. MAKE THE SALAD: To the bowl with the corn, add the bell pepper, onion, cilantro, and jalapeño (if using). Add the dressing to taste (I usually use most of it) and toss to mix well. Fold in the cotija and garnish with the cilantro and more cotija. Serve immediately or cover and refrigerate up to 1 day in advance.

Pro Tips & Tricks

- The silk strands from an ear of corn aren't appealing, so use a bristle brush to remove them from the kernels before cutting them off the cob.

- To cut the corn from the cob without making a mess, set a small bowl upside down inside a larger bowl. Place your corn vertically on top of the smaller bowl and run your knife straight down the sides of the cob (taking care not to hit the bowl with your knife). The kernels will fall right into the larger bowl.

- If you aren't able to find cotija cheese, you can substitute feta and add it to taste.

Orange, Blueberry, and Avocado Salad

My friend Sarah made this salad for a ladies' brunch one afternoon, and I knew I needed the recipe because it was an instant hit. The juicy oranges and bursts of blueberries were like sunshine on a plate, followed by the creamy richness of avocado and goat cheese. But what really puts it over the top are the sweet, crunchy bits of honey-roasted pecans—not to mention the ultimate compliment of Sarah using a dressing recipe from my website! Thank you, Sarah, for this new favorite!

SERVES 6

FOR THE MAPLE DRESSING

¼ cup extra-virgin olive oil

2 tablespoons apple cider vinegar

1 tablespoon real maple syrup

2 teaspoons Dijon mustard

1 small garlic clove, pressed or grated

¼ teaspoon fine sea salt

⅛ teaspoon freshly ground black pepper

FOR THE SALAD

5 ounces spring greens mix

2 navel oranges or 6 clementines, peeled, quartered, and sliced into bite-size pieces (see Pro Tips & Tricks)

1 cup blueberries

1 large avocado, pitted, peeled, and sliced

½ cup Honey-Roasted Pecans (page 69) or unsalted raw pecans, toasted (see Pro Tips & Tricks)

⅓ cup crumbled goat cheese

1. MAKE THE DRESSING: In a measuring cup or resealable jar, combine the oil, vinegar, maple syrup, Dijon, garlic, salt, and pepper. Whisk or cover the jar and shake well until blended. Set aside for the flavors to meld while you assemble the salad.

2. MAKE THE SALAD: In a large serving bowl, create a bed of the spring greens. Top with the oranges, blueberries, avocado, pecans, and goat cheese.

3. Just before serving, drizzle the dressing over the salad to taste (I use all of it), toss gently to combine, and serve.

Pro Tips & Tricks

- For an even more beautiful presentation, use a paring knife to remove as much of the white pith from the oranges as you can.

- If you don't want to make the Honey-Roasted Pecans, it's worth the effort to toast unsalted raw pecans for the flavor. In a small dry skillet over medium heat, toast the pecans, tossing frequently, until they're golden and fragrant, 3 to 5 minutes. Set aside to cool.

Steak Cobb Salad
with Herb Vinaigrette

I first came up with this salad as a solution for what to do with leftover steak. I had just enough to not want to waste it but not quite enough to make a whole meal. Enter lots of fresh greens and veggies, plus a vibrant, herbaceous dressing. The end result was so good that I regularly make steak just to toss it over this salad, although it would also be delicious with other proteins, like shrimp or chicken.

SERVES 4 (OR 6 AS A SIDE)

FOR THE STEAK

1 pound steak, such as New York strip, rib eye, or top sirloin

Fine sea salt and freshly ground black pepper

½ tablespoon extra-light olive oil (if pan-searing)

FOR THE HERB DRESSING

⅓ cup extra-virgin olive oil

3 tablespoons freshly squeezed lemon juice

2 tablespoons finely chopped fresh cilantro leaves

1 tablespoon finely chopped fresh dill

1 garlic clove, pressed or grated

¾ teaspoon fine sea salt

¼ teaspoon freshly ground black pepper

FOR THE SALAD

5 ounces spring greens mix

1 cup cherry or grape tomatoes, halved

1 cup cooked sweet corn (see Pro Tips & Tricks)

½ large English cucumber, sliced

1. MAKE THE STEAK: Remove the steaks from the refrigerator 20 to 30 minutes before grilling or pan-searing them.

2. If grilling: Preheat the grill to medium-high heat. Generously season the steaks with the salt and pepper. Place the steaks on the grill, cover, and reduce the heat to medium. Grill for 4 to 5 minutes, until the first side is browned and charred. Flip and grill for another 4 to 8 minutes, depending on your desired doneness—130°F to 135°F for medium-rare, 140°F to 145°F for medium, or 145°F to 150°F for medium-well. (Note: these are the temperatures for pulling the steaks off the grill; they will continue to cook as they rest.) Transfer the steaks to a cutting board and tent loosely with foil. Let them rest for 10 minutes before slicing them against the grain.

If pan-searing: Season the steaks with the salt and pepper. Heat the extra-light olive oil in a large skillet or cast-iron pan over medium-high heat. When the oil begins to smoke, add the steaks and sear for 4 minutes, until the first side is browned. Flip and cook for another 4 minutes, or until the steaks are cooked to your desired doneness. (See above for temperatures to look for on your instant-read thermometer.) Tent with foil and rest before slicing.

3. MAKE THE DRESSING: In a medium bowl, whisk together the extra-virgin olive oil, lemon juice, cilantro, dill, garlic, salt, and pepper. Set aside for the flavors to meld.

4. MAKE THE SALAD: Add the greens to a large mixing bowl. Top the greens with the steak, tomatoes, corn, cucumber, avocado, feta, and onion. You can either do this in neat rows like a classic cobb salad, or you can scatter them evenly.

5. Just before serving, drizzle with the dressing to taste. (I usually use all of it.) Toss gently to combine and enjoy.

1 large avocado, pitted, peeled, and sliced

⅓ cup crumbled feta, goat, or blue cheese

¼ cup thinly sliced red onion

Pro Tips & Tricks

- You have a number of options for preparing the corn: (1) add the corn kernels to salted boiling water and boil until tender, 2 to 3 minutes, (2) sauté the corn according to the directions on page 210, (3) use frozen corn and cook according to package instructions, or (4) use canned, drained corn.

5

SOUPS

Growing up, my mom made soups all the time. It was partially out of necessity—it was an efficient way to feed a large family, and it was inexpensive. But what I didn't realize until I was an adult—after years of complaining that I didn't want another bowl of borscht!—was that soups were also my mom's way of making us something comforting, nourishing, and delicious. I have so much more appreciation now for how she managed to turn a handful of humble ingredients into a deeply flavorful meal, which I've since used as inspiration when developing recipes for my site and for my own family. And, as it turns out, soup is still going strong in my dinner rotation—including, yes, Classic Ukrainian Borscht (page 122)! From creamy and satisfying Loaded Corn Chowder (page 116) to hearty Zuppa Toscana (page 110) to simple Roasted Tomato Soup with Baked Grilled-Cheese Sandwiches (page 118), we have soup almost every week because it's an easy meal to pull together, but it's also such a welcome moment to sit down to a bowl of Turkey Meatball Soup (page 112) or Homestyle Chicken Soup (page 115) after a long day. Plus, a pot of soup can last for two or three days as leftovers, and it only gets better with time!

Zuppa Toscana

When I was a teenager, one of my favorite hangouts was the Olive Garden. I loved their Zuppa Toscana, which was technically a soup, but with its spicy Italian sausage and hearty potatoes and kale, it seemed more like a complete meal. I knew I had to come up with my own version to make at home, and it turns out that it's just as good as the original (if not better). Add some buttered and toasted sourdough bread, plus plenty of grated cheese, and you can call it lunch or dinner.

SERVES 8

6 slices regular-cut bacon, chopped

1 pound bulk spicy Italian sausage (or links with casings removed; see Pro Tips & Tricks)

1 medium yellow onion, diced

Extra-light olive oil or vegetable oil, as needed

1 medium head of garlic (about 10 large cloves), peeled and minced

2 tablespoons all-purpose flour (optional; see Pro Tips & Tricks)

8 cups Homemade Chicken Bone Broth (page 126) or store-bought low-sodium chicken broth or stock

2 cups filtered water

5 medium Yukon gold or russet potatoes (about 1½ pounds), unpeeled and sliced into ¼-inch-thick pieces

1 bunch of curly kale, leaves stripped, rinsed, and chopped (6 to 7 cups; see Pro Tips & Tricks)

1 cup heavy cream

½ teaspoon fine sea salt, plus more to taste

¼ teaspoon freshly ground black pepper, plus more to taste

Freshly grated Parmesan cheese, for serving

1. In a 5½-quart Dutch oven or large heavy-bottomed pot over medium-high heat, add the bacon and cook for 5 to 7 minutes, stirring frequently, until browned and crisp. Transfer the bacon to a paper towel–lined plate.

2. Pour off all but about 2 tablespoons of the bacon fat from the pot and return the pot to medium-high heat. Add the sausage and cook, breaking it up with the back of a wooden spoon or spatula as you stir, for 6 to 8 minutes, until it has browned. Transfer the sausage to the paper towel–lined plate with the bacon and set aside.

3. Add the onions to the pot, reduce the heat to medium, and cook for 5 minutes, stirring frequently, until soft and golden. If the pan begins to look dry, add the oil as needed. Add the garlic and cook, stirring, until fragrant, about 1 minute. Sprinkle the flour (if using) over the onions and garlic and stir constantly for 1 minute. Stir in the broth and 2 cups water, and bring to a boil.

4. Add the potatoes and cook for 12 to 14 minutes, until the potatoes are just tender. Add the kale and the reserved sausage and bring the soup back up to a gentle boil. Stir in the cream, salt, and pepper, adding more if needed.

5. Remove the pot from the heat. Ladle the soup into bowls and top with the bacon and a sprinkling of Parmesan.

6. Store any leftovers in an airtight container in the refrigerator for up to 4 days.

Pro Tips & Tricks

- Using hot Italian sausage is the closest to the restaurant version and adds a pleasant spiciness to this soup, but if you want to make it more kid-friendly, use a mild Italian sausage.

- To make this gluten-free, simply omit the flour.

- To strip the kale leaves, hold the end of the stem with one hand. With the other hand, pinch just above where the leaves start and run your fingers firmly along the stem, pulling off the leaves as you go.

- Don't peel the potatoes! The skins add texture to the dish and make it feel even more rustic.

- Don't skimp on the garlic. It might look like a lot, but I promise the strong garlic flavor will mellow as the soup simmers, giving you an even richer-tasting broth.

Turkey Meatball Soup

With twelve grandkids between the ages of three and fourteen who all show up hungry after church on Sundays, Baba (my mom) regularly makes this soup because it's as soothing as it is delicious, and the adults are just as excited to smell it simmering on the stove when we walk in the door. I highly recommend making it a meal with Milk Bread Rolls (page 198) and our Salade Maison (page 86).

SERVES 10 TO 12

FOR THE MEATBALLS

1 pound ground turkey

1 large egg

1 teaspoon fine sea salt

1 teaspoon onion powder

¼ teaspoon freshly ground black pepper

¼ teaspoon garlic powder

FOR THE SOUP

2 tablespoons extra-virgin olive oil

2 celery stalks, diced

2 medium carrots, thinly sliced

1 medium yellow onion, diced

8 cups Homemade Chicken Bone Broth (page 126) or store-bought low-sodium chicken broth or stock

2 cups filtered water

6 medium Yukon gold potatoes, peeled, chopped into ¼-inch-thick pieces, and rinsed

1 tablespoon fine sea salt, plus more to taste

⅓ cup orzo (optional; see Pro Tips & Tricks)

1 large egg, lightly beaten

¼ cup finely chopped fresh dill or parsley leaves, plus more for serving (optional)

2 small garlic cloves, grated

Freshly ground black pepper

1. MAKE THE MEATBALLS: In a large bowl, combine the turkey, egg, salt, onion powder, pepper, and garlic powder and mix well. Working with ½- to 1-tablespoon portions, wet your hands and roll each portion into a ball. Transfer the rolled meatballs to a rimmed baking sheet. If the meatballs start to stick to your hands, rinse them again, and continue with clean, wet hands. Set the meatballs aside.

2. MAKE THE SOUP: Heat the oil in a 5- to 7-quart Dutch oven or large soup pot over medium heat. Add the celery, carrots, and onion and cook, stirring occasionally, for 7 minutes, until the vegetables are softened and golden. Add the broth, 2 cups water, the potatoes, and salt. Bring the soup to a boil over high heat and add the orzo (if using). Reduce the heat to medium-low and simmer, uncovered, for about 10 minutes, until the potatoes can be pierced easily with a fork.

3. Carefully add the meatballs to the pot and continue to simmer for 5 minutes, until the meatballs are cooked through. Stir in the egg, followed by the dill and garlic. Simmer just until the egg is cooked, 2 to 3 minutes. Remove the pot from the heat and season with salt and pepper. Sprinkle with more dill (if using) and serve immediately.

4. Store any leftovers in an airtight container in the refrigerator for up to 4 days.

Pro Tips & Tricks

- You can also use ground chicken, pork, or beef for the meatballs. I've tested them all for variety because I make this soup ALL THE TIME.

- You can make this recipe gluten-free by leaving out the orzo or substituting it with jasmine rice. Just note that rice takes longer to cook, so add it with the broth and boil for 5 minutes before adding the potatoes.

- Rinse the potatoes after slicing them to keep them from discoloring and to remove excess starch.

- Stirring a beaten egg into soup is common in Ukrainian cooking. The ribbons of egg essentially poach in the broth and soak up all that flavor, while also adding heartiness and richness to your soup.

Homestyle Chicken Soup

This recipe is what I reach for when I want something comforting and satisfying. It reminds me of a version my mom used to make for us with alphabet-shaped pasta or stelline (star-shaped) pasta, which my sisters and I loved, especially on a chilly afternoon. It's flavorful and hearty, and yet this soup only takes 45 minutes to make. The secret to developing all that flavor is using Homemade Chicken Bone Broth (page 126), although store-bought is OK, too.

SERVES 8

8 cups Homemade Chicken Bone Broth (page 126) or store-bought low-sodium chicken broth or stock

5 cups filtered water

2 skinless, bone-in chicken legs or 2 skinless, bone-in chicken breasts (if you prefer white meat)

2½ teaspoons fine sea salt, plus more to taste

½ teaspoon freshly ground black pepper, plus more to taste

2 dried bay leaves

3 tablespoons extra-light olive oil or vegetable oil

1 medium yellow onion, finely chopped

2 celery stalks, finely chopped

2 medium carrots, sliced into ⅛-inch-thick coins

¾ cup dry ditalini pasta (see Pro Tips & Tricks)

2 tablespoons chopped fresh parsley leaves

2 tablespoons chopped fresh dill

1 large garlic clove, pressed or grated

1. In a 5½-quart Dutch oven or large soup pot over medium-high heat, combine the broth, 5 cups water, the chicken, salt, pepper, and bay leaves. Bring to a boil, reduce the heat to medium-low, and partially cover. Simmer for 25 minutes, skimming off any foam that rises to the surface, until the chicken is just cooked through. (An instant-read thermometer inserted in the center should register 165°F for chicken thigh meat or 155°F for chicken breast meat.)

2. While the soup simmers, heat the oil in a large skillet over medium heat. Add the onion, celery, and carrots and cook for 6 to 8 minutes, until the onions are softened and beginning to turn golden. Transfer the vegetables to the soup pot.

3. When the chicken is cooked, transfer it to a plate and let cool slightly. When it's cool enough to handle, shred the meat into bite-size pieces and discard the bones and fat.

4. Add the pasta to the pot and cook for 5 minutes, until softened but not fully cooked through. Return the shredded chicken to the pot and continue cooking for another 5 minutes, or until the pasta is fully cooked.

5. Stir in the parsley, dill, and garlic and remove the pot from the heat. Season the soup with more salt and pepper if needed, discard the bay leaves, and serve.

6. Store any leftovers in an airtight container in the refrigerator for up to 4 days.

Pro Tips & Tricks

- I love the texture and look of ditalini pasta, but you can use a different small pasta, such as orzo or fideo cut spaghetti.

- Don't be tempted to add more pasta than is called for in the recipe. Pasta continues to absorb liquid as it stands, so the soup will get too thick if you overdo it.

Loaded Corn Chowder

I created this recipe as a way to take advantage of that supersweet summer corn—including the cob. Most people toss the cob once the kernels have been removed, but it's actually the secret to infusing a creamy stock with rich corn flavor. Add tender potatoes and crispy bacon, and you've got a soup that everyone will start requesting the minute the weather gets warmer.

SERVES 6 TO 8

FOR THE CORN STOCK

5 fresh corn cobs, kernels removed and reserved for the chowder (see Pro Tips & Tricks below and on page 102)

4 cups Homemade Chicken Bone Broth (page 126) or store-bought low-sodium chicken broth or stock

1½ cups milk of any kind

1 cup heavy cream

FOR THE CHOWDER

4 slices regular-cut bacon, chopped

3 celery stalks, finely diced

1 large yellow onion, finely diced

1 large carrot, finely diced

4 cups fresh corn kernels (from the 5 corn cobs for the stock)

3 medium Yukon gold potatoes (about 1 pound), peeled and finely diced

2 teaspoons fine sea salt, plus more to taste

¼ teaspoon freshly ground black pepper

¼ teaspoon ground cayenne pepper, plus more to taste

2 tablespoons chopped fresh chives, for garnish

1. MAKE THE CORN STOCK: In a large stockpot over medium-high heat, combine the stripped corn cobs, broth, milk, and cream. Bring to a boil, then reduce the heat to medium-low and simmer, uncovered, for 20 minutes. Remove the pot from the heat and discard the corn cobs.

2. MAKE THE CHOWDER: In a 5- to 7-quart Dutch oven or large pot over medium-high heat, add the bacon and cook, stirring occasionally, for 5 to 7 minutes, until browned. Using a slotted spoon, transfer the bacon bits to a paper towel–lined plate and set aside, reserving the bacon fat in the pot.

3. In the same pot, over medium-high heat, add the celery, onion, and carrot and cook, stirring occasionally, for 7 to 8 minutes, until the onion is soft. Add the corn, potatoes, salt, pepper, and cayenne. Pour in the prepared corn stock and bring the mixture to a gentle boil. Reduce the heat to low and simmer, uncovered, for 10 to 15 minutes, until the potatoes are tender. Taste and adjust the seasoning as needed.

4. Ladle the chowder into bowls and garnish with the reserved bacon and the chives.

5. Store any leftovers in an airtight container in the refrigerator for up to 4 days.

Pro Tips & Tricks

- In order to not end up with any stringy bits in your chowder, it's crucial that you remove all the thread-like silk from the corn before slicing off the kernels. The easiest way to do this is to brush the corn with a firm-bristled brush or even a clean toothbrush. The bristles will catch the silk and it will come off easily.

Roasted Tomato Soup
with Baked Grilled-Cheese Sandwiches

The beauty of this recipe, which involves roasting the tomatoes before blending them into a silky, cozy soup, is that you can either take advantage of all the in-season tomatoes during the summer or you can use more lackluster store-bought tomatoes any time of year. Either way you're going to get the richest, deepest, most naturally sweet tomato flavor out of your ingredients. My kids give me two thumbs-up whenever I make this, especially when I serve my gooey baked grilled-cheese sandwiches on the side.

SERVES 4 TO 6

3 pounds ripe tomatoes (see Pro Tips & Tricks), halved lengthwise if small or medium, or quartered if large

1 large yellow onion, quartered and separated into smaller pieces

8 garlic cloves, peeled and ends trimmed

3 tablespoons extra-virgin olive oil

2 teaspoons fine sea salt, plus more to taste

¼ teaspoon freshly ground black pepper, plus more to taste

2 cups Homemade Chicken Bone Broth (page 126) or store-bought low-sodium chicken stock or broth

4 tablespoons chopped fresh basil, plus more for serving

½ cup heavy cream, plus more to taste

½ cup freshly grated Parmesan cheese, plus more for serving

2 tablespoons tomato paste

2 teaspoons sugar, plus more to taste

Baked Grilled-Cheese Sandwiches, for serving (recipe follows)

1. Preheat the oven to 400°F.

2. On a rimmed baking sheet, arrange the tomatoes, cut side up, with the onions and garlic in a single layer. Drizzle with the oil and sprinkle with ½ teaspoon of the salt and the pepper. Roast for 45 to 50 minutes, until the edges of the tomatoes and onions begin to brown. Set aside to cool for 10 minutes. (This is when I like to get started on the grilled-cheese sandwiches.)

3. In a food processor or blender, add half of the tomato mixture. Add 1 cup of the broth and 2 tablespoons of the basil and blend until smooth. Transfer the mixture to a large soup pot or Dutch oven and set aside.

4. Add the remaining tomato mixture, plus any juices that have accumulated in the pan, to the food processor, along with the remaining 1 cup of broth and 2 tablespoons basil. Blend until smooth and transfer to the pot.

5. Over medium heat, bring the soup to a simmer. Stir in the cream, Parmesan, tomato paste, sugar, and remaining 1½ teaspoons of salt. Continue stirring so the cheese melts evenly into the soup. Taste and season as needed with more cream, sugar, salt, or pepper. (See Pro Tips & Tricks.)

6. Ladle the soup into bowls and garnish with more basil and Parmesan. Pair with Baked Grilled-Cheese Sandwiches for dunking.

7. Store any leftovers in an airtight container in the refrigerator for up to 5 days or in the freezer for up to 3 months.

Pro Tips & Tricks

- You may need to adjust some of your seasonings according to the flavor of your tomatoes. Out-of-season tomatoes may be more acidic, so add more sugar or cream if your soup has a sharp, acidic taste.

Baked Grilled-Cheese Sandwiches

The first time I discovered that you could make grilled cheese sandwiches in the oven instead of babysitting them on the stove, I knew it would be a game changer. It meant that I could effortlessly whip up a big batch to serve alongside a pot of my Roasted Tomato Soup, which is one of my favorite meals to make for my family and to serve when we have guests. It's a satisfyingly complete meal that gives everyone the warm fuzzies.

MAKES 4 SANDWICHES

3 tablespoons unsalted butter, softened

8 slices of your favorite sandwich bread

8 thick slices medium cheddar cheese

4 slices mozzarella cheese

Pro Tips & Tricks

- This recipe is very easy to scale up or down, depending on how many (or how few) people you are feeding.

1. If your oven is not already preheated after roasting the tomatoes, preheat the oven to 400°F.

2. Spread the softened butter over one side of 4 slices of the bread (about 1 teaspoon of butter per slice) and place them butter side down on a rimmed baking sheet.

3. Top each slice of bread with a slice of cheddar, a slice of mozzarella, and another slice of cheddar. Spread the remaining butter over the remaining 4 slices of bread and place the slices on top of the cheese, butter side up.

4. Bake for 10 minutes, flipping about halfway through, until both sides are golden brown.

Country Club French Onion Soup

I started working for my late boss (and friend) Pearl when I was just fourteen years old. I started as an intern at her antiques company, and during the seven years I spent there, she gave me a better education than I ever got in business school. (But that's another story!) She took me under her wing and was always spoiling me by taking me out to eat at her country club, where I fell in love with French onion soup. After that, whenever I would see French onion soup on a menu, I would always order it—but it was never as good. My obsession led me to re-create one I could finally fall in love with again, and every time I make it, I remember my time with Pearl.

SERVES 6

FOR THE SOUP

2 tablespoons extra-virgin olive oil

2 tablespoons (¼ stick) unsalted butter

6 large yellow onions (about 3 pounds), halved and thinly sliced with the grain

½ teaspoon sugar

2 garlic cloves, minced

½ cup dry sherry wine (dry vermouth or dry white wine will work, too)

8 cups beef stock or broth

3 sprigs of fresh thyme, plus more for garnish, or ¼ teaspoon dried

1 dried bay leaf

1 teaspoon fine sea salt, plus more to taste

½ teaspoon freshly ground black pepper

FOR THE CHEESY CROUTON TOPPING

12 (½-inch-thick) slices of baguette

Extra-virgin olive oil, for brushing the toasts

1½ cups shredded Gruyère cheese (8 ounces)

1. MAKE THE SOUP: In a 5½-quart Dutch oven or large heavy-bottomed pot over medium heat, combine the oil and butter. When the butter foams, add the onions and sauté, uncovered, stirring occasionally, for 10 minutes.

2. Sprinkle the onions with the sugar, which will help them caramelize more quickly. Continue cooking, uncovered, for 30 to 40 minutes, stirring occasionally, until the onions are caramelized and browned. Stir more frequently toward the end to prevent scorching or burning the onions.

3. WHILE THE ONIONS COOK, START THE CHEESY CROUTON TOPPING: Preheat the oven to 400°F.

4. Lightly brush both sides of each slice of bread with the oil. Arrange them in a single layer on a rimmed baking sheet and bake for 6 to 8 minutes, until golden brown at the edges. Set aside.

5. When the onions are done caramelizing, add the garlic to the pan and cook, stirring constantly, for 1 minute. Pour in the sherry and deglaze the pan by using a wooden spoon to scrape up the brown bits from the bottom of the pan. Continue stirring until all of the sherry has cooked out, about 3 minutes. Stir in the stock, thyme, bay leaf, salt, and the pepper. Stir to combine. Add more salt, if needed, and remove from the heat. Remove the bay leaf and thyme stems and discard.

6. When ready to serve, preheat the broiler on high. Divide ¾ cup of the Gruyère among the toasts and broil for 2 to 3 minutes, until the cheese melts and turns golden in spots.

7. Ladle the soup into bowls. Divide the remaining ¾ cup of Gruyère between the bowls, top with the hot cheesy toasts and a sprinkle of fresh thyme leaves and serve.

Pro Tips & Tricks

- This soup keeps well in the refrigerator for 3 to 4 days, whether you make it ahead and make the cheesy croutons just before serving or store it as leftovers. You could also freeze the soup without the croutons for up to 3 months.

Classic Ukrainian Borscht

Growing up in a Ukrainian family is pretty much a guarantee that you'll enjoy many, many bowls of borscht. It's an iconic Ukrainian dish, and there are as many versions out there as there are families. But what they each have in common is that every pot is a labor of love. My mom's recipe has evolved over the years to include ingredients and shortcuts better suited for an American kitchen—namely ketchup. Once she discovered this condiment here, she knew that its magical combination of acidic, tangy sweetness would be the perfect addition and save the step of cooking down tomatoes to get the same effect. When I was a kid, I didn't appreciate borscht (and *may* have complained about it on occasion), but now I crave its rich, earthy flavor.

SERVES 8 TO 10

11 cups filtered water

4 cups Homemade Chicken Bone Broth (page 126) or store-bought low-sodium chicken broth or stock

1½ pounds baby back pork ribs (pork riblets will also work)

2 teaspoons fine sea salt, plus more to taste

4 tablespoons extra-light olive oil, divided

3 medium-large beets (1 pound), peeled and coarsely grated (see Pro Tips & Tricks)

2 medium carrots, grated

3 medium potatoes, peeled and chopped into ¼-inch-thick pieces (I like Yukon gold)

1 large yellow onion, diced

2 celery stalks, chopped

¼ cup ketchup

½ small head of green cabbage, cored and shredded or sliced thinly (4 to 5 cups)

Freshly ground black pepper to taste

1 dried bay leaf (optional)

¼ cup finely chopped fresh dill, plus more for garnish

1. In a large soup pot (at least 5½ quarts), combine 11 cups of water, the broth, ribs, and salt. Bring to a boil over medium-high heat, then reduce to a simmer. Cook, uncovered, while you prepare the other components of the soup, skimming off and discarding any foam that rises to the top as soon as you see it form and making sure to avoid a rapid boil. This will help keep your broth from looking murky.

2. Meanwhile, heat 2 tablespoons of the oil in a large skillet over medium heat. Add the beets and carrots and cook for 10 minutes, stirring frequently, until softened. (Sautéing the beets enhances the flavor and color of the soup.) Add the beets and carrots to the pot and cook at a low boil for an additional 20 minutes.

3. Add the potatoes and cook at a low boil for 10 minutes. Meanwhile, heat the remaining 2 tablespoons of oil over medium heat in the same skillet you used for the beets. (No need to wash it!) Add the onion and celery and cook for 8 to 10 minutes, until softened and golden. Stir in the ketchup and cook for another minute then transfer to the pot.

4. Using tongs, transfer the ribs to a large bowl. Once cool enough to handle, separate the meat from the bones and use forks to break up the meat into bite-size pieces. Discard the bones and return the meat to the pot. Add the cabbage, bring the soup to a low boil over medium heat, and cook for 5 minutes. During the last minute of cooking, season with more salt, if needed, and the pepper. Stir in the bay leaf (if using), dill, and garlic. If you want more acidity (it will depend on the sweetness of your beets), add the vinegar to taste, beginning with 1 teaspoon.

5. Remove the bay leaf and discard. Ladle the soup into bowls and serve with a dollop of sour cream and more dill.

6. Cover and refrigerate leftovers for up to 4 days or freeze for up to 3 months.

1 large garlic clove, pressed or grated

1 teaspoon white vinegar, plus more to taste

Sour cream or mayonnaise, for serving

Pro Tips & Tricks

- The fastest way to grate beets is on the large-hole grater attachment on a food processor. You can also use the large holes on your box grater, or use a mandoline or a julienne slicer to cut them into matchstick slices.

- Wear disposable gloves and an apron, and exercise caution when handling beets because their juice will stain your hands, your clothes, and your countertops if you aren't careful.

- I like to do all my chopping and other prep while the broth simmers with the ribs; it makes the cooking process much more relaxed and efficient. If you're prepping while other ingredients are cooking, a pot of borscht should take 65 to 70 minutes from start to finish.

Chicken Tortilla Soup

This recipe combines all the flavors of chili and tacos that you love, wrapped up in a cozy bowl of soup. It's definitely a dish that holds its own as the main event of a meal, especially if you include everyone's favorite toppings—don't skip that part! And while it's very simple to prepare, you can make it even easier by using leftover roasted chicken (page 168).

SERVES 8

2 tablespoons extra-light olive oil or vegetable oil

1 large yellow onion, chopped

2 medium jalapeños, stemmed, seeded, and finely chopped (see Pro Tips & Tricks)

4 garlic cloves, minced

4 cups Homemade Chicken Bone Broth (page 126) or store-bought low-sodium chicken broth or stock

1 (28-ounce) can crushed tomatoes

2 medium boneless, skinless chicken breasts (about 1 pound; see Pro Tips & Tricks)

1 (15-ounce) can black beans, rinsed and drained

1 (15-ounce) can whole kernel corn, rinsed and drained

1½ teaspoons ground cumin

1½ teaspoons chili powder

1 teaspoon fine sea salt, plus more to taste

¼ teaspoon freshly ground black pepper, plus more to taste

⅓ cup fresh cilantro leaves, chopped, plus more for garnish

1½ tablespoons freshly squeezed lime juice (from 1 lime), or to taste

1. In a 5½-quart Dutch oven or soup pot, heat the oil over medium-high heat. When the oil shimmers, add the onion and jalapeño and sauté for 5 minutes, stirring occasionally, until softened and the onion is slightly golden. Add the garlic and cook for 1 minute, until fragrant.

2. Stir in the broth, tomatoes, chicken, beans, corn, cumin, chili powder, salt, and pepper. Bring the mixture to a boil then reduce the heat to a simmer. Cook, uncovered and stirring occasionally to prevent scorching, for about 20 minutes, until the chicken is just cooked through and easy to shred.

3. Use tongs to transfer the chicken to a large bowl. Use forks or a stand mixer to shred the meat. (See Pro Tips & Tricks.) Add the shredded chicken back to the pot and continue simmering for 5 minutes. Remove the pot from the heat.

4. Stir in the cilantro and lime juice. (I usually use the full 1½ tablespoons, but if your tomato broth is on the acidic side, you may want to add less.) Season with more salt and pepper, if needed.

5. Ladle the soup into soup bowls and serve with the cheese, avocado, tortilla strips, sour cream (if using), and more cilantro. If adding cheese, sprinkle it on the soup first so it melts, and finish with the sour cream and cilantro so they stay cool and fresh tasting.

6. To freeze this soup, let it cool completely—without adding the toppings—and store in an airtight container in the freezer for up to 3 months.

FOR SERVING (OPTIONAL)

Shredded Mexican cheese

Diced avocado

Tortilla strips or crushed
tortilla chips

Sour cream

Pro Tips & Tricks

- When handling spicy jalapeño peppers, you may want to wear disposable gloves.

- If using leftover cooked chicken or rotisserie chicken, use 3 cups of shredded chicken in place of the chicken breasts. Add the shredded chicken to the soup after it has simmered for 20 minutes.

- To easily shred the chicken, transfer the hot chicken breasts to the bowl of a stand mixer fitted with the paddle attachment. Use a fork to break the breasts into quarters, then mix on low speed to shred the chicken.

Homemade Chicken Bone Broth

Ever since I learned about how good bone broth is for gut health, I pretty much always have a batch in my fridge or freezer. I'll either ladle it into a mug with a sprinkle of salt and pepper and drink it like tea, or I'll use this rich, flavorful broth any time I need it for a recipe. Whether you make it on the stovetop or in a slow cooker or instant pot, it's an almost entirely hands-off recipe, which means it's beyond simple to make a big potful to keep on hand for whenever the need, or appetite, arises. It will make all your dishes taste that much better and leave your belly feeling oh so good.

MAKES 8 TO 12 CUPS

2½ pounds chicken bones (from 2 roasted or rotisserie chickens)

10 to 16 cups water, amount and temperature dependent on the cooking method used

1 tablespoon apple cider vinegar

1 teaspoon fine sea salt

1 medium yellow onion, halved

2 celery stalks, leaves attached, cut into thirds

2 medium carrots, halved

2 garlic cloves, smashed and peeled

1 dried bay leaf (optional, but nice)

STOVETOP METHOD: This method is best if you have a huge stockpot and will be home to keep an eye on the broth as it cooks.

1. In an 8-quart stockpot, add the bones, 16 cups of water, the vinegar, and salt. Bring to a boil over medium-high heat, then reduce to a simmer. Use a ladle or spoon to skim off any foam or impurities that rise to the top and discard. Cover the pot and cook for 6 hours.

2. Add the onion, celery, carrots, garlic, and bay leaf (if using). Continue simmering, covered, for 9 hours (for a total of 15 hours). Be sure not to let the broth come to a hard boil or your broth will look foggy. If needed, you can pause the cooking overnight, leaving the broth covered on the stove, and continue the following day.

3. Strain the broth through a fine-mesh sieve into a second pot, extracting as much liquid as possible from the cooked vegetables. Discard the solids. Let the broth cool to room temperature. Transfer it to an airtight container and store in the refrigerator for up to 5 days or freeze for up to 3 months. (Be sure to leave room in the container for expansion.)

SLOW-COOKER METHOD: This is the set-it-and-forget-it method that can simmer away while you sleep. I also like this method because the broth is richer in color and flavor since it's never stirred or vigorously boiled.

1. In a 6-quart slow cooker, add the bones, 12 cups of warm to hot water, the vinegar, and salt. Set the heat to low and cook for 6 hours.

2. Add the onion, celery, carrots, garlic, and bay leaf (if using). Continue cooking on low for another 9 hours (for a total of 15 hours). If needed, you can let it go longer overnight.

3. See the **Stovetop Method** for straining and storage recommendations.

INSTANT-POT METHOD: This method is not only incredibly easy—it's so fast, which is why it's the one I use most often.

1. In a 6-quart instant pot, add the bones, vinegar, salt, onion, celery, carrots, garlic, and bay leaf (if using). Add enough water (10 to 11 cups) to cover the contents, but do not exceed the max fill line.

2. Cook on high pressure for 2 hours. Allow the instant pot to depressurize on its own for 30 minutes, then release the pressure. (I always use an oven mitt to protect my hand in case the valve sputters.)

3. See the **Stovetop Method** for straining and storage recommendations.

Pro Tips & Tricks

• Bone broth is best when it is cooked until you can easily break a chicken bone in half with your hands. This means the amazing nutrients from the marrow are in your broth. You also know if you cooked it long enough when it thickens after refrigeration—which is totally normal. The broth turns to liquid again when it is heated.

6

PASTA AND GRAINS

I have always been the biggest pasta and grains lover in my family. There's something so warming and satisfying about these dishes, mainly because they remind me of my childhood in Ukraine. From my grandmother's jumbo-size Potato Pierogi (page 145)—you can't spend hours making a zillion tiny ones when you're trying to feed twelve children!—to Pelmeni (page 141) stuffed with chicken and beef, you could taste the care put into every little doughy packet. As an adult, I still find so much comfort in a steaming bowl of Baked Mac and Cheese (page 154) or Creamy Chicken and Rice (page 148). I'm frequently serving these dishes for dinner because they're so easy and versatile, and when we do go out to eat, I can never resist ordering a pasta dish off the menu—then re-creating it at home (like my Shrimp Scampi Alfredo, page 131). So, you can imagine how happy it makes me that my son, David, now shares my love of pasta and has his own signature dish, which you'll have to check out on page 152!

Shrimp Scampi Alfredo

Shrimp was one of those foods that I couldn't get enough of growing up—literally, because my mom was allergic. But my dad and I were obsessed, which is why we now look for any opportunity to eat it. Every year for his birthday, I make him a big batch of shrimp that he (and I) can feast on. One year, I re-created this creamy shrimp pasta after trying it at a restaurant because I loved the idea of combining the flavors of shrimp scampi and classic Alfredo sauce. My kids were licking their plates clean; meanwhile, I took the more sophisticated route of soaking up every drop with a piece of crusty bread.

SERVES 6

1 (12-ounce) package of spaghetti or fettuccine

½ cup reserved pasta water

1 pound large (21/25) raw shrimp, peeled and deveined

½ teaspoon fine sea salt, plus more to taste

¼ teaspoon freshly ground black pepper, plus more to taste

¼ teaspoon paprika, plus more to taste

1 tablespoon extra-virgin olive oil

2 tablespoons (¼ stick) unsalted butter

1 teaspoon onion powder

½ cup dry white wine, such as sauvignon blanc (see Pro Tips & Tricks)

2 garlic cloves, minced

2 cups heavy cream

⅛ teaspoon crushed red pepper flakes (optional)

⅓ cup shredded Parmesan cheese, plus more for serving

3 tablespoons finely chopped fresh parsley leaves, plus more for serving

1. Bring a large pot of well-salted water to a boil over high heat. Add the pasta and cook according to the package instructions until al dente. Reserve ½ cup of the pasta cooking water and then drain the pasta, but do not rinse.

2. While the pasta cooks, season the shrimp with the salt, pepper, and paprika. In a large nonreactive skillet, heat the oil over medium-high heat. Add the shrimp in a single layer and cook for 1 to 2 minutes per side, until opaque and just cooked through. Use a slotted spoon or tongs to transfer the shrimp to a plate.

3. In the same pan over medium heat, melt the butter. Add the onion powder and whisk for 30 seconds. Add the wine, using a whisk to scrape up any browned bits from the bottom of the pan. Let the wine reduce until only about a quarter of the liquid remains, 2 to 3 minutes. Add the garlic and cook for another minute, until fragrant.

4. Whisk in the cream and the red pepper flakes (if using). While continuing to whisk, bring the cream to a gentle simmer and reduce the heat to low. Cook for 2 minutes, until the sauce thickens slightly. Sprinkle the Parmesan over the sauce and whisk to combine. Remove the pan from the heat, stir in the parsley, and season with more salt, pepper, and paprika, if needed. If the sauce looks too thick, add the reserved pasta water 1 tablespoon at a time until you've achieved the desired consistency. Return the shrimp to the pan, add the pasta, and toss to combine.

5. Top with more parsley and Parmesan and serve.

Pro Tips & Tricks

- White wine adds depth of flavor to this sauce, but don't worry—most of the alcohol cooks out! Use a bottle that you'd drink but that isn't too expensive.

Creamy Pesto Pasta

Some things are meant to be refreshingly simple, and pesto pasta is one of them. Pesto is one of the easiest sauces to make, and when you blend in a little bit of pasta cooking water, it magically transforms into a creamy, luxurious sauce with vibrant lemon and basil flavor. You could serve this as a vegetarian main dish or a side or toss in some cooked chopped chicken or shrimp for protein.

SERVES 4 (OR 6 AS A SIDE)

FOR THE PESTO

½ cup pine nuts (or walnuts or peeled almonds)

2 cups tightly packed fresh basil leaves

¾ cup shredded Parmesan cheese

½ cup extra-virgin olive oil

2 garlic cloves, roughly chopped

¼ cup freshly squeezed lemon juice (from 1 large or 2 small lemons)

½ teaspoon fine sea salt

¼ teaspoon freshly ground black pepper

FOR THE PASTA

1 tablespoon fine sea salt

16 ounces fusilli pasta (or your favorite pasta)

½ cup reserved pasta water

1½ cups cherry tomatoes, halved (optional)

¼ cup pine nuts (optional)

Freshly grated Parmesan cheese, for serving

1. MAKE THE PESTO: In a small dry skillet over medium heat, toast the pine nuts, tossing frequently, until they are golden and fragrant, 3 to 5 minutes.

2. In the bowl of a food processor fitted with the blade attachment, add the basil, Parmesan, oil, nuts, garlic, lemon juice, salt, and pepper—in that order. Blend on high for 2 to 3 minutes, until the mixture is finely minced and mostly smooth, stopping to scrape down the bowl with a spatula as needed. Set aside.

3. MAKE THE PASTA: Bring a large pot of water to a boil over high heat. Add the salt and pasta and cook according to the package instructions, until al dente. Reserve ½ cup of the pasta cooking water and then drain the pasta.

4. Transfer the pasta to a large bowl. Starting with about ½ cup, spoon the pesto over the pasta. Drizzle in about ¼ cup of the reserved pasta water, or enough to make the sauce smooth and creamy. Stir to combine, adding more pesto, if desired. Store any leftover pesto in an airtight container in the refrigerator for up to 5 days.

5. Sprinkle the pasta with the tomatoes and nuts (if using), plus more Parmesan cheese. Serve immediately.

Pro Tips & Tricks

- This pesto recipe makes slightly more than you'll need for the pasta, which is a major bonus because you can keep it in the fridge for up to 5 days and scoop it onto steaks or chicken or spread it on sandwiches.

The Most Amazing Lasagna (page 136)

The Most Amazing Lasagna

I couldn't think of another name for this dish that would do it justice; it's truly the only lasagna recipe you'll need. Between the three-cheese sauce and Italian-sausage meat sauce, it's sure to become a most-requested staple in your dinner rotation the way it is in ours. Add in the fact that I can prep this a day ahead or earlier in the day and bake it off when we're ready to eat (perfect for weeknights or after-church Sunday lunch), and I can honestly say that everybody wins.

SERVES 8 TO 10

FOR THE MEAT SAUCE AND LASAGNA NOODLES

1 tablespoon extra-light olive oil or vegetable oil, plus more for greasing

1 pound (80/20 or 85/15) ground beef

½ pound bulk sweet Italian sausage (or links with casings removed)

1 medium yellow onion, chopped

3 garlic cloves, minced

1 (28-ounce) can crushed tomatoes

1 (14-ounce) can whole peeled tomatoes, with their juice

¼ cup chopped fresh parsley leaves, plus more for garnish

1 teaspoon dried oregano leaves

2 tablespoons plus 1 teaspoon fine sea salt, divided, plus more to taste

½ teaspoon freshly ground black pepper

Pinch of granulated sugar

10 dry lasagna noodles (see Pro Tips & Tricks)

1. MAKE THE MEAT SAUCE: Heat the oil in a 5½-quart Dutch oven or large deep skillet over medium-high heat. Add the beef and sausage and cook, breaking up the meat with the back of a wooden spoon or spatula, for about 5 minutes, until it is just cooked through and has rendered all its fat. Drain off all but about 2 tablespoons of the fat. Add the onion to the skillet and cook, stirring, for about 5 minutes, until softened. Add the garlic and cook for just another minute, stirring frequently, until fragrant.

2. Stir in the crushed tomatoes, whole peeled tomatoes with their juice, parsley, oregano, 1 teaspoon of the salt, and the pepper, pressing on the whole tomatoes with a wooden spoon or spatula to break them up. Reduce the heat to low, cover, and simmer for 25 minutes, stirring occasionally. Season with the salt, pepper, and sugar, if needed. Remove the pot from the heat and cover to keep the sauce warm.

3. WHILE THE MEAT SAUCE IS SIMMERING, COOK THE LASAGNA NOODLES: Grease two rimmed baking sheets with oil and set aside. Fill a large pot with water and add the remaining 2 tablespoons of salt. Bring to a boil over high heat. Add the lasagna noodles and stir continuously for the first 2 minutes to keep them from sticking together. Cook the noodles according to the package instructions, until they are al dente. Drain the noodles and immediately arrange them in a single layer on the prepared baking sheets.

4. WHILE THE PASTA IS COOKING, MAKE THE CHEESE SAUCE: In a large bowl, add the ricotta, mozzarella, Parmesan, cream, egg, parsley, and salt and stir well until the mixture is smooth. Set aside.

5. ASSEMBLE THE LASAGNA: Preheat the oven to 375°F.

15 ounces part-skim ricotta cheese

1 cup shredded mozzarella cheese

1 cup shredded Parmesan cheese

⅓ cup heavy cream

1 large egg

2 tablespoons chopped fresh parsley leaves

½ teaspoon fine sea salt

TO ASSEMBLE

3 cups shredded mozzarella cheese, divided

6. In the bottom of a 9 × 13-inch casserole dish, spread ½ cup of the meat sauce. Arrange 3 noodles side by side and spread about a third of the remaining meat sauce over the top. Sprinkle with 1 cup of the mozzarella, then spoon half of the cheese sauce over that. Follow with another layer of 3 noodles, a third of the meat sauce, 1 cup of mozzarella, and the remaining half of the cheese sauce. Finish with a final layer of 3 noodles, using pieces of the tenth noodle to patch any gaps (see Pro Tips & Tricks), the remaining third of the meat sauce, and the remaining 1 cup of mozzarella.

7. Poke 9 to 12 toothpicks halfway into the lasagna. (This will keep the cheese from sticking to the foil—there's nothing worse than losing a big hunk of melty mozzarella to the foil!) Cover with foil and bake for 30 minutes. Uncover and bake for another 25 minutes, or until the lasagna is bubbling at the edges and the cheese is golden. Let cool for 15 minutes before serving, which will help keep the slices tidy. Sprinkle with more parsley and serve.

Pro Tips & Tricks

- The recipe calls for 10 lasagna noodles because I use 9 whole noodles, then chop the tenth into pieces to fit them into any small gaps as I build the lasagna. I call for traditional dry lasagna noodles (versus no-boil) because I love the classic look of curly edges on my noodles, they're nice and substantial, and they make the best lasagna.

- **Make ahead:** To make this ahead, fully assemble the lasagna, cover with foil, and refrigerate it overnight or up to 1 day. You will likely need to add another 5 minutes or so to the cook time because you're baking it cold.

Tuscan Pizza
with White Sauce

I frequently make this recipe for Vadim, who loves the combination of our family's favorite white pizza sauce with a heap of Tuscany-inspired toppings. And what makes it even more special is the crust, which is made from what I can honestly tell you is the best pizza dough ever. It ferments overnight to develop tons of flavor and gives you a thin-crust center with a lovely chewy edge, plus those nice air bubbles when it bakes—just like in an Italian pizzeria. Oh, and it makes two ten-inch pizzas, which means you can make this pizza plus a cheese pie for the "traditionalists" (aka the kids).

MAKES TWO 10-INCH PIZZAS

FOR THE PIZZA DOUGH

1¼ cups warm water (105°F to 110°F)

1 teaspoon honey

½ tablespoon fine sea salt

½ teaspoon active dry yeast

3⅓ cups all-purpose flour (see How to Measure Flour Properly on page 20), plus more for dusting

Vegetable or neutral oil, for greasing

FOR THE WHITE SAUCE

2 tablespoons (¼ stick) unsalted butter

1½ tablespoons all-purpose flour

1¼ cups whole or 2-percent milk

2 garlic cloves, finely pressed or grated

½ teaspoon fine sea salt

¼ teaspoon freshly ground black pepper

1. MAKE THE PIZZA DOUGH: In a small bowl, stir together the water, honey, and salt. Sprinkle the yeast over the mixture and let it sit for 5 minutes to activate the yeast; you should see some foam form at the top. After 5 minutes, stir to combine.

2. Add the flour to a large bowl and form a well in the center. Pour in the yeast mixture and stir with a firm spatula until the dough comes together. Knead by hand in the bowl for 2 minutes; the dough will be sticky. Cover the bowl with plastic wrap and let the dough rise at room temperature for 4 to 5 hours, or until doubled in size.

3. Transfer the dough to a floured surface and turn to lightly coat it in flour so it isn't sticky. Divide the dough in half. Fold each piece of dough in half eight times, gently pulling the sides over the center like you're closing a book, rotating the dough 90 degrees each time. Form each piece into a ball and transfer each one to its own lightly oiled bowl, seam side down. Cover and refrigerate overnight (18 hours) or up to 1 week.

4. MAKE THE WHITE SAUCE: In a small saucepan over medium heat, melt the butter. Whisk in the flour and continue whisking for 1 to 2 minutes. Be careful not to let the mixture brown.

5. Continue whisking as you slowly stream in the milk. Whisk until smooth, thickened, and bubbly. Whisk in the garlic, salt, and pepper. Add the Parmesan and whisk for another 30 seconds. Be careful not to let the sauce boil after adding the cheese or it may clump together. Remove the pan from the heat and continue whisking just until the cheese is melted and the sauce is smooth. Set the sauce aside to cool before using it for the pizza. Alternatively, you could let the sauce cool completely and store it in an airtight container in the refrigerator for up to 5 days.

INGREDIENTS CONTINUE

RECIPE CONTINUES

⅓ cup shredded Parmesan cheese

FOR THE TOPPINGS

Shredded mozzarella cheese

Baby spinach

Sliced tomatoes

Thinly sliced brown or white mushrooms

Jarred quartered artichokes, drained and coarsely torn

Sliced salami or pepperoni

Pepperoncini (or yellow banana peppers)

Sliced black olives

Dried oregano leaves

Kosher salt

6. MAKE THE CRUST AND ASSEMBLE THE PIZZA: Before using the dough, let it come to room temperature for 1 hour.

7. Before forming your crust, place a pizza stone or inverted baking sheet on the center rack of your oven and preheat the oven to 550°F. (I do this about 30 minutes into letting my dough come to room temperature so the dough doesn't proof for too long, which will make it more difficult to work with.) Lightly flour a pizza peel, prep the toppings, and set aside.

8. When the dough is about room temperature and the oven is preheated, transfer one piece of the dough to a floured surface, turning to lightly coat in flour. Pat the center of the dough gently with your fingertips. Do not pop any bubbles! Lift the dough over the knuckles of both hands and roll your knuckles under the center of the dough, working outward as you rotate the dough along your knuckles, leaving a thicker crust at the edge. Take care not to make the center too thin. Continue working the dough until it's 10 to 12 inches in diameter.

9. Place the dough on the prepared pizza peel. Give the peel a little shake to make sure the pizza is not sticking to the peel.

10. Lightly spread half of the sauce over the dough, leaving a 1-inch border. Sprinkle the sauce with the cheese and then layer on the spinach, tomatoes, mushrooms, artichokes, salami, pepperoncini, and olives. Finish with a sprinkling of the oregano and kosher salt, plus a drizzle of the oil. Give the pizza one more shake to make sure it slides easily on the peel; you don't want it to stick while transferring it to the oven. Slide the pizza onto the hot pizza stone and bake for 8 to 10 minutes, or until the crust is golden brown and some of the larger bubbles on the crust are lightly scorched to ensure a crisp crust.

11. Slide the peel underneath the pizza and transfer it to a cutting board to cool slightly before slicing and serving. Repeat with the remaining dough, sauce, and toppings to make the second pizza.

Pro Tips & Tricks

- Feel free to mix and match your toppings or use what you have on hand to make it your own specialty pizza.

- Be careful not to weigh down the dough too much with sauce and toppings, which can make it difficult to get the pie neatly into the oven.

Pelmeni

Pelmeni are the Siberian version of meat-filled dumplings, like Italian ravioli or tortellini. They are popular throughout Eastern Europe and when tossed in butter, they are the definition of comfort food—which is why it's no wonder that this is my dad's favorite dish.

Having a helper to make these will make the process faster and more fun, or you can follow my lead and park yourself on a barstool in the kitchen, put on your headphones, and watch an episode of *The Office*. It's well worth it.

SERVES 4 TO 6
(MAKES 60 TO 65 PELMENI)

1 batch Pierogi Dough (page 147)

1 tablespoon extra-light olive oil

½ medium yellow onion, finely diced (about ½ cup)

1 large garlic clove, minced

1 pound ground meat of your choice (see Pro Tips & Tricks)

1 teaspoon fine sea salt, plus more for boiling

½ teaspoon freshly ground black pepper

1 tablespoon water

All-purpose flour, for dusting

FOR SERVING

3 tablespoons unsalted butter, melted

Chopped fresh dill (optional)

Sour cream (optional)

White distilled vinegar (optional)

Ketchup (optional)

1. Make the dough, cover, and let it rest for 30 minutes at room temperature while you prepare the meat filling.

2. Heat the oil in a medium skillet over medium heat. Add the onion and sauté, stirring occasionally, for 5 minutes, until soft and golden. Add the garlic and stir until fragrant, about 1 minute.

3. Transfer the mixture to a large bowl and add the meat, salt, pepper, and water. Use your hand to mash the mixture until just combined. Don't overmix or the meat can become tough. Set aside.

4. Cut the dough in half and cover one piece in plastic wrap. Set the other half on a lightly floured surface. Use a rolling pin to roll out the dough until thin, less than ⅛ inch thick. (Periodically move the dough around on the table to make sure it's not sticking, adding more flour if needed but taking care not to get too much flour on the surface of the dough.) Use a 2½-inch cookie cutter to cut out about 25 circles, or as many as you can get. Collect the scraps and add them to the covered dough to repurpose. Keep the remaining dough covered.

5. Line two rimmed baking sheets with parchment paper or lightly dust them with flour.

6. In the center of each dough round, add 1 teaspoon of the meat mixture. Note that there are a few options for how to stuff the pelmeni: You could go old-school by using two small spoons to help scoop the filling without using your fingers. Or you could speed things up a touch by piping the meat filling onto the dough rounds. You can use a disposable pastry bag or large plastic zip-top bag with the corner snipped off for piping. Lastly, you could use a mold for these, called a pelmenitsa, which you can order online.

RECIPE CONTINUES

7. Fold the dough over the meat and tightly pinch the edges together. Bring the two corners to the center and pinch them together to make a little ear shape. Add the finished pelmeni to the prepared baking sheets in a single layer as you repeat with the remaining dough and filling.

8. To cook the pelmeni, bring a large pot of well-salted water to a boil over medium-high heat. Add half of the dumplings to the water and stir a couple times to prevent them from sticking to one another. Once they float to the top, reduce the heat, keeping the pot at a medium boil, for 6 minutes, until the meat cooks through. Use a skimmer or strainer to remove the pelmeni and transfer them to a large serving bowl. Repeat with the remaining pelmeni, then drizzle with the butter, sprinkle with the dill (if using), and serve with sour cream, vinegar, and ketchup (if using), for dipping.

Pro Tips & Tricks

- For the filling, you can use ground pork or an equal-parts combination of chicken and beef or chicken and pork. The only meat I wouldn't use on its own is ground beef, which can be a little dry, but when paired with another meat it becomes tender and flavorful.

- **Make ahead:** To freeze the pelmeni, leave the uncooked pelmeni on the prepared baking sheets and freeze for about 2 hours, or until frozen solid. Add them to a freezer-safe zip-top bag and freeze for up to 3 months. You can cook them from frozen in boiling water. Cook as directed above.

Potato Pierogi (Vareniki)

This recipe is dedicated to my late grandma Marina, who cooked every meal from scratch for her children using her woodstove, without the conveniences of packaged foods, well-stocked grocery stores, or the occasional break to dine out or order in. Plus, my grandma had twelve children (my mom was her only daughter), so you can imagine how it was no small task to feed her family. One of her secrets was to make her pierogi (or *vareniki*, as we called them) extra-large, so that she didn't have to spend all day making four times as many small and dainty ones. My mom fondly remembers the pierogi being so big that Grandma would cut them in half to feed two kids, and that Grandma would also sprinkle them with browned salo, an old-school version of bacon bits.

SERVES 5 TO 6
(MAKES 25 TO 28 PIEROGI)

1 batch Pierogi Dough (recipe follows)

4 to 5 medium Yukon gold potatoes (about 1 pound), peeled and quartered

½ cup lightly packed shredded mozzarella cheese

2 tablespoons plain cream cheese

2 tablespoons (¼ stick) unsalted butter, divided

2 tablespoons plus ¼ teaspoon fine sea salt

All-purpose flour, for dusting

6 slices regular-cut bacon, chopped

1 small yellow onion, finely chopped

Sour cream, for serving

1. Make the pierogi dough and let it rest at room temperature for 30 minutes.

2. In a large saucepan, add the potatoes and enough water to cover them by an inch. Set the pan over medium-high heat and bring to a boil. Reduce the heat to a low boil and cook the potatoes for 18 to 20 minutes, until they can be easily pierced with a fork. Drain the potatoes and return them to the pan. Use a potato masher to mash them right in the pot. (You can also use a potato ricer or electric hand mixer if you want the potatoes supersmooth.)

3. Mash in the mozzarella, cream cheese, 1 tablespoon of the butter, and ¼ teaspoon of the salt. Cover the pan until you're ready to use the filling.

4. Lightly flour a rimmed baking sheet and set aside.

5. To form the pierogi, cut the dough in half and cover one piece in plastic wrap. Set the other half on a lightly floured surface. Use a rolling pin to roll out the dough until thin, less than ⅛ inch thick. Use a 3-inch cookie cutter or glass to cut as many circles as you can out of the dough. Collect the scraps and add them to the covered dough to repurpose.

6. In the center of each dough round, add a scant 1 tablespoon of the potato mixture. Avoid getting the potatoes on the edges of the dough or it won't seal properly. Gather up the edges of the dough over the potato and tightly pinch them together. To ensure a tight seal and for a traditional pattern, crimp the edges a second time, using a pinch-and-twist motion.

INGREDIENTS CONTINUE

RECIPE CONTINUES

7. Arrange the finished pierogi in a single layer on the prepared baking sheet. Loosely cover the pierogi with plastic wrap to keep them from drying out. Repeat with the remaining dough and potato filling and set aside.

8. In a large cast-iron or nonstick skillet over medium heat, add the bacon and cook, stirring, for 1 minute to release some of the fat. Add the onions and continue cooking, stirring occasionally, for about 6 to 8 minutes, until the bacon is browned and the onion is golden. Remove the pan from the heat and melt in the remaining 1 tablespoon of butter. Set aside.

9. To cook the pierogi, fill a large pot with water and the remaining 2 tablespoons of salt. Bring to a rapid boil over medium-high heat. Add half of the pierogi to the pot, gently dropping them in two at a time so they don't stick together. Give them a gentle stir, then return the water to a boil. Cook the pierogi for about 2 minutes, just until they float to the top.

10. Use a slotted spoon or skimmer to transfer the cooked pierogi to a large serving bowl. Immediately drizzle them with half of the bacon mixture; the bacon fat will keep the pierogi from sticking. Repeat with the remaining pierogi and bacon mixture.

11. Serve the pierogi warm with dollops of the sour cream.

Pro Tips & Tricks

- When I have time, I love to double this recipe and make a second batch for the freezer—a fun weekend project, especially if you have helpers lend a hand with the molding.

- **Make ahead:** To freeze the pierogi, arrange them in a single layer on a generously floured baking sheet and freeze about 2 hours, until firm. Transfer the pierogi to a freezer-safe zip-top bag and freeze for up to 3 months. You can cook them from frozen in boiling water. Gently stir immediately after adding them to the water so they don't stick to the bottom. They are done when they float to the top, approximately 2 minutes.

Pierogi Dough

The secrets for soft dough that's easy to work with are: (1) don't over-knead it, (2) avoid adding too much flour (see How to Measure Flour Properly on page 20), and (3) rest the dough before shaping it to allow it to relax and soften.

**MAKES ENOUGH DOUGH FOR
1 BATCH PIEROGI OR PELMENI**

2 cups all-purpose flour, plus more as needed (see How to Measure Flour Properly on page 20)

¾ teaspoon fine sea salt, plus more as needed

½ cup warm water

2 tablespoons extra-light olive oil or vegetable oil

1 large egg

1 tablespoon sour cream

1. In a large bowl, whisk together the flour and salt until well combined. Form a well in the center and set aside.

2. In a measuring cup (I do this in the same cup I use to measure the water) or a small bowl, use a fork to lightly beat together the warm water, oil, egg, and sour cream. Pour the mixture into the well of flour and, using a wooden spoon to stir, form a dough. If the dough is sticky, add more flour 1 tablespoon at a time until it's no longer sticking to your hands.

3. Turn out the dough onto a lightly floured surface. Knead the dough by hand for about 2 minutes, just until the dough is smooth and elastic. Don't go beyond that or your dough will get tough. Cover the dough with a sheet of plastic wrap and let it rest at room temperature for 30 minutes.

Creamy Chicken and Rice

Personally, I'm not a big fan of standing over the stove and endlessly stirring in order to enjoy perfectly creamy risotto. That said, I *am* a big fan of rich, cheesy, perfectly tender rice with a bold pop of fresh herbs. So, I developed this recipe, which has risotto-like texture without all the fuss. Plus, I add chicken to make it the ultimate one-pot meal. Whether you're making this ahead and reheating it or serving it straight from the pot with a fresh salad, it's the ideal weeknight dinner.

SERVES 8 TO 10

1 whole garlic head

¼ cup extra-light olive oil or vegetable oil

¼ cup (½ stick) unsalted butter

1 medium yellow onion, finely diced

2 large carrots, coarsely grated on the large holes of a box grater

2 teaspoons fine sea salt, plus more to taste

1½ pounds boneless, skinless chicken thighs, trimmed and cut into 1-inch pieces

2 dried bay leaves (optional)

¼ teaspoon freshly ground black pepper, plus more to taste

1 cup dry white wine, such as sauvignon blanc (see Pro Tips & Tricks)

5 cups Homemade Chicken Bone Broth (page 126) or store-bought low-sodium chicken broth or stock, warmed

2 cups medium-grain white rice (see Pro Tips & Tricks)

½ cup shredded Parmesan cheese, plus more for serving

⅓ cup chopped fresh Italian parsley leaves, plus more for serving

1. Slice off the tip of the garlic head to expose the cloves inside, leaving the root end intact. Set aside.

2. In a 5½-quart Dutch oven or large pot over medium-high heat, heat the oil and 2 tablespoons of the butter. Add the onion, carrots, and 1 teaspoon of the salt and cook for 8 to 10 minutes, until the vegetables are soft and golden. Add the chicken, bay leaves (if using), pepper, and the remaining 1 teaspoon of salt. Cook, stirring occasionally, for about 5 minutes, until the chicken is golden on all sides.

3. Increase the heat to high and add the wine. Cook, using a wooden spoon or spatula to scrape up any browned bits from the bottom of the pot, for 3 to 5 minutes, until most of the wine has evaporated. Add the broth and rice, and place the garlic head, sliced side down, in the center of the rice. Bring the mixture to a boil, reduce the heat to low, and cover. Simmer for about 15 minutes, until the rice is fully cooked.

4. Remove the pot from the heat and remove and discard the bay leaves. Take out the garlic head. You can either discard the garlic cloves or squeeze them from their skins and stir them into the rice. Add the remaining 2 tablespoons of butter, plus the Parmesan and parsley, and stir until the butter is fully melted and incorporated. Season with more salt and pepper, if needed.

5. Serve immediately with more Parmesan and parsley or cover to keep the rice warm until ready to serve.

Pro Tips & Tricks

- You'll notice that I call for adding whole cloves of garlic. I prefer to do this because of how it infuses garlic flavor without being too overpowering.

- This recipe calls for white wine, which gives the dish even deeper flavor, but you can substitute it with more chicken broth, if you prefer.

- Do not rinse the rice for this dish. We want all the good, creamy starch we can get!

FAN FAVORITE

Shrimp Fried Rice

As a busy mama, I know firsthand that it doesn't get any better than a one-pan dinner, complete with a protein and veggies. What I love about this recipe in particular is that it's a great way to use up cooked rice, and I always have the veggies in my freezer. Plus, leftovers keep well and reheat nicely. You could also substitute the shrimp for just about any other protein (I love diced leftover ham), or just skip the shrimp altogether for a simple but scrumptious vegetarian option.

SERVES 6

1 pound (26/30) raw shrimp, peeled and deveined

1 teaspoon cornstarch

¼ teaspoon fine sea salt

¼ teaspoon freshly ground black pepper

3 tablespoons extra-light olive oil or vegetable oil

4 large eggs, beaten

¼ cup thinly sliced green onions (white and green parts)

5 cups leftover white rice, chilled (see Pro Tips & Tricks)

1 (12-ounce) bag of frozen peas and carrots, thawed

2 tablespoons soy sauce or coconut aminos, plus more to taste

1½ teaspoons sesame oil

1. In a medium bowl, toss the shrimp with the cornstarch, salt, and pepper. Let sit at room temperature for 10 minutes.

2. Heat a large (preferably 12-inch) nonstick skillet over medium-high heat until very hot. Add 2 tablespoons of the olive oil, swirl the pan so the oil coats the bottom, and add the shrimp in a single layer. Cook the shrimp for 1 minute per side, or until cooked through and opaque. Transfer the shrimp to a bowl.

3. In the same skillet over medium heat, add the eggs, breaking them up with a spatula to roughly scramble. Transfer the eggs to the same bowl as the shrimp.

4. Wipe out the skillet with a paper towel and return the pan to medium-high heat. Add the remaining 1 tablespoon of olive oil, swirl the skillet to coat the bottom, and add the green onions. Cook, stirring, for 1 minute, until the green onions are fragrant and softened.

5. Stir in the rice and spread it evenly in the pan. Let it cook undisturbed for 1 to 2 minutes, until the rice is sizzling and beginning to crisp in some places. Stir the rice, then leave it alone once again to sizzle and crisp, another 1 to 2 minutes.

6. Add the peas and carrots, soy sauce, and sesame oil and stir well. Return the shrimp and eggs to the pan and continue cooking, stirring frequently, for 1 to 2 minutes, until the rice is sizzling and the flavors have combined. Add more soy sauce, if needed, and serve immediately.

Pro Tips & Tricks

- Start with COLD rice. Refrigerated leftover rice works best because it's slightly dried out and won't get sticky or mushy. That said, if you don't have any leftover rice, you can make some for this dish. First, be sure to rinse the rice well before cooking it to remove any extra starch. Cook the rice according to the package instructions, then let it cool to room temperature. Spread the rice over a rimmed baking sheet or the bottom of a casserole dish and refrigerate until chilled.

David's Fettuccine Alfredo

This recipe is my son's specialty. It's been his favorite dish since he was little, and when he turned ten, he insisted on learning how to make it himself. I certainly didn't object! I love how proud he is when he serves it to our family, which is well deserved—it tastes like it could be from a fancy restaurant. And yes, it's so simple that even a ten-year-old can do it!

SERVES 6

1 (16-ounce) package of fettuccine (see Pro Tips & Tricks)

¼ cup reserved pasta water

2 tablespoons (¼ stick) unsalted butter

2 garlic cloves, pressed or grated, or ½ teaspoon garlic powder

½ teaspoon onion powder

2 cups heavy cream

1 cup shredded Parmesan cheese, plus more for serving

½ teaspoon fine sea salt, plus more to taste

¼ teaspoon freshly ground black pepper, plus more to taste

Finely chopped fresh parsley leaves, for serving (optional)

1. Bring a large pot of well-salted water to a boil over high heat. Add the pasta and cook according to the package instructions until al dente, stirring occasionally. Reserve ¼ cup of the pasta cooking water and drain the pasta. Transfer the pasta back to the pot and cover to keep warm.

2. While the pasta cooks, in a small saucepan over medium heat, melt the butter. Add the garlic and onion powder and whisk for 30 seconds, just until fragrant. Whisk in the cream and bring the mixture to a bare simmer. Reduce the heat to low and add the Parmesan. Whisk just until the cheese is melted into the sauce, 1 to 2 minutes. Be careful not to let the sauce boil, otherwise the cheese will clump. (You can pull the pan off the heat for a few seconds, if needed.) If the sauce looks too thick, add the reserved pasta water 1 tablespoon at a time until you've achieved the desired consistency. Remove the pan from the heat and season with the salt and pepper. Season with more salt and pepper, if needed.

3. Pour the sauce over the pasta and toss thoroughly to coat, adding more of the pasta water if needed to thin out the sauce. Garnish with more Parmesan and parsley (if using) and serve immediately.

Pro Tips & Tricks

- You can use the Alfredo sauce with any pasta variety, long or short, so feel free to go with whatever is in your pantry or sounds fun that night! But we especially love how this sauce coats fettuccine noodles.

- Make the sauce as the pasta boils so that you can combine them as soon as they're both done. This timing also means that you can have this dish on the table in 15 minutes flat.

Baked Mac and Cheese

When most people think of baked mac and cheese, they usually picture a big gooey slab with a crunchy breadcrumb crust on top. I'm all for great texture, but I've found that this kind of topping can dry out the pasta—plus, not all kids are fans of it. (And I was tired of scraping the top off my daughter's portion every time!) So, I came up with a version that features a *cheesy* crust instead, which gives you that irresistible cheese pull when lifting it out of the pan while also sealing in the creamy pasta underneath. I call that a major win-win.

SERVES 10 TO 12

6 tablespoons (¾ stick) unsalted butter, plus more for greasing

1 tablespoon plus ½ teaspoon fine sea salt, plus more as needed

1 pound elbow noodles

½ cup reserved pasta water

1 tablespoon extra-light olive oil or other neutral oil

6 cups shredded medium cheddar cheese (16 ounces)

2 cups shredded mozzarella cheese (6 ounces; see Pro Tips & Tricks)

⅓ cup all-purpose flour

3 cups whole milk

1 cup heavy cream

1 teaspoon paprika

1 teaspoon mustard powder or 2 teaspoons Dijon mustard

1 teaspoon garlic powder

½ teaspoon onion powder

¼ teaspoon freshly ground black pepper, plus more to taste

1. Preheat the oven to 350°F. Butter a 3-quart or 9 × 13-inch casserole dish and set aside.

2. Bring a large pot of water to a boil over high heat. Add 1 tablespoon of the salt and the pasta and cook according to the package instructions, until al dente. Reserve ½ cup of the pasta cooking water and then drain the pasta. Immediately drizzle the noodles with the oil to prevent sticking and set aside.

3. In a large bowl, stir together the cheddar and mozzarella and set aside (you should have about 8 cups total).

4. In a 5½-quart Dutch oven or large pot over medium heat, melt the butter. When the butter foams, whisk in the flour. Continue whisking for about 2 minutes, until the flour just starts to turn golden in color.

5. While whisking, slowly stream in the milk, cream, and reserved pasta water. Continue whisking until the mixture is creamy, smooth, and just beginning to boil.

6. Add the paprika, mustard powder, garlic powder, onion powder, the remaining ½ teaspoon of salt, and the pepper. Whisk to combine, then reduce the heat to low and simmer, continuing to whisk, for 2 to 3 minutes, until the sauce has thickened to a light gravy consistency.

7. Add 3 cups of the cheese mixture to the pan and stir until melted. Add another 3 cups of the cheese mixture (you should have about 2 cups remaining for topping the dish) and stir until melted. Stir in the pasta to coat. Turn off the heat and season with more salt and pepper, if needed.

8. Pour the mac and cheese evenly into the prepared casserole dish. Sprinkle the remaining 2 cups of cheese over the top and bake for 15 minutes, until the cheese is melted and bubbly. For an even more golden-brown topping, set the oven to broil for the last 2 to 3 minutes of baking. Serve warm.

Pro Tips & Tricks

- If you want to "dress up" your mac, try swapping out the mozzarella for Gruyère.

- This reheats well in the microwave. I add a portion to a microwave-safe bowl, then sprinkle a little bit of water over the top to keep the pasta moist. Microwave on high, stirring every 20 seconds, until warmed through and creamy.

7

MEAT AND SEAFOOD MAINS

Cooking meals for my family is rooted in something much deeper than just putting something delicious on the table. I saw how hard my parents had to work to provide for me and my sisters, and it was not lost on me how their resourcefulness, gratitude, and ability to turn a little into a lot made our lives so much richer than money ever could. Particularly watching my mother in the kitchen day after day, producing the most mouthwatering, nourishing meals from whatever she could piece together was so inspiring. And what made it so special was all the love she put into it. Now that I have a family of my own, I do my best to channel that same care and can-do spirit into the meals that I make for them. And I'd like to think that when I do, I'm also honoring the people who had to sacrifice so much so that I could be here doing just that. I especially think about my grandpa Peter (my father's father), who was drafted into the Soviet army during World War II at age 18.

Grandpa Peter was captured and escaped from German concentration camps *twice*—once by rolling under a passing train James Bond–style and another time by blending in with civilians who were allowed into the camp to trade with the prisoners. When he realized he was free, he stood outside of the camp's barbed wire fences and cried—for what he had experienced and for all the others who were suffering. When he got married, he knew he needed to do whatever it took to lift himself and his new wife out of poverty. He took note of an elderly woman selling flowers at the market, realizing that she was making a good living. So, he conducted a little "market research"—observing her pricing and following her home one day to see how she grew her flowers. He took what he learned, built his own greenhouse, and started growing chrysanthemums to sell. He taught my mom and dad the same trade, and eventually they were able to build a livable

home and put food on the table. They went on to teach other relatives, friends, and neighbors the same business, so that they, too, could support their families. For my family, there was more than enough success to go around.

The recipes in this chapter, maybe more so than any other section of this book, were inspired by my grandparents and my parents. They were created in the spirit of generosity, of bringing people together, and of not requiring you to spend a lot of money—or time—to make something special. My goal is to show you how easy it can be to make the humblest ingredients taste delicious and indulgent. But more than that, to give you the tools to make something with love for the people in your life who matter most.

Chicken Pot Pie

Just when I thought people didn't make their own from-scratch chicken pot pies anymore, this recipe garnered over 3 million views on YouTube and 6.1 million views on Facebook and has now earned over nine hundred 5-star reviews. It goes to show that people will always crave the comfort foods they love, and chicken pot pie is at the top of that list. Plus, store-bought versions have nothing on juicy chicken and perfectly cooked vegetables in a rich, creamy gravy hugged by a flaky, homemade crust.

SERVES 8

1 batch The Only Pie Dough You'll Need (recipe follows), chilled

6 tablespoons (¾ stick) unsalted butter

1 cup chopped yellow onion (from 1 medium onion)

1 cup thinly sliced carrots (from 2 medium carrots)

8 ounces button or cremini mushrooms, sliced

3 garlic cloves, minced

⅓ cup all-purpose flour, plus more for dusting (see How to Measure Flour Properly on page 20)

2 cups Homemade Chicken Bone Broth (page 126) or store-bought low-sodium chicken broth or stock

½ cup heavy cream

2 teaspoons fine sea salt

¼ teaspoon freshly ground black pepper, plus more to taste

4 cups shredded cooked chicken

1 cup frozen peas

¼ cup chopped fresh parsley leaves, plus more for serving

1 large egg, beaten

Kosher salt, for sprinkling

1. Make the pie dough. Preheat the oven to 425°F.

2. In a 5½-quart Dutch oven or large soup pot over medium heat, melt the butter. Add the onions and carrots and cook for 8 minutes, until soft. Add the mushrooms and garlic and cook for another 5 minutes, until the mushrooms are softened. Add the flour and cook, stirring constantly, for 2 minutes. Stir in the broth and cream and bring the mixture to a simmer. Simmer for 1 minute, or until the mixture thickens to a gravy-like consistency. Season with the salt and pepper. Fold in the chicken, peas, and parsley and remove the pot from the heat. Set aside to cool slightly while you roll out the crusts.

3. On a floured surface, use a rolling pin to roll one of the pie crust disks into a 12-inch circle. Carefully transfer the dough to a 9-inch pie dish. Spoon the filling into the crust.

4. Roll the second pie crust disk into a 10-inch circle and place it over the pie filling. Fold the excess dough under the bottom crust and crimp the pie crusts together to seal. To do this, hold your thumb and index finger an inch apart on the outside edge of the crust and press between them with the index finger of the other hand. Repeat this motion around the edges of the pan, which will create a fluted rim.

5. Use a paring knife to cut five 1-inch slits in the top crust. Brush the crust with the beaten egg and sprinkle lightly with kosher salt and pepper.

6. Bake for 30 to 35 minutes, or until the top crust is golden brown. If it looks like the edges are browning too quickly, cover them with a pie shield or make one by cutting a 4-inch circle out of the center of a 12 × 12-inch sheet of foil and placing the sheet with the hole removed over the pie.

7. Let the pie rest for at least 15 minutes before slicing and serving.

RECIPE CONTINUES

The Only Pie Dough You'll Need

You can always tell a homemade crust from a frozen premade one—the buttery taste and flaky texture are dead giveaways. It also only takes ten to fifteen minutes to come together. Whether you're making your Thanksgiving pies, my savory Chicken Pot Pie (page 159), or looking for a way to use up a bumper crop of peaches, berries, or apples, this crust will make all the difference between a pie that is good and one that gets all the compliments.

MAKES 2 SINGLE OR
1 DOUBLE CRUST

2½ cups all-purpose flour, plus more for dusting (see How to Measure Flour Properly on page 20)

1½ teaspoons sugar

½ teaspoon fine sea salt

1 cup (2 sticks) very cold unsalted butter, diced into ¼-inch pieces (see Pro Tips & Tricks)

½ cup ice water

1. In the bowl of a food processor, add the flour, sugar, and salt and pulse a few times to combine. Add the butter and pulse again, just until coarse crumbs form. The mixture should be dry and powdery. Dribble in about 7 tablespoons of the ice water, 1 tablespoon at a time, pulsing between each addition, just until moist clumps form. Press a piece of dough between your fingers—if the dough sticks together, you're done adding water. If not and you've already added all 7 tablespoons, add more water 1 teaspoon at a time, until the dough feels just moist enough.

2. Dust a work surface with flour and turn out the dough. Gather it together with your hands as best you can into a large clump. (It won't be smooth, and you'll need to resist the temptation to knead or fuss with it.) Divide the dough in half and flatten each half to form a disk. Wrap each disk tightly with plastic wrap and refrigerate for at least 1 hour before using.

Pro Tips & Tricks

- The key to perfectly flaky crust is using *supercold* butter and *ice-cold* water. It's pretty much the only time when people with cold hands have the advantage. (I'll take my wins where I can!)

- **Make ahead:** After tightly wrapping each disk with plastic wrap, store them in the refrigerator for up to 3 days. Or seal them in a zip-top bag to store them in the freezer for up to 3 months. Allow them to thaw overnight in the fridge or at room temperature for 1 hour, or until softened enough to roll out, before using. If you let the disks thaw in the fridge, let them soften at room temperature for 30 minutes before using.

Smothered Chicken Tenders
with Pan Gravy

Chicken tenders are one of the easiest cuts of chicken to work with. There's virtually no prep or trimming required, and they are very forgiving if you slightly overcook them. If you sear them in a pan, which is both quick and easy, then with just a few more ingredients you'll be able to whip up a quick pan gravy using all those flavorful drippings. I highly recommend serving these over Whipped Mashed Potatoes (page 201) or with a side of Baba's Cucumber Spears (page 213).

SERVES 4
(MAKES 8 TO 10 TENDERS)

½ cup plus 2 tablespoons all-purpose flour

1 teaspoon fine sea salt, plus more to taste

½ teaspoon freshly ground black pepper, plus more to taste

1 teaspoon paprika

½ teaspoon garlic powder

1 large egg

1 pound chicken tenders (8 to 10 tenders)

2 tablespoons extra-light olive oil, plus more as needed

2 tablespoons (¼ stick) unsalted butter

1 cup Homemade Chicken Bone Broth (page 126) or store-bought low-sodium chicken broth or stock

½ cup low-fat or whole milk

2 tablespoons finely chopped fresh parsley leaves, for garnish

1. In a medium bowl, whisk together ½ cup of the flour with the salt, pepper, paprika, and garlic powder.

2. In another medium bowl, use a fork to thoroughly beat the egg until foamy. Dip a tender into the egg wash, then transfer it to the flour mixture. Turn the tender in the mixture so it is fully coated on all sides. Transfer the tender to a plate and repeat with the remaining tenders.

3. Line a plate with a paper towel and set aside. Heat the oil in a large nonstick or cast-iron skillet over medium heat. Working in batches if necessary, so as not to crowd the pan, add the tenders in a single layer. Cook for 4 to 5 minutes per side, until both sides are golden brown and an instant-read thermometer inserted into the thickest part of each tender registers 165°F. Transfer the finished tenders to the paper towel–lined plate.

4. In the same skillet over medium heat, melt the butter. Add the remaining 2 tablespoons of flour and whisk constantly for about 2 minutes, until golden. Whisk in the broth followed by the milk, then bring the mixture to a simmer over medium heat. Reduce the heat to low and continue cooking at a simmer for about 3 minutes, until the sauce has thickened to a light gravy consistency. Season with more salt and pepper, if needed.

5. Add the tenders back to the pan and spoon the gravy over them. Remove the pan from the heat and garnish with the parsley.

Thank-You-Mom Chicken Schnitzel

The first time I made this, my daughter—who was six at the time—got up from the table mid-dinner to give me a hug. She said, "Thank you for making me this chicken, Mom." I just about melted. Later that night, she remembered the tasty chicken in her prayers, thanking God for it in true six-year-old fashion. It's been making regular appearances at our table ever since, whether it's served as a main course with potatoes and veggies, layered on a bun and topped with coleslaw and pickles, or sliced into strips and tossed onto salads.

SERVES 4

2 large boneless, skinless chicken breasts (about 1½ pounds)

¼ cup all-purpose flour

2 teaspoons garlic salt

½ teaspoon paprika

½ teaspoon freshly ground black pepper

2 large eggs

1½ cups panko breadcrumbs

Extra-light olive oil or vegetable oil, for frying

Fine sea salt

Fresh parsley, for serving

Lemon wedges, for serving

1. Line a cutting board with plastic wrap. Cut each chicken breast in half lengthwise to make 4 thin cutlets. Place the chicken in a single layer on the cutting board and cover with a second sheet of plastic wrap. Use a meat mallet, rolling pin, or the bottom of a heavy saucepan to pound the chicken thin, about ¼ inch thick. Cut each cutlet in half for 8 cutlets total.

2. Set up three medium bowls: In the first, whisk together the flour, garlic salt, paprika, and pepper. In the second, add the eggs and thoroughly beat with a fork. In the third, add the panko.

3. Dredge both sides of 1 cutlet in the flour to coat well, then in the egg, letting any excess drip back into the bowl before breading the chicken in the panko. It helps to use a fork or tongs for this process to keep your hands clean. Transfer the breaded cutlet to a platter or baking sheet. Repeat with the remaining cutlets, keeping them in a single layer on the platter. If you have time, let the breaded chicken rest for 10 minutes, which will help the coating stick better.

4. Heat a large nonstick pan over medium heat and add just enough oil to coat the bottom, about 3 tablespoons. When the oil shimmers, add a few cutlets to the pan, being careful not to crowd them. Cook for 3 to 4 minutes per side, until crispy and golden and an instant-read thermometer registers 165°F. (You can also slice one open; the juices should run clear and the meat should no longer be pink.) Reduce the heat if the cutlets are browning too quickly. Transfer the cutlets to a paper towel–lined plate and immediately sprinkle the cutlets with the salt. Repeat with the remaining cutlets, adding more oil to the pan as needed.

5. Serve immediately with a sprinkle of parsley and the lemon wedges.

Pro Tips & Tricks

- The key to getting the most flavor out of any fried food is to sprinkle it with salt as soon as it comes out of the oil. We also love a squeeze of fresh lemon juice over the crispy cutlets to add brightness.

Spice-Rubbed Pork Tenderloin

In my opinion, pork tenderloin doesn't get enough credit. When it's prepared correctly, it can be impressively juicy and flavorful, not to mention the fact that it's one of the least expensive cuts of meat you can buy. The trick I've developed is to pierce the meat all over with a fork so that the herbs and seasonings infuse into the pork as it roasts—and that's it. No marinating or fancy footwork required. You'll have the perfect quick dinner one night and delicious sandwiches using the leftovers the following day.

SERVES 4

1 teaspoon fine sea salt, plus more to taste

1 teaspoon Italian seasoning

1 teaspoon garlic powder

1 teaspoon ground coriander

½ teaspoon freshly ground black pepper

1 (1½-pound) pork tenderloin, trimmed of fat and silver skin (see Pro Tips & Tricks)

2 tablespoons extra-light olive oil or vegetable oil, divided

1. Place an oven rack in the center of the oven and preheat the oven to 400°F.

2. In a small bowl, stir together the salt, Italian seasoning, garlic powder, coriander, and pepper.

3. Pat the tenderloin dry with a paper towel and pierce it all over with a fork. Rub the tenderloin evenly with 1 tablespoon of the oil, followed by the spice mixture.

4. In a large cast-iron or oven-safe skillet over medium-high heat, heat the remaining 1 tablespoon of oil. Add the pork and sear it on all sides, about 2 minutes per side, until golden brown.

5. Transfer the pan to the oven and roast the tenderloin for 8 minutes. Flip the pork and roast for another 5 to 7 minutes, until the center registers 145°F on an in-oven or instant-read thermometer. Transfer the pork to a cutting board and let it rest for 5 to 10 minutes before slicing.

Pro Tips & Tricks

- The secret to making the meat as tender as possible is to first remove the tough white membrane known as "silver skin" from the tenderloin. Simply insert the tip of your knife between the silver skin and the meat and then slide the blade of your knife along the meat while pulling the silver skin away at the same time.

- This recipe calls for cooking the tenderloin to the USDA-recommended internal temperature of 145°F, which will be slightly pink in the middle.

Roasted Chicken and Gravy

Whoever said you have to wait for Thanksgiving to make gravy? Just as you would use the deliciously browned bits and all the juices from your roasted turkey to make a deeply flavorful pan sauce, you can do the exact same thing when making chicken. Pouring the gravy over a crispy, golden chicken breast or leg makes it so much more decadent, and yet the entire meal takes barely any time to pull together.

SERVES 6

FOR THE ROASTED CHICKEN

1 (5½-pound) whole chicken, giblets removed, patted dry with paper towels

2½ teaspoons fine sea salt, divided

¾ teaspoon freshly ground black pepper, divided

6 garlic cloves, halved

1 lemon, halved

2 sprigs of fresh rosemary

2 tablespoons (¼ stick) unsalted butter, melted

FOR THE GRAVY

1¾ cups Homemade Chicken Bone Broth (page 126) or store-bought low-sodium chicken broth or stock, or as needed

3 tablespoons unsalted butter

3 tablespoons all-purpose flour

¼ teaspoon fine sea salt

¼ teaspoon freshly ground black pepper

Pinch of paprika (optional)

1. MAKE THE CHICKEN: Place an oven rack in the bottom third of the oven so the chicken will sit right in the center. Preheat the oven to 425°F.

2. Set the chicken in a 10-inch cast-iron skillet or other large oven-proof pan. Season the inside cavity of the chicken with ½ teaspoon of the salt and ¼ teaspoon of the pepper. Stuff the chicken with the garlic, lemon, and rosemary. Twist and tuck the wings under the chicken and tie the legs together with oven-safe kitchen string. Brush the butter all over the top and sides of the chicken and season generously with the remaining 2 teaspoons of salt and ½ teaspoon of pepper.

3. Roast the chicken, uncovered, for 80 to 90 minutes, until the internal temperature of the deepest part of the thigh and the thickest part of the breast registers 165°F on an in-oven or instant-read thermometer, or until the juices run clear when you cut between the leg and thigh.

4. Transfer the chicken to a platter, tent loosely with foil, and let rest for at least 15 minutes before slicing and serving. Be sure to use any additional juices collected on the platter to add to the gravy.

5. MAKE THE GRAVY: Scrape the pan drippings out of the skillet into a 2-cup measuring cup. Spoon off and discard any excess fat that rises to the top. Add enough broth for 2 cups of liquid total.

6. Return the pan to medium heat and melt the butter. Whisk in the flour and continue whisking for 1 minute, until the mixture is golden brown. While whisking, slowly stream in the drippings mixture and bring it to a slight boil. Reduce the heat to low and simmer for 3 to 5 minutes, until the gravy has thickened to your desired consistency. Season with the salt, pepper, and paprika (if using).

7. Carve the chicken as desired and serve with the warm gravy.

Pro Tips & Tricks

- Use an in-oven thermometer so you can track the temperature of your chicken without needing to open the oven. Insert the thermometer into the deepest part of the chicken breast.

- If you have hot spots in your oven and see uneven browning, rotate your chicken halfway through baking.

- As a general rule of thumb, roasting estimates are 75 minutes for a 5-pound bird, 80 minutes for a 5½-pound bird, and 90 minutes for a 6-pound bird.

- If you're lucky enough to have leftovers, try reheating the chicken in a skillet with leftover gravy—a trick we use on Thanksgiving, too. Simmering the meat in the sauce makes it taste more like a dish you whipped up fresh than something reheated from the fridge.

Baked Salmon
with Garlic and Dijon

According to my readers, this salmon dish has saved marriages, impressed in-laws, and left many picky eaters smiling. With more than seven hundred 5-star reviews on my site and my kids' stamp of approval (they always ask for seconds), it's safe to say that this is *the* recipe to try if you're new to cooking fish and looking for where to start. Olive oil whisked with lemon, garlic, and Dijon is the secret to juicy, perfectly cooked fish while also providing complex, sophisticated flavor without complex or sophisticated techniques.

SERVES 4

1 (1½-pound) salmon fillet, pin bones removed (see Pro Tips & Tricks)

3 garlic cloves, minced

2 tablespoons chopped fresh parsley leaves

2 tablespoons extra-light olive oil or vegetable oil

2 tablespoons freshly squeezed lemon juice

1½ teaspoons Dijon mustard

½ teaspoon fine sea salt

⅛ teaspoon freshly ground black pepper

½ lemon, sliced into 4 rings

1. Preheat the oven to 450°F. Line a rimmed baking sheet with parchment paper or foil.

2. Cut the salmon into 4 equal portions and arrange them, skin side down, on the prepared baking sheet.

3. In a small bowl, combine the garlic, parsley, oil, lemon juice, Dijon, salt, and pepper. Generously spread the mixture over the top and sides of the salmon pieces and top each piece with a slice of lemon.

4. Bake for 12 to 15 minutes, or until just cooked through and flaky. Serve immediately.

Pro Tips & Tricks

- To remove the pin bones from the salmon, run your fingers across the surface of the fish to feel for the bones. If you find any, use a pair of kitchen tweezers to gently pull out the bones.

- Don't marinate the fish in the sauce—the acid from the lemon will actually cook the fish. Trust me, slathering the fish just before it bakes will give it plenty of flavor.

Philly Cheesesteak Sandwiches

I'm all for a good, juicy cheeseburger, but give me a gooey, beefy cheesesteak with caramelized onions on a toasted garlic-butter hoagie roll and I'm in *heaven*. Our favorite way to make these is on our grill's flat cooktop because we can make a bunch of sandwiches at once, including when we take our cooktop out to the woods when we're camping. But you could also make these on the stove. No matter which way you go, this recipe is perfect for quickly whipping up sandwiches for the whole family. Let's just say this one gets a lot of love from my readers. Since the salmon already has tons of flavor, it doesn't need more than a simple side of fluffy white rice or roasted veggies.

SERVES 4

2 tablespoons (¼ stick) unsalted butter, softened

1 garlic clove, pressed

4 hoagie rolls, sliced three-quarters through longways

2 tablespoons extra-light olive oil or vegetable oil, divided

1 large sweet onion, diced

1 pound rib eye steak, fat trimmed and meat thinly sliced (see Pro Tips & Tricks)

½ teaspoon fine sea salt

½ teaspoon freshly ground black pepper, or to taste

8 slices mild provolone cheese

¼ cup mayonnaise, or to taste

1. In a small bowl, stir together the butter and garlic. Spread the garlic butter onto the cut sides of the hoagie rolls.

2. In a large skillet or on a griddle or flat cooktop over medium heat, lay the rolls flat, buttered side down. Toast for 1 to 2 minutes, until golden brown. Transfer the rolls to a plate and set aside.

3. In the same skillet over medium heat, heat 1 tablespoon of the oil. Add the onions and cook, stirring frequently, for 8 to 10 minutes, until softened and golden brown. Transfer the onions to a bowl and set aside.

4. In the same skillet, increase the heat to high and add the remaining 1 tablespoon of oil. Add the steak in an even layer and let cook, undisturbed, for about 2 minutes, or until starting to brown. Flip, season with the salt and pepper, and cook for another 2 to 3 minutes, until cooked through. Stir in the onions.

5. Divide the mixture into 4 equal portions in the pan and turn off the heat. Top each portion with 2 slices of the cheese.

6. Spread a thin layer of mayo on the toasted side of each roll. Place a roll over one of the cheesesteak portions and use a large spatula to scrape the cheesy beef into the roll, as you flip it over. Repeat with the remaining rolls and cheesesteak mixture. Serve warm.

Pro Tips & Tricks

- Rib eye is the traditional steak of choice for these sandwiches, and its marbling makes it nice and tender when cooked. Another cut I like to use is flank steak, which is leaner than rib eye but gets tender when sliced against the grain.

- For easier slicing, cover and freeze your steak for 30 minutes before cooking.

Baked Teriyaki Salmon

When we were kids, my parents saved up to buy a Sea Ray sport boat. We'd take it to Elliott Bay in Seattle to go fishing, which was one of our favorite activities. Once, we were out trolling for salmon when a dense fog rolled in. It eventually got so thick that we couldn't see two feet in front of us, and my parents had to stop the boat. Suddenly, out of nowhere, there was a loud blast, and what seemed like a fifty-foot wall rolled by as a massive barge missed us by about twenty feet. We retreated as quickly as we could while water poured into our boat from the ship's wake. Thankfully, we made it out OK—and even managed to catch two gorgeous salmon that day, each as long as my arm. It was definitely an unforgettable trip.

I've always loved cooking salmon, and this dish gets top marks with everyone in my family. The kids love the sweetness of the glaze, while the adults appreciate the layers of Asian-inspired flavor. Since the salmon already has tons of flavor, it doesn't need more than a simple side of fluffy white rice or roasted veggies.

SERVES 6 TO 8

⅓ cup (packed) light brown sugar

3 tablespoons teriyaki sauce

3 tablespoons hoisin sauce

3 tablespoons soy sauce

1 tablespoon distilled white vinegar

1 tablespoon sesame oil

1 tablespoon minced garlic (from 2 large cloves)

2 teaspoons peeled and grated fresh ginger or ½ teaspoon ground ginger

1 (2- to 3-pound) salmon fillet, sliced into 6 to 8 portions (see Pro Tips & Tricks)

2 tablespoons sliced green onions (green parts only)

2 teaspoons sesame seeds

1. In a medium bowl, combine the sugar, teriyaki sauce, hoisin sauce, soy sauce, vinegar, oil, garlic, and ginger and whisk until the sugar is dissolved.

2. Carefully place the salmon portions in a large zip-top bag. Pour about half of the marinade over the salmon and lightly massage the bag to coat the salmon. Gently press out the excess air from the bag, seal it, and place in the refrigerator for 30 minutes to 1 hour to marinate. Reserve the remaining marinade in an airtight container in the refrigerator.

3. Preheat the oven to 400°F. Line a large rimmed baking sheet with foil.

4. Using tongs, transfer the salmon to the prepared baking sheet skin side down and discard the marinade in the bag. Bake for 12 to 16 minutes, or until the salmon is flaky and an in-oven or instant-read thermometer registers 145°F at the thickest part of the salmon. (Bake times will vary depending on the thickness of the salmon.)

5. In a small saucepan over medium heat, add the remaining half of the marinade. Bring to a simmer and reduce the heat to low. Cook, stirring occasionally, for 3 to 4 minutes, until the sauce is slightly thickened. Remove the pan from the heat.

6. Brush the salmon with the sauce, sprinkle with the green onions and sesame seeds, and serve.

Pro Tips & Tricks

- When choosing salmon at the fish counter, keep in mind that thicker and fattier pieces of salmon tend to be juicier and more forgiving if slightly overbaked. Wild-caught salmon tends to be leaner and thinner (unless it's a wild king salmon, which is thick, rich, and fatty), while farm-raised salmon tends to be thicker with more fat.

- The type of salmon you use in this recipe can also make a difference in bake time. Leaner, thinner fillets will bake more quickly, while thicker or fattier fillets will take longer.

Beef and Broccoli Stir-Fry

My readers love copycat recipes of beloved takeout dishes that they can re-create at home, so it's no wonder this is one of my most popular recipes. I love how saucy and satisfying this dish is, that it's a one-pan meal, that it doesn't require a ton of ingredients, and that it's done in thirty minutes, complete with beef and veggies. All you need is a pot of fluffy white rice and you have a meal that will also hit the spot the next day.

SERVES 4

FOR THE STIR-FRY SAUCE

½ cup hot water

6 tablespoons low-sodium soy sauce

3 tablespoons (packed) light brown sugar

2 tablespoons sesame oil

1½ tablespoons cornstarch

2 teaspoons minced or grated garlic (from about 3 cloves)

1 teaspoon peeled and grated fresh ginger

¼ teaspoon freshly ground black pepper

FOR THE BEEF AND BROCCOLI

2 tablespoons extra-light olive oil or vegetable oil, divided

6 cups broccoli florets (from about 1 large head of broccoli)

1 pound flank steak, thinly sliced into bite-size strips (see Pro Tips & Tricks)

Cooked white rice, for serving (I like jasmine)

Sesame seeds, for serving

1. MAKE THE SAUCE: In a medium bowl, add the hot water, soy sauce, sugar, sesame oil, cornstarch, garlic, ginger, and pepper and whisk until the sugar is dissolved. Set aside.

2. MAKE THE BEEF AND BROCCOLI: In a large skillet over medium heat, heat 1 tablespoon of the olive oil. Add the broccoli and cook, partially covered, for 4 to 5 minutes, stirring or tossing several times until the broccoli is bright green and crisp-tender. Transfer the broccoli to a plate.

3. In the same skillet over high heat, heat the remaining 1 tablespoon of olive oil. Add the beef in a single layer and cook for about 2 minutes per side, until just cooked through. Add the sauce and reduce the heat to medium-low. Simmer for 3 to 4 minutes, until the sauce thickens slightly. Add the broccoli and stir to combine. If needed, add 1 to 2 tablespoons of water to thin the sauce. It should easily coat the beef and broccoli.

4. Serve immediately over the rice and top with the sesame seeds.

Pro Tips & Tricks

- For easier slicing, cover and freeze your steak for 30 minutes before cooking.

- If you prefer softer broccoli, add 2 tablespoons of water in step 2 before covering with the lid. This will steam the broccoli.

- **Make ahead:** This is a great dish for making ahead or for packing up for work or school lunches because the meat reheats so nicely in the sauce.

Cheeseburger Sliders

These have all the things you love about juicy, cheesy burgers combined with everything you could want in an appetizer that feeds a crowd (or a hungry family!)—and with virtually none of the effort. Instead of standing over a hot grill flipping individual patties and then assembling dozens of individual burgers, this recipe calls for the brilliant hack of topping a sleeve of rolls with a seasoned ground beef mixture and cheese. We serve them with dill pickle spears, french fries, and all the classic burger condiments.

MAKES 24 SLIDERS

- 2 tablespoons (¼ stick) unsalted butter, melted, plus more for greasing
- ½ tablespoon extra-light olive oil or vegetable oil
- 2 pounds lean (90/10 or 93/7) ground beef
- ½ large yellow onion, finely chopped
- 1 teaspoon fine sea salt
- 1 teaspoon freshly ground black pepper
- 1 teaspoon garlic powder
- ¼ cup mayonnaise
- 1 (24-pack) white Hawaiian sweet rolls
- 16 slices medium cheddar cheese, divided
- 1 tablespoon sesame seeds

1. Preheat the oven to 350°F. Grease a rimmed baking sheet with butter and set aside.

2. In a large skillet over medium-high heat, heat the oil. Add the beef and onion, breaking up the meat with a spoon or spatula. Season with the salt, pepper, and garlic powder and cook for about 8 minutes, until the meat is just cooked through. Remove the pan from the heat.

3. Carefully tilt the skillet to spoon off and discard any excess fat. Stir the mayo into the beef mixture and set aside.

4. Keeping the rolls connected, use a large serrated knife to carefully slice them in half widthwise. Place the bottom half of the rolls on the prepared baking sheet. Line the rolls with 8 of the cheese slices. Spread the beef mixture evenly over the cheese, using the back of a spatula to square off the edges. Top the beef with the remaining 8 slices of cheese. Place the tops of the buns over the burgers and brush with the butter. Sprinkle the sesame seeds over the buns and bake for 12 to 15 minutes, until the cheese is melted and the buns are golden brown. Serve immediately.

Pro Tips & Tricks

- A fun twist on the sesame-seed topping is to use everything-but-the-bagel seasoning instead.

- This recipe is party sized, but you can halve it to feed a smaller crowd.

- **Make ahead:** You can assemble these a day ahead, cover, and refrigerate them. Then bake as directed.

- If reheating leftovers, microwave the burgers for 20 to 30 seconds, until warm.

Shrimp Avocado Tostadas

I took one of our all-time favorite appetizers, ceviche, and made a meal out of it so we could have it for lunch! Ceviche is a South American dish in which raw fish is "cured" in a bright, fresh citrus marinade, tossed with a chunky salsa and avocado, and heaped onto a crispy tostada. I love using sautéed shrimp because I prefer my seafood cooked, and it takes literally two minutes in the pan, but it's still the same light yet filling dish that's especially nice in the summer.

SERVES 4 TO 6
(MAKES 12 TOSTADAS)

FOR THE SHRIMP

1½ pounds large (21/25) shrimp, peeled and deveined

½ teaspoon ground cumin

½ teaspoon ground cayenne pepper

½ teaspoon fine sea salt

¼ teaspoon freshly ground black pepper

1 tablespoon extra-light olive oil

FOR THE PICO DE GALLO AND GUACAMOLE

4 Roma tomatoes, cored and diced

½ English cucumber, diced

½ medium red onion, finely chopped

4 tablespoons freshly squeezed lime juice (from about 2 limes), divided

2 tablespoons extra-virgin olive oil

¼ cup chopped fresh cilantro leaves, plus more for garnish

2 large avocados

¼ teaspoon fine sea salt, plus more to taste

1. COOK THE SHRIMP: In a medium bowl, combine the shrimp with the cumin, cayenne, salt, and pepper. Toss to combine.

2. In a large skillet over medium-high heat, heat the extra-light olive oil. Working in batches if necessary, so as to not crowd the pan, add the shrimp in a single layer. Cook for 1 minute per side, or until just cooked through and opaque white. Transfer the shrimp to a cutting board and coarsely chop. Set aside to cool.

3. MAKE THE PICO DE GALLO: In a large bowl, combine the tomato, cucumber, onion, and shrimp. Drizzle the mixture with 2 tablespoons of the lime juice, the extra-virgin olive oil, and cilantro. Gently toss to combine and set aside.

4. MAKE THE GUACAMOLE: Halve the avocados and use a spoon to scoop the flesh into a small bowl. Add the remaining 2 tablespoons of lime juice and the salt, then use a fork to coarsely mash the mixture. Season with more salt, if needed.

5. ASSEMBLE THE TOSTADAS: Spread the guacamole over each tostada. Add some of the shredded lettuce and then the shrimp mixture. Garnish with more cilantro and serve with the hot sauce and lime wedges for squeezing over the tostadas.

Pro Tips & Tricks

- You can use smaller shrimp (31/40 count) if that is what you have or can find. You just won't have to chop the shrimp.

- You can use store-bought tostadas—which is a great shortcut!—or you can make your own, which is what I do when we already have corn tortillas on hand from making Famous Fish Tacos (page 263). Here's how you do it: Arrange taco-size corn tortillas on a rimmed baking sheet in a single layer. Spray both sides with cooking spray, lightly sprinkle with salt, and bake at 425°F for 5 minutes per side, flipping halfway through. Remove from the oven and let cool on a wire rack.

FOR ASSEMBLY

12 corn tostadas (see Pro Tips
    & Tricks)

½ head iceberg lettuce,
    shredded (about 3 cups)

Your favorite hot sauce

Lime wedges

Garlic-Crusted Beef Tenderloin

Yes, a tenderloin is spendy, but it's also one of those stunning holiday dishes that is impressive and memorable. Plus, the last time I made this, I calculated that our family enjoyed an entire steakhouse-style meal—this tenderloin, Whipped Mashed Potatoes (page 201), and Green Beans Almondine (page 206)—for about how much we'd pay for *one* plate at a nice restaurant. With its beautiful garlicky crust and juicy, perfectly cooked center, this is the dish Vadim and I are referring to whenever we go out for steak and say to each other, "We make it better at home."

SERVES 4 TO 6

1 (2-pound) beef tenderloin (to make a larger roast, see Pro Tips & Tricks)

1½ teaspoons fine sea salt, divided

2 tablespoons extra-light olive oil

2 tablespoons minced garlic (from 4 to 5 cloves)

1 teaspoon freshly ground black pepper

1 teaspoon minced fresh rosemary leaves or ½ teaspoon dried rosemary

½ teaspoon minced fresh thyme leaves or ¼ teaspoon dried thyme

1. Use a sharp knife to trim away any silver skin or white connective tissue on the surface of the tenderloin (see Pro Tips & Tricks on page 167). If the tenderloin has a thin end, fold it under to create a uniform thickness. Use kitchen twine to tie the tenderloin in 1-inch intervals.

2. Place the tenderloin in a roasting pan and season all over with 1 teaspoon of the salt. Loosely cover the meat with plastic wrap and let it rest at room temperature for 1 hour. This will ensure even cooking.

3. Place an oven rack in the center of the oven and preheat the oven to 500°F.

4. In a small bowl, add the oil, the remaining ½ teaspoon of salt, the garlic, pepper, rosemary, and thyme. Stir to combine. Rub the garlic mixture evenly over the tenderloin, coating it well on all sides.

5. Bake on the center rack for 28 to 30 minutes, until an in-oven or instant-read thermometer inserted in the thickest part of the meat registers 130°F. (This is for medium doneness; if you prefer your meat less or more well done, see Pro Tips & Tricks.)

6. Transfer the meat to a cutting board and tent loosely with foil. (Don't leave the tenderloin in the pan or it will overcook one side.) Let the meat rest for 10 minutes, which will bring the roast to a final medium temperature of 135°F to 140°F. Remove the string and slice the tenderloin into ½-inch-thick medallions. Serve right away, topped with any pan juices.

Pro Tips & Tricks

- To make a 4-pound roast, cut the tenderloin in half and roast the two pieces side by side in the oven about 2 inches apart.

- To cook the tenderloin to your desired doneness, the general rule of thumb is to roast it to 5° to 10° less than your ideal final temperature, as it will continue to cook as it rests. Here are cook times for other doneness options:

  - Medium-rare: Bake 24 to 26 minutes to 120°F, for a final resting temperature of 125°F to 130°F.

  - Medium-well: Bake 30 to 32 minutes to 135°F, for a final resting temperature of 140°F to 145°F.

Salmon Piccata

When I was learning how to cook, I quickly realized what a huge difference a few solid techniques could make in my repertoire. This dish is the perfect example—by pan-searing the salmon, you're creating a crisp, golden crust that seals in the fish's juicy center. All that's left to do is swirl in some butter, lemon, and capers to make a beyond-easy pan sauce that tastes like it came from a nice restaurant. Serve this with Whipped Mashed Potatoes (page 201), Perfect Parmesan Asparagus (page 202), or Green Beans Almondine (page 206) for a quick and polished meal.

SERVES 4

1½ pounds skin-on or skinless salmon, cut into 4 fillets (see Tips & Tricks on page 175)

½ teaspoon fine sea salt, plus more to taste

¼ teaspoon freshly ground black pepper, plus more to taste

¼ cup (½ stick) unsalted butter, softened, divided

1 tablespoon extra-light olive oil

½ small yellow onion, very finely chopped (about ⅓ cup)

¾ cup Homemade Chicken Bone Broth (page 126) or store-bought low-sodium chicken broth or stock

¼ cup freshly squeezed lemon juice (from 1 large or 2 medium lemons)

3 tablespoons capers, rinsed and drained

1 tablespoon finely chopped fresh parsley leaves, for garnish

4 lemon slices, for garnish (optional)

1. Use paper towels to pat the salmon dry. Season both sides of each fillet with the salt and pepper.

2. In a large nonstick, nonreactive skillet over medium-high heat, combine 1 tablespoon of the butter and the oil, swirling the pan as the butter melts to prevent splatter. When the butter has melted and is done foaming, add the salmon skin side up (if your fillets are skin-on) and sauté for 3 to 4 minutes, until the first side is seared and golden brown. Flip the fish, reduce the heat to medium, and sauté for another 3 to 4 minutes, until browned, flaky, and done to your liking. Transfer the fish to a plate and tent loosely with foil to keep the salmon warm as you make the pan sauce.

3. In the same skillet over medium-low heat, add the onion and cook for 3 minutes, until just softened. Stir in the broth, lemon juice, and capers using a wooden spoon to scrape up any browned bits from the bottom of the skillet. Increase the heat to medium and bring the mixture to a boil. Cook for 3 to 5 minutes, until the sauce has thickened into a glaze.

4. Remove the skillet from the heat and stir in the remaining 3 tablespoons of butter, 1 tablespoon at a time. Stir constantly until the butter is emulsified and incorporated.

5. Season the sauce with salt and pepper. Return the salmon to the skillet and spoon the sauce over the top. Garnish with the parsley and lemon slices (if using). Spoon the sauce over the fish to serve.

Pro Tips & Tricks

- You know it's time to flip the salmon over when you slide a spatula underneath and it releases easily. If the salmon is sticking to the pan, it's probably not quite ready to flip.

- For perfectly cooked salmon, use an instant-read thermometer and sauté until the salmon reaches 145°F at the thickest part of the fish.

Pan-Seared Cod
in White Wine, Tomato, and Butter Sauce

What I love about this dish is that it doesn't overcomplicate the simplicity that is cooking fish. All that's required is searing the fillets until they're tender, flaky, and golden brown, then stirring together a deeply flavorful pan sauce. This recipe also works well with different varieties of white, flaky fish. If you're feeling fancy or planning a special-occasion dinner, try this with halibut (the sauce is halibut worthy), sea bass, sole fillets, or grouper. Serve with simple rice or buttered pasta and a fresh green salad.

SERVES 4

4 (6- to 8-ounce, 1-inch-thick) boneless, skinless cod fillets (see Pro Tips & Tricks)

1 teaspoon fine sea salt, divided

¾ teaspoon freshly ground black pepper, divided

2 tablespoons extra-light olive oil, plus more as needed

¼ cup (½ stick) unsalted butter

¼ cup dry white wine (see Pro Tips & Tricks)

3 cups cherry or grape tomatoes

2 garlic cloves, minced (about 1 tablespoon)

2 tablespoons chopped fresh basil leaves, for garnish

1. Use paper towels to thoroughly pat dry the fish. Season the fillets all over with ¾ teaspoon of the salt and ½ teaspoon of the pepper.

2. In a large nonstick, nonreactive skillet, heat the oil over medium-high heat. When the oil is shimmering, add the fish top side down and sauté, undisturbed, for 3 to 4 minutes, until golden brown and seared on the first side.

3. Flip the fish, reduce the heat to medium, and continue cooking for 2 to 4 minutes, until the fish is seared on the second side, adding more oil if the skillet looks dry. The fish should be just cooked through and opaque in the center, and an instant-read thermometer inserted in the thickest part of the fish should register 145°F. (Cook time will depend on the thickness of your fillets.) Transfer the fish to a plate in a single layer and tent loosely with foil to keep warm.

4. In the same skillet over medium-high heat, add the butter, wine, tomatoes, and garlic. Use a wooden spoon to scrape up any browned bits from the bottom of the skillet and cook for 3 to 4 minutes, until the liquid is reduced by half and the tomatoes start to soften and burst. Season the sauce with the remaining ¼ teaspoon of salt and ¼ teaspoon of pepper, or to taste. Remove the pan from the heat.

5. Add the fish back to the pan, and spoon the tomatoes and sauce over the top. Garnish with the basil and serve.

Pro Tips & Tricks

- If using frozen fish, thaw it in the refrigerator overnight to ensure that it isn't watery and sears properly.

- Use any inexpensive dry white wine, such as sauvignon blanc, pinot gris, chardonnay, or Riesling. Avoid using "cooking wine," which may contain additives that will affect the overall flavor of the dish.

- To ensure tender fish, be careful not to overcook the fish and use a nonstick pan to keep the fish from sticking and falling apart.

Perfect Grilled Steak
with Mustard-Pepper Sauce

It's nice to have go-to recipes in your arsenal that make dinner a little more special, and this is one of those recipes. A perfectly cooked steak served with a rich, complex sauce feels like such an indulgence, and yet neither component on its own requires much time or expertise. So long as you season the steaks generously before putting them on the grill (with more salt than you think you should!) and use an instant-read thermometer to nail your ideal doneness, you'll always be just minutes away from the perfect steak dinner.

SERVES 4

FOR THE STEAKS

2 (16-ounce, 1¼- to 1½-inch-thick) New York strip steaks (see Pro Tips & Tricks)

2 teaspoons kosher salt

1 teaspoon freshly ground black pepper

FOR THE MUSTARD-PEPPER SAUCE

½ cup (1 stick) unsalted butter, cut into 8 pieces

1½ tablespoons stone-ground mustard

1 tablespoon freshly squeezed lemon juice

1 tablespoon coarsely ground black pepper

Pinch of fine sea salt

2 sprigs of fresh rosemary

1. MAKE THE STEAKS: Remove the steaks from the refrigerator 20 to 30 minutes before grilling to take the chill off. Preheat the grill to medium-high heat.

2. Season the steaks all over with the salt and pepper. Place your steaks on the grill and reduce the heat to medium. Cover and grill for 4 to 5 minutes, until the first side is browned and charred. Flip and grill, covered, for another 4 to 8 minutes, depending on your desired doneness. (See Pro Tips & Tricks.) Insert an instant-read thermometer into the thickest part of the steak and remove the steaks from the grill once they are 5° to 10° under your desired doneness.

3. Transfer the steaks to a plate and tent loosely with foil. Let the steaks rest for 10 minutes while you make the sauce.

4. MAKE THE SAUCE: In a small saucepan over low heat, combine the butter, mustard, lemon juice, pepper, and salt. Whisk constantly for 2 to 3 minutes, until the butter is melted, the ingredients are combined, and the sauce is just beginning to steam (do not boil or the sauce will separate!). As soon as you see wisps of steam, remove the pot from the heat. Add the rosemary sprigs and stir for 30 seconds, then discard the rosemary and cover the sauce to keep warm until ready to serve, or up to 1 hour.

5. Slice the steak against the grain and arrange the slices on a serving platter. Spoon the sauce over the top and serve right away.

Pro Tips & Tricks

- You can substitute with a different or more affordable cut of steak, if you prefer, but keep in mind that the cooking time will vary with the thickness of your steak. Rib eye and top sirloin are also great choices.

- Steak doneness: For medium-rare, remove steaks at 130°F to 135°F (to serve at 140°F); for medium, remove at 140°F to 145°F (to serve at 150°); and for medium-well, remove at 145°F to 150°F (to serve at 155°F).

Grilled Salmon Sandwiches
with Lemon Aioli

I'm always looking for ways to make salmon a little more exciting. I wasn't sure how it would go over served as a sandwich on a brioche bun, but to my surprise, everyone in my family loved it! I think what sold them on it was the vibrant, creamy lemon aioli that brings together the juicy salmon, fresh spring greens, and thick-sliced cucumber. It's a whole meal on a bun.

SERVES 4

FOR THE GRILLED SALMON SANDWICHES

High-heat cooking oil, such as grapeseed or vegetable oil, for greasing

1½ tablespoons unsalted butter, softened at room temperature

4 burger buns, preferably brioche

4 (6-ounce) boneless, skinless salmon fillets

1 tablespoon extra-light olive oil

Fine sea salt and freshly ground black pepper to taste

Spring greens mix

Thickly sliced cucumber

FOR THE LEMON AIOLI

½ cup mayonnaise

1 teaspoon lemon zest (from 1 lemon)

1 tablespoon freshly squeezed lemon juice

1 garlic clove, pressed or grated

1. MAKE THE SANDWICHES: Preheat the grill to medium-high heat (350°F to 400°F) and grease the grates with the high-heat cooking oil.

2. Spread the butter over the cut sides of the buns and set aside.

3. Rub the salmon fillets with the olive oil and season with salt and pepper on both sides. Place the salmon on the grill and cook, covered, for 3 minutes per side, or until cooked through. An instant-read thermometer inserted into the thickest part of the fish should register 140°F to 145°F. Transfer the fish to a plate and tent loosely with foil to keep warm while you prepare the remaining components.

4. Place the buns, cut side down, on the grill for about 1 minute, until grill marks form. Transfer each bun to individual serving plates and set aside.

5. MAKE THE LEMON AIOLI: In a small bowl, stir the mayo to remove any lumps. Add the lemon zest, lemon juice, and garlic and stir to combine. Set aside.

6. ASSEMBLE THE SANDWICHES: Spread the aioli over the grilled sides of the buns. Add a generous amount of greens to the bottom buns, topped by the cucumber slices. Set the grilled salmon over the top and cover with the top buns. Serve immediately.

Pro Tips & Tricks

- Assemble and add the sauce just before serving so your buns don't get soggy.
- Follow these salmon grilling guidelines for cooking over medium heat (350°F):
  - 1-inch-thick fillets = 3 minutes per side
  - ¾-inch-thick fillets = 2 to 3 minutes per side
  - ½-inch-thick fillets = 2 minutes per side

Cowboy Burgers

Burgers are in our regular dinner rotation in the summer, so we're always looking for ways to up our game. But once we tried this souped-up version, we realized it would be pretty tough to beat. With a third-pound patty, crispy onion rings, bacon, and a barbecue aioli, it's decidedly a two-hander of a sandwich with a Western spin (hence its name). Don't even bother with flimsy napkins; you'll want paper towels for these towering saucy burgers!

MAKES 4 BURGERS

FOR THE BARBECUE AIOLI

⅓ cup mayonnaise

2 teaspoons sweet barbecue sauce, plus more to taste

FOR THE CRISPY ONION RINGS

Grapeseed or other high-heat cooking oil, for frying

1 cup milk of any kind

1 tablespoon distilled white vinegar

½ cup sour cream

1 cup all-purpose flour

½ tablespoon fine sea salt

1 teaspoon garlic powder

¼ teaspoon freshly ground black pepper

1 large sweet or yellow onion, sliced into ½-inch rings

1. MAKE THE AIOLI: In a small bowl, stir together the mayo and barbecue sauce and set aside.

2. MAKE THE CRISPY ONION RINGS: In a 5½-quart Dutch oven or large pot over medium heat, add 1 inch of the oil. It should be enough to fully submerge the onion rings. You could also use a deep fryer if you have one.

3. While the oil heats, prepare the batter. In a medium bowl, whisk together the milk and vinegar. Let the mixture sit for 5 minutes, then whisk in the sour cream. Set aside.

4. In another medium bowl, whisk together the flour, salt, garlic powder, and pepper.

5. Separate the onion rings and dip each ring into the sour-cream mixture, then dredge with the flour. (I use a fork to transfer the onions from the wet ingredients to the dry, so my hands don't get gunky.) Dip the onions in the wet mixture a second time, followed by the dry mixture. Place the battered onion rings on a plate until ready to fry.

6. When the oil reaches 375°F, add 3 to 4 of the battered onion rings in a single layer and fry for about 3 minutes total, until the exterior is crisp and light golden brown on each side. Transfer the cooked onion rings to a paper towel–lined plate to soak up any excess oil, then repeat with the remaining onion rings.

7. MAKE THE BURGERS: Preheat the grill to medium heat. Prepare all the toppings for the burgers and set aside.

8. Spread the cut side of the buns with the butter and toast in a dry skillet or on the grill over medium heat for about 1 minute, until golden brown. Set aside.

9. Divide the beef into four equal portions and form patties that are roughly ½ inch thick and 1 inch wider than the burger buns. Indent the center of each patty with a spoon, which will prevent the center from puffing. Season the patties generously on one side with the

FOR THE BURGERS

½ cup sliced dill pickle

8 iceberg lettuce leaves

1 large tomato, sliced into 8 rounds

8 slices cooked bacon (see page 98)

4 burger buns (I love brioche)

1½ tablespoons unsalted butter, softened at room temperature

1⅓ pounds (80/20) ground chuck beef

Fine sea salt and freshly ground black pepper to taste

4 thick slices of medium cheddar cheese

salt and pepper. Grill the patties indent side up, covered, for 3 to 5 minutes, until juices begin accumulating on the top of the burger and the first side has a nice sear. Flip the burgers and cook for another 3 minutes. Add a slice of cheese to each patty and cook, covered, for 1 to 2 minutes, until an instant-read thermometer inserted into the thickest part of the patty registers 150°F to 155°F. The temperature of the meat will continue to rise as the meat rests, bringing the final temperature closer to 160°F (the USDA recommendation for a well-done burger with no pink in the center).

10. ASSEMBLE THE BURGERS: Slather both cut sides of the buns with the aioli. On the bottom buns, add the pickles, then the lettuce, tomatoes, burger patty, and bacon. Finish with the onion rings and the top buns. Serve immediately.

Pro Tips & Tricks

- Toast the buns and have all the toppings ready before grilling the burger patties. That way the burgers can be enjoyed hot, juicy, and fresh off the grill. Don't skip toasting the buns—it adds great flavor and prevents them from getting soggy.

- If you're short on time, you can swap the fried onion rings for sliced raw onion. This burger will still be pretty epic!

Chicken in Mushroom Wine Sauce

This recipe is the kind of dish that would be right at home in a good Italian restaurant, and yet it's quick and easy to make. I've put it to the test with my own family for many weeknight dinners, and when the kids argue over who gets the bigger piece of chicken and then completely clean their plates, you know that you're onto something! Between the juicy, tender chicken and the rich, creamy sauce, I can't say it comes as a surprise. Serve this over Whipped Mashed Potatoes (page 201), rice, or pasta, plus a simple salad.

SERVES 4

2 large boneless, skinless chicken breasts (1½ pounds total)

⅓ cup all-purpose flour

1 teaspoon fine sea salt, divided

¾ teaspoon freshly ground black pepper, divided

3 tablespoons unsalted butter, divided

2 tablespoons extra-light olive oil, divided, plus more as needed

8 ounces cremini or baby bella mushrooms, thickly sliced

½ cup finely diced yellow onion (from ½ medium onion)

3 garlic cloves, minced

¼ teaspoon dried thyme or 1 teaspoon fresh thyme leaves

½ cup dry white wine (see Pro Tips & Tricks on page 186)

1 cup Homemade Chicken Bone Broth (page 126) or store-bought low-sodium chicken broth or stock

½ cup heavy cream

1 tablespoon finely chopped fresh parsley leaves, for garnish (optional)

1. Line a cutting board with plastic wrap. Cut each chicken breast in half lengthwise to make 4 cutlets. Place the chicken in a single layer on the cutting board and cover with a second sheet of plastic wrap. Use a meat mallet, rolling pin, or the bottom of a heavy saucepan to pound the chicken thin, about ⅓ inch thick. Set aside.

2. In a shallow bowl, stir together the flour, ½ teaspoon of the salt, and ½ teaspoon of the pepper. Dip the cutlets into the flour mixture, turning to coat, and tap off any excess.

3. In a large nonreactive skillet over medium heat, combine 1 tablespoon of the butter and 1 tablespoon of the oil. When the butter foams, add the chicken in a single layer. (You will most likely need to work in batches.) Cook for 3 to 4 minutes per side, until the cutlets are golden brown on both sides and cooked through (an instant-read thermometer inserted into the center should register 165°F). Transfer the cutlets to a plate and tent loosely with foil to keep warm. Repeat with the remaining cutlets, adding more oil to the pan if needed.

4. In the same skillet over medium heat, add the remaining 2 tablespoons of butter, the mushrooms, and onion and sauté, stirring frequently, for 6 to 8 minutes, until the onions are soft and the mushrooms are lightly browned.

5. Add the garlic, thyme, the remaining ½ teaspoon of salt, and the remaining ¼ teaspoon of pepper and stir for 30 seconds, until fragrant. Pour in the wine and broth and bring to a boil over high heat, stirring frequently and using a wooden spoon to scrape up any browned bits from the bottom of the skillet. Continue boiling for 7 to 10 minutes, until most of the liquid has evaporated and turned syrupy. (This process will go more quickly in a larger skillet.)

6. Stir in the cream, reduce the heat to medium-low, and simmer for 1 to 2 minutes, until the sauce begins to thicken. Season with more salt and pepper, if needed. Return the cutlets to the pan and spoon the sauce over the top. Serve garnished with parsley (if using).

Pro Tips & Tricks

- Use a nonreactive skillet when working with wine so your sauce doesn't break when you add the cream.

8

ON THE SIDE

When I polled my audience about what they most wanted to see in my cookbook, one of the most frequent answers I got was "interesting sides." As a mom, I can relate to that because I'm always thinking about how I can use side dishes to keep our regular meal rotation feeling fresh and well-rounded. So, I focused my attention on developing recipes—particularly veggie recipes—that everyone, including your kids, will want to go back to for a second helping. While everyone's busy cleaning their plates, you'll have the satisfaction of knowing that you made them something special with fresh, seasonal ingredients—and that it took minimal time to throw it together. But you can just let them go on *mmm*ing and *aaaah*ing over dinner.

Milk Bread Rolls

You've been forewarned: you'll never want to settle for store-bought rolls after making a batch of these. They're irresistibly soft and have a light, airy center that pulls apart like cotton candy thanks to the combination of milk and butter. They're also considered a quick bread and for a good reason—your mixer does most of the work, and they rise while you're preparing the rest of your meal. Serve them alongside just about any dish, with honey for dipping (which my daughter LOVES) or slathered in jam for breakfast (my personal favorite).

MAKES 12 ROLLS

1 cup low-fat or whole milk, warmed to 105°F to 110°F

3 tablespoons warm water (115°F)

3 tablespoons sugar

2¼ teaspoons active dry yeast (0.25 ounces)

1 large egg, room temperature

6 tablespoons (¾ stick) unsalted butter, melted and cooled to 110°F, divided, plus more for greasing

1½ teaspoons fine sea salt

3½ cups bread flour, divided, plus more as needed (see How to Measure Flour Properly on page 20)

Vegetable or other neutral oil, for greasing

1. In the bowl of a stand mixer fitted with the whisk attachment or in a medium bowl with a hand mixer, whisk together the milk, water, and sugar. Sprinkle the top of the mixture with the yeast and mix just to combine. Set aside, uncovered, for 7 minutes to activate the yeast. Mix in the egg, 5 tablespoons of the butter, and the salt.

2. Attach the dough hook to the mixer and add 2 cups of the flour. Mix on low speed (or speed level 2 if your mixer has this setting) until the flour is incorporated. Add the remaining 1½ cups of flour in thirds, letting it incorporate with each addition and scraping down the sides of the bowl as needed. Continue adding flour about 1 tablespoon at a time, until the dough feels moist to the touch but not sticky. (I usually end up adding about ¼ cup more flour in total.)

3. On the same low speed, let the mixer knead the dough for 10 minutes, or you can knead by hand. The dough should pull away from the sides of the bowl as it's mixed and will be smooth and elastic.

4. Lightly coat the inside of a large bowl with the oil and transfer the dough to the bowl. Turn the dough to coat it in the oil and cover with plastic wrap. Let the dough rise in a warm place (about 100°F) for 1 hour or at room temperature for 2 hours, or until doubled in size.

5. Turn out the dough onto a clean work surface; you should not need any additional flour at this point. Use a bench scraper or knife to divide the dough into 12 even pieces. Cup your hand over a piece of dough and roll it over the work surface to form a ball. Repeat with the remaining dough balls.

6. Generously butter a 9 × 9-inch square nonstick metal baking pan or a 10-inch round cake pan and arrange the rolls seam side down. Oil a sheet of plastic wrap and place the oiled side loosely over the rolls. Let the rolls rest in a warm place (about 100°F) for 30 to 45 minutes or at room temperature for 1 hour, until visibly puffed.

7. While the dough is rising, place an oven rack in the center of the oven and preheat the oven to 350°F.

8. Bake the rolls for 22 to 25 minutes, until the tops are golden brown and the center of the middle roll registers 190°F on an in-oven or instant-read thermometer. Brush the rolls with the remaining 1 tablespoon of butter. Let the rolls cool in the pan for 10 minutes before transferring them to a cooling rack. The rolls can be enjoyed warm or at room temperature.

Pro Tips & Tricks

- These rolls are best enjoyed within 2 days of making them, though they'll last for up to 5 days when stored in an airtight container at room temperature.

- The secret to enjoying fresh baked bread and rolls any time without having to make them from scratch is to freeze them the day you bake them. If you know you're not going to eat the whole batch—or you make extra to enjoy another time—wrap the bread in foil once it has cooled and store in the freezer for up to 3 months.

Whipped Mashed Potatoes

This is my go-to mashed potato recipe because it's so easy to make and yet luxuriously creamy. The little bit of sour cream adds just the right amount of zip, and I've also perfected how much seasoning to add. (It's easy to underseason your potatoes.) My only rule is that you can't save this recipe for the holidays! If your family is anything like mine, they'll love having this on the table for weekday meals.

SERVES 6

12 medium russet potatoes (about 4 pounds), peeled and quartered

1½ cups heavy cream, warmed, plus more as needed

¼ cup sour cream

1½ teaspoons fine sea salt, plus more to taste

2 tablespoons (¼ stick) unsalted butter, melted

2 tablespoons finely chopped fresh parsley leaves or chives (optional)

1. In a large pot, add the potatoes and enough cold water to cover by 1 inch. Set the pot over high heat and bring to a boil. Reduce the heat to medium-low and simmer for 13 to 15 minutes, until you can easily pierce the potatoes with a fork.

2. Drain the potatoes, return them to the pot, and set the pot over low heat to evaporate any excess water, about 1 minute. Whip the potatoes with a hand mixer (or use a potato masher) and drizzle in the cream as you whip, adding more cream as needed depending on your desired texture. Add the sour cream and salt and mix until combined. Taste and adjust the seasoning with more salt, if desired.

3. Transfer the potatoes to a serving bowl, drizzle with the melted butter, and top with the parsley (if using). Serve immediately.

Pro Tips & Tricks

- The trick to getting the creamiest potatoes is two-fold. First, use *heavy* cream (which will also give you richer flavor). Make sure your cream is warmed before adding it. It will incorporate more easily, and it will also keep your potatoes from cooling too quickly. And second, mash the potatoes with an electric hand mixer, which is easier and will incorporate more air into the potatoes, making them even fluffier. That said, a potato masher will work just fine.

Perfect Parmesan Asparagus

In my opinion, asparagus doesn't need much fuss in order to really shine. After all, you want to taste the natural sweetness of the vegetable. The key is to cook it just right—until it's crisp-tender and vibrant green—and to keep the other ingredients simple. In this case, it's a sprinkling of Parmesan that makes a delectable, cheesy crust over the asparagus. My son and I are always going after all the little browned bits of cheese on the baking sheet!

SERVES 6 TO 8

2 pounds asparagus, rinsed, dried, and ends trimmed (see Pro Tips & Tricks)

2 tablespoons extra-virgin olive oil

½ teaspoon fine sea salt

¼ teaspoon garlic powder

¼ teaspoon freshly ground black pepper

½ cup shredded Parmesan cheese

Lemon wedges, for serving (optional)

1. Place an oven rack in the center of the oven and preheat the oven to 400°F.

2. On a nonstick, rimmed baking sheet, arrange the asparagus in a single layer. Drizzle the oil over the top and roll the asparagus to coat. Season with the salt, garlic powder, and pepper and toss or roll again to coat in the seasonings. Bake for 10 to 15 minutes, until the asparagus is tender but still crisp.

3. Sprinkle the Parmesan evenly over the asparagus and return to the oven for 2 minutes, just until the cheese is melted.

4. Transfer the asparagus to a serving platter and serve immediately (so the asparagus doesn't wilt) with the lemon wedges (if using).

Pro Tips & Tricks

- If you don't want to fuss with peeling the ends of your asparagus, a trick I learned years ago was to just snap off the ends. The asparagus will naturally break between the tender stalk and the tougher, fibrous end.

- If you don't have a nonstick baking sheet, line a regular baking sheet with parchment paper for easy cleanup.

Crispy Roasted Potatoes
with Garlic and Rosemary

One of the staples of Ukrainian cooking is potatoes. I also live in Idaho (aka potato land), so I could probably write an entire book on potatoes. Instead, I had to choose just a few of my favorite potato dishes, and this one absolutely makes the cut. It's a recipe that not only delivers perfectly crisp-on-the-outside, buttery-soft-on-the-inside potatoes every single time, but it also features olive oil that's infused with garlic and rosemary—a genius hack that doesn't take any extra effort and yet makes this dish seem elegant and sophisticated.

SERVES 6

¼ cup extra-light olive oil or vegetable oil

4 garlic cloves, minced (about 1½ tablespoons)

2 tablespoons minced fresh rosemary leaves or 2 teaspoons dried rosemary

1½ teaspoons fine sea salt, plus more to taste

½ teaspoon freshly ground black pepper, plus more to taste

1 (3-pound) bag small Yukon gold or red-skinned potatoes (or a combination of both)

1. Place an oven rack in the center of the oven and preheat the oven to 425°F.

2. In a measuring cup (I like to use the same cup I use to measure the oil) or a small bowl, whisk together the oil, garlic, rosemary, salt, and pepper. Set aside for at least 10 minutes for the flavors to meld.

3. Wash and thoroughly pat dry the potatoes. (If they're still damp when you cook them, they'll steam in the oven instead of crisping up.) Cut the potatoes into halves or quarters—roughly bite-size pieces about ½ inch thick—and place them in a large bowl.

4. Toss the potatoes with the oil-and-garlic mixture. Transfer the potatoes to a large rimmed baking sheet and arrange them cut side down in a single, even layer.

5. Roast the potatoes for 45 minutes, or until they are fork tender and the bottoms are crisp and golden brown. Season with more salt and pepper, if needed, and serve hot.

Pro Tips & Tricks

- The secret to nailing perfectly crispy-yet-tender potatoes is to roast them cut side down without flipping them.

- You can easily scale this recipe up or down, making it perfect for larger gatherings. Figure that you'll need ½ pound of potatoes per serving.

- For easy cleanup, line your baking sheet with parchment paper or use a nonstick baking sheet.

- **Make ahead:** To make this dish ahead, keep the roasted potatoes uncovered in a warm oven until ready to serve. They also reheat well in a skillet on the stove.

Green Beans Almondine

This is the green bean recipe for people who *think* they don't like green beans. The secret is in the buttery pan sauce, crunchy almonds, and bright pop of lemon zest. I've been making this dish for years and bringing it to family gatherings—oftentimes with a doubled recipe's worth because it goes so quickly!—especially because I can pull this dish together in about ten minutes.

SERVES 4

- 1 tablespoon plus ¼ teaspoon fine sea salt, divided, plus more to taste
- 1 pound green beans (preferably French green beans, also called *haricots verts*), trimmed
- ¼ cup (½ stick) unsalted butter, divided
- ½ cup slivered or sliced almonds
- ⅛ teaspoon freshly ground black pepper, plus more to taste
- 2 garlic cloves, minced
- 1½ teaspoons lemon zest (from 1 lemon), plus more for garnish (optional; see Pro Tips & Tricks)

1. Fill a 3-quart saucepan two-thirds full of water. Add 1 tablespoon of the salt and bring to a boil over high heat. Add the green beans, return the pot to a boil, and cook, uncovered, for 3 to 7 minutes, until the beans are crisp-tender (this will depend on the thickness of your beans). Using a colander, drain the beans and immediately rinse them with cold water to stop the cooking process. Drain well and set aside.

2. In a large skillet over medium-low heat, melt 3 tablespoons of the butter. When the butter is foaming, add the almonds, the remaining ¼ teaspoon of salt, and the pepper and stir constantly for 2 to 3 minutes, until the nuts are golden and toasted. They'll toast up quickly—be careful not to burn them!

3. Add the garlic and stir for 30 seconds, until fragrant but not brown. Turn off the heat and add the remaining 1 tablespoon of butter, stirring until melted. Add the beans to the pan and toss to coat with the almonds and butter. The residual heat from the skillet will rewarm the beans. Season with more salt and pepper, if needed.

4. Sprinkle the beans with the lemon zest and gently toss to coat. Transfer the beans to a serving platter and top with any remaining sauce. Serve garnished with more lemon zest (if using).

Pro Tips & Tricks

- Use a microplane grater, citrus zester, or the fine holes of a box grater to remove the zest from the lemon peel, making sure to avoid the bitter white pith underneath.

- If scaling up this recipe or if using a larger pot to cook the green beans, be sure to salt the water sufficiently. As a rule of thumb, the water should taste as salty as ocean water.

Skillet Parm Zucchini

My mom grows zucchini in her enormous garden every year—and has a tendency to overplant pretty much everything—which means that most of the summer we have more zucchini than we know what to do with. That's when we reach for this recipe, which pairs simply sautéed zucchini with deeply flavored caramelized onions and savory Parmesan cheese. It's the perfect side dish with just about any meal, and I never have to remind my kids to eat their veggies.

SERVES 4

2 tablespoons extra-light olive oil or vegetable oil

3 medium or 1 large zucchini (1¼ pounds), cut into ¼-inch-thick half-moons (see Pro Tips & Tricks)

½ medium yellow onion, thinly sliced

½ teaspoon fine sea salt, plus more to taste

⅛ teaspoon freshly ground black pepper, plus more to taste

¼ cup freshly grated Parmesan cheese

1. In a large skillet over medium heat, heat the oil. Add the zucchini, onion, salt, and pepper and stir to combine. Cook, stirring occasionally, for 10 to 12 minutes, until the zucchini and onion are softened and golden brown. (I like to give the zucchini a chance to brown between stirring.)

2. Season with more salt and pepper, if needed. Sprinkle the Parmesan over the top and remove the pan from the heat. Serve hot.

Pro Tips & Tricks

- You could use yellow squash in place of zucchini or use a mix of squash and zucchini.

- The zucchini will shrink significantly as it cooks, so it's easy to oversalt. Don't add more than the recipe calls for! You can always adjust the seasoning later.

Ba-Corn
(Sautéed Corn with Crispy Bacon)

I wanted to challenge myself to come up with a dish that felt nice and fresh for warm weather, and sweet, juicy corn immediately came to mind. Sautéing the kernels brings out that natural sweetness, and that goes double when you add the contrasting saltiness of bacon. Plus, it's done in about fifteen minutes, which is just about all the time you want to spend at a hot stove in the summer. When my niece Lily tried it for the first time, she coined it "ba-corn." It was so clever, it stuck!

SERVES 4 TO 6

4 ears of corn (see Pro Tips & Tricks)

4 slices of bacon, chopped

½ teaspoon fine sea salt

Pinch of freshly ground black pepper

1 large garlic clove, finely minced or grated

2 tablespoons finely chopped fresh chives, plus more for garnish (optional)

1. Peel the husks and remove the silk from the corn. (See Pro Tips & Tricks on page 116.) Use a knife to remove the kernels from the cobs, trying to cut as close to the cobs as possible. (See Pro Tips & Tricks on page 102.)

2. In a large heavy-bottomed skillet over medium heat, cook the bacon, stirring frequently, for 5 to 7 minutes, until browned and crisp. Transfer the bacon to a paper towel–lined plate and reserve 1½ to 2 tablespoons of bacon drippings in the skillet.

3. Return the skillet to medium heat and add the corn kernels. Season with the salt and pepper and cook, uncovered and stirring frequently, for 5 to 6 minutes, until the corn is tender but still crisp. You want all of the corn's starchy flavor to have cooked off. During the last minute of cooking, add the garlic and stir constantly for about 1 minute, until the garlic is fragrant. Stir in the chives and remove the skillet from the heat.

4. Transfer the corn to a serving dish and top with the bacon and more chives (if using).

Pro Tips & Tricks

- Four ears of corn produce about 2½ cups of corn kernels. You can also substitute a 10- to 12-ounce bag of frozen corn. In a colander, give the corn a quick rinse to thaw and melt any ice. Drain well and cook as you would fresh corn.

Baba's Cucumber Spears

Not only do my parents grow a ton of cucumbers in their garden, but this is also one of the most requested dishes at our family gatherings. So now my mom, whom the kids call Baba (which is Ukrainian for *grandma*), is known for it. Dressing the cucumbers in garlic and vinegar complements their fresh flavor and crisp texture, which is a perfect way to showcase them when they're in season. And you can easily scale up the recipe for a picnic or barbecue, which is a good thing because an outdoor gathering just wouldn't be the same without a big bowl of Baba's cucumber salad!

SERVES 4

5 to 7 small cucumbers (about 1¼ pounds; see Pro Tips & Tricks)

2 tablespoons finely chopped fresh dill

2 tablespoons extra-virgin olive oil

2 garlic cloves, finely minced or grated

1 tablespoon white wine vinegar or distilled white vinegar

¼ teaspoon fine sea salt, plus more to taste

¼ teaspoon freshly ground black pepper, plus more to taste

1. Cut the cucumbers into quarters lengthwise. If your cucumbers are on the larger side, cut them into sixths. Place the cucumbers in a large mixing bowl.

2. Add the dill, oil, garlic, vinegar, salt, and pepper. Toss the cucumbers to coat well and season with more salt and pepper, if needed. Cover and refrigerate the cucumbers for 30 minutes, then serve. These are best enjoyed the day they are made.

Pro Tips & Tricks

- If you scale up the recipe, go lighter on the vinegar and add it to taste.
- Any small or mini cucumber variety will work for this recipe. Try garden, Kirby, cocktail, or Persian cucumbers.

Honey-Glazed Carrots

This is a deceptively simple dish that tastes way more complex than it actually is. The honey brings out the natural sweetness of the carrots and helps them caramelize as they bake, which will also change the mind of any carrot skeptic. This would be right at home next to a weeknight meal, but it definitely feels special enough for a holiday table, especially if you use pretty multicolored carrots.

SERVES 4 TO 5

10 to 12 medium carrots (about 2 pounds), halved or quartered if large (see Pro Tips & Tricks)

2 tablespoons extra-virgin olive oil

3 tablespoons honey (see Pro Tips & Tricks)

½ teaspoon fine sea salt, plus more to taste

¼ teaspoon freshly ground black pepper, plus more to taste

1 tablespoon unsalted butter, cut into pieces

1 tablespoon chopped fresh parsley leaves, for garnish (optional)

1. Place an oven rack in the center of the oven and preheat the oven to 400°F. Line a rimmed baking sheet with parchment paper.

2. Place the carrots on the prepared baking sheet, drizzle them with the oil and honey, and sprinkle them with the salt and pepper. Roll or toss the carrots so they are evenly coated.

3. Dot the carrots with the butter and bake them for 30 to 35 minutes, stirring after 20 minutes. The cook time will depend on the thickness of your carrots, but you're looking for them to be golden brown in spots and fork tender.

4. Transfer the carrots to a serving dish and drizzle them with any juices from the pan. Season with more salt and pepper, if needed. Garnish with the parsley (if using) and serve.

Pro Tips & Tricks

- You can make this recipe with whole carrots or cut them into quarters. If your carrots are very large and thick, you'll want to at least halve them lengthwise, or else they will take forever to bake. Baby carrots aren't ideal because their high water content prevents them from caramelizing.

- You can substitute maple syrup for the honey to make maple-roasted carrots.

9

SOMETHING SWEET

Since this chapter is dedicated to dishes that make you feel all the warm, fuzzy feelings, it seemed very fitting that I share the story of how I met my husband, Vadim. Well actually, how we almost *never* met. When I was fifteen, I was determined not to date until I turned eighteen. Instead, I focused on school, my family, and my church. But one weekend at a fundraising car wash my church youth group had organized, a car full of boys pulled up. I pretended not to notice Mr. Tall, Dark, and Handsome in the front seat, but something about him made my stomach flutter. I secretly hoped I'd see him again and even told my sister Svetlana.

What I didn't realize was that Vadim wasn't from Meridian, or even from Idaho. He lived in California and was on a camping trip with a couple of his cousins. At the last minute, they decided to stop in town because his third cousin lived there . . . and happened to belong to our church. So, imagine the Divine intervention at play when our youth group went out later that evening to Delsa's Ice Cream Parlour—and there he was. We were both shy, but we managed to say hello. Then, after ice cream—rocky road for me, huckleberry cheesecake for him—a group of us headed up to Table Rock, a mountain peak where our youth group would occasionally go to sing worship songs and hang out. On the way back, I somehow ended up riding with Vadim, squished between two of his travel companions in the back seat. (I later learned that this was Svetlana's ploy; she had told him that I liked him!) He asked for my number, I wrote it on a sheet of paper on his back before he continued on his trip, and the rest was history. When I was eighteen and he was twenty-two, we were married. (Which wasn't considered that

Here's our first photo together, taken just after Vadim asked me for my phone number. I wrote it on a sheet of paper over his back just before he drove back to California.

young in our Ukrainian community! Plus, I'd like to think that I was mature for my age . . .) A few months later, we bought our first house, and we've been inseparable ever since.

Just as it was in 2000 in that ice cream parlor when our romance was blossoming, dessert is a universal love language. There's no more effective way to show someone how much you care than to treat them to something sweet, delicious, and homemade. This chapter is full of the recipes I reach for when I want to spread a little extra love, whether it's the Cranberry-Apple-Almond Crisp (page 243) for Vadim, the chocolate cake for my daughter (Diana's Chocolate Birthday Cake, page 229, is named for her), or the Cinnamon-Sugar Donuts (page 234) for my son. Whether it's for a celebration, or to mark the end of a long week, or for no reason at all, these dishes are here for you to make for the special people in your life.

Strawberry Panna Cotta

I thought I made the best panna cotta ever . . . until I tried adding fresh strawberry puree. *Then* I knew that I had a winning recipe, especially when my husband ate two of them and then talked about it for days. The tartness of the strawberries balances the sweetness of the cream, and when you add in the pretty pink presentation and individual portions, you have a dish that's perfect for a restaurant menu . . . or company. (But between you and me, it's really just a no-bake dessert that takes less than thirty minutes to whip up and can be made up to three days ahead.)

SERVES 6

1 pound strawberries, hulled and quartered, plus more for garnish

⅔ cup plus 2 tablespoons sugar, divided

½ cup whole milk

2½ teaspoons unflavored gelatin

2 cups heavy cream

1 teaspoon pure vanilla extract

Pinch of fine sea salt

1 cup sour cream

1. In a food processor or blender, combine the strawberries and 2 tablespoons of the sugar and blend until smooth. Set a fine-mesh strainer over a medium bowl and strain the mixture, using a spatula to push and extract as much puree as you can, then discard the seeds. You should end up with a little more than 1 cup of puree. Set aside.

2. In a medium saucepan, add the milk and sprinkle the gelatin over the top. Let stand for 4 to 5 minutes, until the gelatin has softened. Set the pan over medium-low heat and whisk constantly for 4 to 5 minutes, until the gelatin dissolves and the mixture is steaming. Take care not to let the mixture boil.

3. While whisking constantly, slowly add the heavy cream, the remaining ⅔ cup of sugar, the vanilla, and salt. Continue cooking and whisking for 5 minutes, until the sugar is fully dissolved and the mixture is steaming. Again, be careful to avoid boiling. Remove the pan from the heat and let the mixture cool for 5 minutes.

4. In a large bowl, whisk together the sour cream and ⅔ cup of the strawberry puree. Whisking constantly, slowly stream in the warm cream mixture until fully incorporated. Divide the mixture between 6 ramekins or wine glasses, cover with plastic wrap, and refrigerate for at least 6 hours, until fully set, or up to 3 days. Cover and refrigerate the remaining strawberry puree.

5. To serve, spoon the reserved strawberry puree evenly over the individual panna cottas. Garnish each panna cotta with a fresh strawberry half.

Honey Baklava

I've always loved traditional Greek baklava with its flaky layers of phyllo and sticky honey-nut filling, but store-bought versions are always too sweet. My secret is adding a dash of lemon juice to the honey syrup, which brightens up the baklava and cuts the sweetness. And using store-bought phyllo makes this dessert surprisingly easy, too. It's actually a great recipe for making ahead because that gives the layers of dough a chance to absorb the syrup and soften. All you need to focus on is assembling, baking, and then taking in all the compliments on your (very impressive) homemade baklava.

MAKES ABOUT 30 PIECES

1¼ cups (2½ sticks) unsalted butter, melted, plus more for greasing

16 ounces phyllo dough, thawed according to package instructions (see Pro Tips & Tricks)

1 cup sugar

¾ cup water

½ cup honey

2 tablespoons freshly squeezed lemon juice

4 cups (1 pound) unsalted raw walnuts, pulsed in a food processor until finely chopped, plus more for garnish

1 teaspoon ground cinnamon

Melted chocolate, for garnish (optional)

1. Preheat the oven to 325°F. Butter the bottom and sides of a 9 × 13-inch nonstick cake pan. Set aside.

2. Trim the phyllo dough to fit your baking dish, if needed, one stack at a time and cover the trimmed dough with a damp towel to keep it from drying out. Discard any scraps.

3. In a medium saucepan over medium-high heat, combine the sugar, water, the honey, and lemon juice. Bring the mixture to a boil while stirring. Reduce the heat to medium-low and simmer the syrup for 4 minutes, undisturbed. Remove the pan from the heat and set aside to let the syrup cool.

4. In a medium bowl, combine the walnuts and cinnamon.

5. Line the bottom of the pan with 1 phyllo sheet and brush it with the butter. Repeat with 9 more sheets, brushing each with the butter before adding the next, for a total of 10 sheets in the bottom layer. Spread about ¾ cup of the nut mixture over the top.

6. Add 5 more sheets of phyllo, buttering each sheet before adding the next. Follow with another layer of ¾ cup of the nut mixture. Repeat three more times, layering and buttering 5 sheets of dough followed by ¾ cup of the nut mixture. For the final layer, add 10 sheets of phyllo, again buttering each sheet before adding the next. Then brush the very top with more butter.

7. Use a sharp knife to cut the pastry lengthwise into 1½-inch strips, then cut diagonally to form roughly 1½-inch-wide diamond shapes. Bake for 1 hour and 15 minutes, or until the top is golden brown.

8. Immediately spoon the syrup evenly over the hot baklava—you'll hear it sizzle, and that's what you want! Let the baklava cool completely at room temperature. For best results, cover the baklava with a tea towel once it has cooled and let the baklava sit for 4 to 6 hours, or overnight, at room temperature so the syrup can saturate and soften the layers of dough.

9. Garnish the baklava with more walnuts and drizzle with the chocolate (if using). Store at room temperature covered with a tea towel for 1 to 2 weeks or wrap in several layers of plastic wrap and freeze for up to 3 months. Thaw at room temperature before serving. You'll find that because the diamonds are precut, they'll separate easily.

Pro Tips & Tricks

- You can find phyllo dough in the freezer section of most major grocery stores. You want to look for a product that has 2 rolls with a total of 40 sheets. Don't try to sub in puff pastry or the recipe won't work.

- I recommend using a metal cake pan that is squared off at the edges. If the ends are sloped, like many glass or ceramic casserole dishes, then you're likely to get syrup pooling there, rather than inside of your baklava.

Best-Ever Brownies

This is one of my all-time most popular blog recipes for a reason: it yields the ultimate fudgy, super chocolatey brownies. I love enjoying these warm out of the oven with a big scoop of ice cream that gets all melty, or better yet, bringing a batch when we go camping. We pass them around the campfire for everyone to tuck between two graham crackers with their toasted marshmallows. Or skip all of the above and enjoy these on their own, hot or cold. No matter which way you go, they're perfection.

MAKES ABOUT 9 BROWNIES

1 cup (2 sticks) unsalted butter, softened, plus more for greasing

16 ounces semisweet chocolate chips (2½ cups), divided

4 large eggs

1¼ cups sugar

1 tablespoon instant coffee granules

3 tablespoons extra-light olive oil or vegetable oil

1 tablespoon pure vanilla extract

⅔ cup all-purpose flour (see How to Measure Flour Properly on page 20)

½ cup unsweetened natural cocoa powder (not Dutch processed)

1½ teaspoons aluminum-free baking powder

½ teaspoon fine sea salt

1. Preheat the oven to 350°F. Butter a 9 × 9-inch baking dish, line with parchment paper, and set aside.

2. In a medium saucepan over low heat, combine the butter and 2 cups of the chocolate chips. Whisk continually as the butter melts, until the mixture is combined. Remove the pan from the heat and set aside to cool for 15 minutes.

3. In a large bowl, whisk together the eggs, sugar, instant coffee, oil, and vanilla. Add the cooled chocolate mixture and whisk to combine. Set aside.

4. In a medium bowl, whisk together the flour, cocoa, baking powder, and salt. Using a spatula, fold the dry mixture into the chocolate mixture until just combined.

5. Transfer the batter to the prepared pan and sprinkle the remaining ½ cup chocolate chips evenly over the top. For fudgy brownies, bake for 35 to 37 minutes; a knife or toothpick inserted into the center should come out fudgy. For soft and moist brownies, bake for closer to 40 minutes; a knife or toothpick inserted into the center should come out with moist crumbs attached.

6. Cool until the brownies are nearly at room temperature. Cut into squares and serve.

Pro Tips & Tricks

- **Make ahead:** Once the brownies have cooled, cover them with plastic wrap and store in an airtight container. They will stay nice and moist for up to 5 days.

Cinnamon Apple Cake

I knew I was on to something when I crossed a French apple cake and a classic Russian *sharlotka* and hundreds of people raved about it. This cake is different than most American cakes in that it isn't overly sweet, and it relies on beaten eggs to give it rise. With just a handful of simple ingredients, the result is a soft, moist, and tender crumb that's dotted with sweet-tart apples and a perfect sprinkle of cinnamon sugar to finish.

SERVES 8

Unsalted butter, for greasing

4 large eggs, room temperature

1 cup plus 1 tablespoon granulated sugar, divided

1 cup all-purpose flour (see How to Measure Flour Properly on page 20)

½ teaspoon aluminum-free baking powder

¼ teaspoon fine sea salt

1 teaspoon pure vanilla extract

4 large Granny Smith apples (about 2 pounds), peeled, cored, quartered, and sliced into ¼-inch-thick pieces

¼ teaspoon ground cinnamon

1. Preheat the oven to 350°F. Grease the bottom (only the bottom!) of a 9-inch springform pan with the butter and line it with a round of parchment paper. Set aside.

2. In the bowl of a stand mixer fitted with the whisk attachment or in a large bowl with a hand mixer, add the eggs. Beat on high speed for 1 minute, until foamy. With the mixer running, gradually add 1 cup of the granulated sugar and continue beating on high for 6 to 8 minutes, until thick and fluffy ribbons form. You're looking for when a ribbon of batter can drizzle from the whisk and sit on top of the surface of the batter below for a moment before incorporating back in.

3. In a medium bowl, whisk together the flour, baking powder, and salt. Sift the flour mixture into the egg batter in three increments, folding with a spatula between each addition and scraping from the bottom of the bowl to pick up any rogue pockets of flour. Fold just until no streaks of flour remain. Fold in the vanilla until just incorporated. Set aside ½ cup of the apples, then fold in the remaining apples until just incorporated. Do not overmix.

4. Transfer the batter to the prepared pan and smooth the top with the spatula. Scatter the reserved apple slices in an even layer over the top. Bake for 60 minutes, or until the top of the cake is golden brown and a knife or toothpick inserted into the center comes out clean.

5. When the cake comes out of the oven, stir together the remaining 1 tablespoon of granulated sugar plus the cinnamon and sprinkle it over the top.

6. Let the cake cool in the pan for 15 minutes. Slide a thin spatula or knife around the edges of the pan to loosen the cake, remove the springform collar, and transfer the cake to a platter to cool to room temperature.

Pro Tips & Tricks

- Don't be tempted to grease the entire pan with the butter. The cake needs to "hold" the sides of the pan in order to rise evenly with a nice flat top instead of caving in at the center.

- Because the eggs are what will help the cake rise, it's critical that you beat the eggs and sugar together with a high-powered mixer. If using an electric hand mixer, add 2 additional minutes of mixing time.

Berry Cheesecake Bars

When my family gathers every Sunday for brunch, my favorite part is watching all the kids' eyes light up when they see my dessert carrier—which is usually packed with something I've been testing for my website. When I was working on these cheesecake bars, I ended up bringing them two weeks in a row—so you can imagine how happy I was to hear that my nieces were even more excited about them the second time because they remembered how good they were. These bars are just as satisfying as classic New York–style cheesecake, but they bake more quickly and don't require a water bath.

MAKES 12 TO 16 BARS

FOR THE CRUST

2 cups graham cracker crumbs (from 14 to 18 whole graham crackers)

½ cup (1 stick) unsalted butter, melted

1 tablespoon sugar

Pinch of fine sea salt

FOR THE CHEESECAKE FILLING

2 pounds (four 8-ounce blocks) plain cream cheese, room temperature

1¼ cups sugar

5 large eggs, room temperature

2 tablespoons sour cream

Zest of 1 large lemon

1½ teaspoons pure vanilla extract

⅛ teaspoon fine sea salt

FOR THE MIXED BERRY SAUCE

2 tablespoons sugar

1 tablespoon cornstarch

1 tablespoon freshly squeezed lemon juice

¼ to ⅓ cup water

4 cups fresh or frozen berries, such as blueberries, blackberries, raspberries, or sliced strawberries

1. MAKE THE CRUST: Preheat the oven to 350°F. Line a 9 × 13-inch metal cake pan with parchment paper, making sure there is at least a few inches of overhang on two opposite sides. Set aside.

2. In a medium bowl, add the graham cracker crumbs, butter, sugar, and salt and stir until the crumbs are moistened. Transfer the mixture to the prepared baking pan and press it evenly into the bottom of the pan. Bake for 8 minutes and set aside to cool to room temperature.

3. MAKE THE CHEESECAKE FILLING: Reduce the oven temperature to 325°F.

4. In the bowl of a stand mixer fitted with the paddle attachment or in a large bowl with a hand mixer, beat together the cream cheese and sugar on medium-high speed for 5 minutes, until whipped and fluffy. Scrape down the sides of the bowl with a spatula as needed.

5. Reduce the mixer speed to medium and add the eggs one at a time, mixing well between each addition and scraping down the sides of the bowl as needed. Reduce the speed to low and add the sour cream, zest, vanilla, and salt. Mix until incorporated. Scrape down the sides of the bowl one last time and mix until smooth.

6. Pour the filling over the cooled crust and bake for 40 to 45 minutes, until the filling is just barely set in the center. Let the cake cool to room temperature, about 2 hours, then cover with plastic wrap and refrigerate for at least 4 hours, until set, or overnight.

7. MAKE THE BERRY SAUCE: In a medium saucepan, stir together the sugar, cornstarch, and lemon juice with ⅓ cup water if using fresh berries (or ¼ cup water if using frozen). Set the pan over medium heat and stir until the mixture starts to thicken, about 1 minute. Add the berries and stir gently as they cook for 5 to 6 minutes, until the berries release some of their juices and begin to boil. Remove the pan from the heat and let the sauce cool before serving.

8. To serve, use the parchment paper "handles" to carefully remove the chilled cheesecake from the pan and transfer it to a cutting board.

Slice the cake into 12 to 16 bars, wiping your knife with a damp paper towel between slices to get nice, neat bars. Drizzle with the berry sauce and serve.

Pro Tips & Tricks

- If you're short on time, you can serve the bars with fresh berries instead of the sauce or even top them with canned cherry pie filling.

- **Make ahead:** Both the cheesecake and the berry sauce can be made up to 2 days in advance. Cover and refrigerate them until ready to serve. If using plastic wrap, be careful that it doesn't lie directly over the surface of your cheesecake, or it will stick to the top.

Diana's Chocolate Birthday Cake
with 6-Minute Chocolate Buttercream

When my daughter requested a chocolate cake for her birthday, I knew I had to come up with something really special. After weeks of research and testing, I came up with this three-layer cake that can only be described as a big chocolate hug. It's decadent, chocolatey, and moist—everything you want in a chocolate cake, and it's definitely fitting for a celebration. It has since been requested three years in a row and is still going strong! I also love this recipe because the cake keeps well at room temperature, so you can make it a day ahead.

**MAKES ONE 9-INCH
3-LAYER CAKE**

FOR THE CAKE

Unsalted butter, softened, for greasing

3 cups all-purpose flour (see How to Measure Flour Properly on page 20)

2½ cups granulated sugar

1 teaspoon fine sea salt

⅔ cup natural unsweetened cocoa powder (not Dutch processed)

2 teaspoons baking soda

2 large eggs, room temperature

2 cups warm coffee (decaf is OK)

⅔ cup extra-light olive oil or vegetable oil

2 tablespoons distilled white vinegar

1 tablespoon pure vanilla extract

Sprinkles, for decorating (optional)

1. MAKE THE CAKE: Place your oven racks in the bottom third and upper third of the oven. Preheat the oven to 350°F. Grease three 9-inch round cake pans with the butter, line the bottoms with a circle of parchment paper, and set aside.

2. In a large bowl, combine the flour, granulated sugar, and salt. Sift in the cocoa powder and baking soda and whisk to combine. Set aside.

3. In a second large bowl, lightly beat the eggs. Add the coffee, oil, vinegar, and vanilla and whisk until smooth. Pour the wet mixture into the dry mixture and whisk until the batter is well-combined and no streaks of flour remain. Use a rubber spatula to scrape the bowl all the way down, pulling up any pockets of flour that might be hiding. The batter will be loose and lumpy—and that's OK!

4. Divide the batter evenly between the prepared pans. Bake the cake layers in the center of each rack for 25 to 30 minutes, until a knife or toothpick inserted into the center comes out clean. Let the cakes cool for 15 minutes in their pans. Run a thin spatula or knife around the edges of the pan to loosen the cakes and transfer them to a wire rack to cool completely.

5. WHILE THE CAKES COOL, MAKE THE BUTTERCREAM: In the bowl of a stand mixer fitted with the whisk attachment or in a large bowl with a hand mixer, beat the butter on high speed for about 3 minutes, scraping down the bowl as needed, until creamy and light in color.

6. Add the confectioners' sugar, cocoa powder, ¼ cup of the cream, the vanilla, and salt. Beat on low speed until the sugar is incorporated, then increase the speed to medium-high. Beat for 3 minutes, scraping down the bowl several times to ensure everything

INGREDIENTS CONTINUE

RECIPE CONTINUES

Diana's Chocolate Birthday Cake with 6-Minute Chocolate Buttercream *continued*

FOR THE CHOCOLATE
BUTTERCREAM

1½ cups (3 sticks) unsalted
butter, softened

4½ cups confectioners' sugar,
plus more to taste

¾ cup natural unsweetened
cocoa powder (not Dutch
processed)

¼ to ½ cup heavy cream

1 tablespoon pure vanilla
extract

½ teaspoon fine sea salt

is well blended. If the frosting is still too thick to be easily spread over the cake, add more cream, 1 tablespoon at a time, until the ideal consistency is reached. Taste and adjust the sweetness with more confectioners' sugar, if needed.

7. The tops of the cakes should be level, but if needed, you can trim them with a serrated knife. Spread a quarter of the frosting over one of the cooled cakes. Place the second cake upside down on top of the first layer and spread another quarter of the frosting to cover the top. Add the third cake upside down on top of the second layer. Spread a quarter of the frosting over the top and the remaining quarter of frosting over the sides. Decorate with the sprinkles (if using) and serve. To serve later that day, you can keep the cake at room temperature, covered by a cake keeper or an overturned large stockpot.

Pro Tips & Tricks

- If you only have two 9-inch cake pans, you can divide the batter between them and bake for about 35 minutes, or until a knife or toothpick inserted into the center comes out clean. You could also use a nonstick springform pan for the third pan.

- The cake and frosting taste best at room temperature. If you make the cake ahead of time and have to refrigerate it, bring it back to room temperature before serving.

- To keep any leftover cake from drying out, place a sheet of plastic wrap directly on the cut portion of the cake to keep the air out, then cover the cake and refrigerate for up to 3 days.

That Yummy Fruit Salad

Years ago, I was at my cousin Alex's house for a barbecue when his wife, Alla, served the most delicious fruit salad I'd ever had. It wasn't just chopped fruit tossed into a bowl as an afterthought. No, this was fresh, seasonal fruit that had been drizzled with a bright, citrusy honey syrup. I asked Alla how she made "that yummy fruit salad," and it's been my signature potluck dish ever since. The citrus syrup works with just about any fruit and keeps it from browning, and everyone always asks me for the recipe.

SERVES 8

3 tablespoons honey

1 teaspoon lemon zest

1 tablespoon freshly squeezed lemon juice

1 teaspoon lime zest

1 tablespoon freshly squeezed lime juice

8 cups chopped fresh fruit (see Pro Tips & Tricks)

1. In a small bowl, whisk together the honey, lemon zest, lemon juice, lime zest, and lime juice.

2. In a large serving bowl, gently toss the fruit with the honey dressing. Serve immediately. Store leftovers in an airtight container in the refrigerator for up to 2 days.

Pro Tips & Tricks

- You can use any fruit you like in this salad, but I recommend sticking with what's in season. In the summer, go with berries, kiwi, grapes, watermelon, pineapple, or mango. In the winter, pears, apples, bananas, citrus, and pomegranate seeds are great.

- You can use only lemon juice, only lime juice, or both in the dressing.

- Don't skip the zest—it takes the salad's flavor to the next level.

- If you have leftover fruit salad, cover and refrigerate it overnight, then serve it over yogurt for a delicious breakfast or snack parfait.

Strawberry-Coconut Ice Pops

My daughter, Diana, and I came up with these when we were craving strawberry ice cream, but we wanted something handheld that she could share with her friends and cousins when they came over (and that just so happens to be way tastier and healthier than anything you could buy in the store). The resulting pops reminded me of a Ukrainian dessert that I enjoyed growing up, which wasn't more than blended strawberries and sour cream with a little sugar. My husband, Vadim, was immediately smitten with the nostalgic flavor, as was the rest of my family.

Using coconut milk makes these pops dairy-free but with a surprisingly creamy texture. And the little bits of strawberry are like bursts of summer in every bite.

MAKES SIX 4-OUNCE OR EIGHT 3-OUNCE ICE POPS

2½ cups fresh strawberries, hulled and quartered

1¼ cups canned unsweetened full-fat coconut milk

¼ cup honey, plus more to taste

1 tablespoon freshly squeezed lemon juice

1. In a food processor or blender, combine the strawberries, coconut milk, honey, and lemon juice and blend until the mixture is nearly smooth but still has small bits of berries. Adjust the sweetness with more honey, if desired.

2. To keep mess to a minimum, use a funnel or measuring cup with a pouring lip to fill your molds. Set the ice-pop molds on their base. If using molds that have sticks attached to their lids, insert them at this point. If using loose wooden sticks, freeze the pops for 1 hour before inserting the sticks. Freeze for about 6 hours, until fully set, or overnight.

3. To remove the pops from the molds, briefly run warm water over the outside of the molds until the pops easily slide out.

Cinnamon-Sugar Donuts

When the craving for fresh donuts strikes, I personally don't want to wait half the day for dough to proof and rise—I mean, they're just going to disappear in five minutes! That's where these tasty little cinnamon-sugar donut holes come in. They're made with the same dough that you'd use to make churros, éclairs, and cream puffs; they come together in about thirty minutes; and they're light, fluffy, and sweet—exactly what you want in a donut.

MAKES ABOUT 45 DONUT HOLES

½ cup water

½ cup whole milk

½ cup (1 stick) unsalted butter

½ cup plus 1 teaspoon sugar, divided

¼ teaspoon fine sea salt

1 cup all-purpose flour (see How to Measure Flour Properly on page 20)

4 large eggs, room temperature

1 teaspoon ground cinnamon

Peanut or vegetable oil, for frying

1. In a large saucepan over medium heat, combine ½ cup water, the milk, butter, 1 teaspoon of the sugar, and the salt. Bring to a boil, stirring frequently. Remove the pan from the heat and use a wooden spoon to stir in the flour until well incorporated.

2. Return the pan over medium heat and continue stirring for another 1½ to 2 minutes to release extra moisture from the mixture and to partially cook the flour. The dough will look smooth and a thin film will form on the bottom of the pan.

3. Transfer the dough to the bowl of a stand mixer fitted with the whisk attachment or a large bowl with a hand mixer and beat on medium speed for 1 minute to cool the mixture slightly. Beat in the eggs one at a time, allowing each to fully incorporate before adding the next. Once all the eggs have been added, use a spatula to scrape down the sides of the bowl and beat the mixture for 1 minute, until the dough is smooth and forms a thick ribbon when you lift the whisk. Set aside.

4. In a medium bowl, stir together the remaining ½ cup of sugar and the cinnamon. Line a plate with a paper towel and set aside.

5. In a 5½-quart Dutch oven or large heavy-bottomed pot over medium heat, add 1½ inches of the oil. Heat the oil until it registers 375°F (see Pro Tips & Tricks). Carefully drop the batter by the teaspoonful into the oil as close to the surface as possible so it doesn't splatter. (A second spoon can be helpful for scooting the batter into the oil.) Take care not to crowd the pot, or the temperature of the oil will drop and your donuts won't get nice and brown. You will most likely need to do this in three to four batches.

6. Fry the dough for about 4 minutes, turning the donuts over halfway through if they don't flip on their own, until they are golden brown on all sides. Use a strainer or slotted spoon to transfer the donuts to the prepared plate to soak up the extra oil and to cool for just a minute or two. Roll the warm donuts in the cinnamon-sugar mixture until well coated. Repeat with the remaining batter.

7. Transfer the finished donuts to a serving dish and serve warm or at room temperature.

Pro Tips & Tricks

* Anytime you're frying, I highly recommend using a clip-on pot thermometer to gauge the temperature of your oil. If the oil is too cool, the donuts will soak up too much oil and get greasy. And if it's too hot, your donuts will brown too quickly without fully cooking through in the center.

Berry Tartlets
with Vanilla Cream

Vibrant, beautiful fruit tarts always steal the show when it's time to serve dessert. But cutting into a fruit tart can be tricky—the tough shell tends to crumble, and it's not long before your work of art starts looking like a mess. The solution is to make these individual tartlets, which take no more effort than a full-size tart but look equally impressive. The dough is so easy to pull together, and you can make both the shells and the pastry cream ahead. Just assemble and serve!

MAKES 12 TO 15 TARTLETS

FOR THE VANILLA CREAM

1 large egg

2 large egg yolks

½ cup sugar

3 tablespoons cornstarch

⅛ teaspoon fine sea salt

2 cups whole milk

2 tablespoons (¼ stick) unsalted butter

2 teaspoons pure vanilla extract

FOR THE DOUGH

1 large egg, room temperature

⅓ cup sugar

5 tablespoons unsalted butter, room temperature, cut into pieces

1 tablespoon mayonnaise

⅛ teaspoon fine sea salt

1½ cups all-purpose flour (see How to Measure Flour Properly on page 20), plus more for dusting

INGREDIENTS CONTINUE

1. MAKE THE VANILLA CREAM: In a medium bowl, combine the egg, egg yolks, sugar, cornstarch, and salt. Whisk vigorously for 2 minutes, until the mixture is completely smooth and lightened in color. Set aside.

2. In a large saucepan over medium heat, heat the milk and butter for about 2 minutes, stirring occasionally to prevent it from scalding, until it's barely at a simmer. (Keep a close eye on it!) Remove the pan from the heat.

3. Whisking constantly, slowly drizzle a third of the milk into the egg mixture. By doing this slowly, you're tempering the eggs to make sure they won't scramble when mixed with the hot milk.

4. Continue whisking as you pour the egg mixture back into the saucepan with the remaining milk. Set the saucepan over medium heat and whisk constantly for about 2 minutes, until the mixture has thickened. Stop mixing for a few seconds to see if bubbles are forming. Once the mixture starts boiling, reduce the heat to medium-low and whisk constantly at a low boil for 1 minute more to cook off the cornstarch so the pastry cream doesn't separate. The pastry cream should be thickened, smooth, and glossy. Stir in the vanilla and remove the pot from the heat.

5. Transfer the pastry cream to a shallow bowl and cover with plastic wrap. Press the plastic wrap to the surface of the cream, which will prevent a skin from forming. Allow the cream to cool to room temperature and then chill in the refrigerator for at least 2 hours or up to 3 days.

6. MAKE THE DOUGH: In the bowl of a stand mixer fitted with the paddle attachment or in a large bowl with a hand mixer, beat together the egg and sugar on medium speed for 30 seconds, until well blended. Add the butter and increase the speed to high. Mix for 2 minutes, until creamy and thick, like buttercream. Add the mayo and salt and mix until blended.

RECIPE CONTINUES

FOR ASSEMBLY

⅓ cup apricot jam (see Pro Tips & Tricks)

1 cup berries, such as sliced strawberries, blueberries, or raspberries; or sliced fruit of choice

7. Add the flour in thirds, mixing to incorporate between each addition. The dough should have a soft, cookie dough–like consistency and should not stick to your fingertips.

8. Generously dust a clean work surface with flour. Turn out the dough and use a rolling pin to roll it to ⅛ inch thick. Use a 3-inch cookie cutter, large glass, or the ring from a mason jar to cut out 12 rounds. Gather up the dough scraps and reroll them to get a few more rounds, if possible.

9. Place each round in the well of a nonstick cupcake tin, using your fingertips to gently push the dough into the bottom and mold the dough so it comes three-quarters of the way up the sides of the cup. Use a fork to poke the bottom of each round of dough three to four times. Refrigerate the cupcake tin for 30 minutes. (This will help the dough keep its shape and produce a taller cup.)

10. Meanwhile, place an oven rack in the center of the oven and preheat the oven to 350°F.

11. Bake the tartlet cups for 10 to 12 minutes, until the edges of the dough are golden. Let them cool in the pan for 15 minutes, then transfer them to a cooling rack to cool completely; they should be easy to remove from the pan. At this point, you could store the cups in an airtight container at room temperature for up to 2 days.

12. ASSEMBLE: In a small microwave-safe bowl, combine the jam and 1 tablespoon water and microwave on high for 30 seconds just to loosen the mixture. (You could also do this in a small pan on the stove.)

13. Fill each tartlet cup with about 2 tablespoons of the pastry cream. Top the cream with the berries, then lightly coat the fruit with the jam glaze. These are best enjoyed the day they are assembled. Keep them chilled until ready to serve.

Pro Tips & Tricks

- You can also make these into 36 mini tartlets. Roll gumball-size pieces of dough and mold them to the cups of a mini muffin tin. Proceed as directed in the recipe, baking for about 10 minutes.

- To speed set the pastry cream, place the bowl of cream over a bowl of ice water for 30 minutes, then refrigerate for 30 minutes or until ready to use.

- If your apricot jam has bits of fruit, you can strain them out for a smoother glaze. You can also substitute it with another light-colored jam.

Fresh Peach Pie

There's nothing like baking a pie with fresh summer peaches to make you feel like a domestic superhero. The sweet aroma of the fruit's juices bubbling and the buttery, flaky crust turning golden has a way of drawing everyone into the kitchen. I'd say the hardest part of this recipe is waiting for it to cool for a couple of hours before you dig in—but don't be tempted to skip that step! You want to give the filling a chance to thicken and settle for easier slicing (and not burn your mouth—not that I know anything about being too impatient to take a taste . . .). Serve with vanilla ice cream, of course.

MAKES ONE 9-INCH PIE

1 batch The Only Pie Dough You'll Need (page 160)

⅓ cup all-purpose flour (see How to Measure Flour Properly on page 20) or 3 tablespoons cornstarch or potato starch, plus more for dusting

2 handfuls of ice

7 to 8 peaches (about 2½ pounds; see Pro Tips & Tricks)

1½ tablespoons freshly squeezed lemon juice

1 teaspoon pure vanilla extract

⅔ cup granulated sugar (see Pro Tips & Tricks)

¼ teaspoon ground nutmeg

⅛ teaspoon fine sea salt

1 large egg

1 tablespoon water

1 teaspoon coarse turbinado or granulated sugar, for finishing

Vanilla ice cream, for serving (optional)

1. Make the pie dough and chill for 1 hour.

2. Remove the first piece of prepared dough from the refrigerator and dust a clean work surface with flour. Use a rolling pin to roll the dough into a 13-inch circle. Scoot the dough around every now and then to ensure that it isn't sticking to the surface, sprinkling more flour under the dough if needed. Transfer the rolled-out dough to a 9-inch, deep-dish pie pan by carefully rolling it onto your rolling pin and unrolling it over the pan. Gently mold the dough to the pan, leaving some overhang, then transfer it to the refrigerator to chill until ready to use.

3. Remove the second piece of dough from the refrigerator. Sprinkle a 12-inch-long sheet of parchment paper with flour and place the dough on top. Roll the dough into a 12-inch circle. Transfer the dough, on the parchment paper, to the refrigerator to chill until ready to use.

4. Place the oven racks in the center and lower third of the oven and preheat the oven to 425°F.

5. Next, make the filling. Fill a large bowl with the ice and some cold water and set aside. Bring a large pot of water to a boil over medium-high heat. Add the peaches and boil for 1 minute, or until the skins begin to loosen. Use a slotted spoon to transfer the peaches to the ice water to cool.

6. When cool enough to handle, halve the peaches to remove the pits, then peel the peaches and cut them into ½-inch-thick slices. You should have about 6½ cups of peach slices. Transfer the peaches to a large bowl, drizzle them with the lemon juice and vanilla and lightly toss to coat. Add the granulated sugar, flour, nutmeg, and salt and gently stir the mixture until the flour and sugar are moistened with peach juices. Transfer the filling to the prepared pie dish and set aside.

RECIPE CONTINUES

7. Slice the second piece of dough with a pizza cutter to create eight 1-inch-wide strips. Arrange four of the strips evenly over the peaches, using any longer strips at the center and shorter strips toward the edges. Pull back every other strip just past the halfway point. Lay one long strip over the center of the pie, perpendicular to the other strips. Unfold the strips, then fold back the alternating strips. Repeat with the remaining strips. (You're creating a lattice pattern.) Next, fold back the alternating strips from the other side of the pie and finish weaving in the remaining strips.

8. Fold any excess dough under the bottom crust and pinch together. Flute the edges of the crust. In a small bowl, beat together the egg and the water. Brush the egg wash over the crust and sprinkle with the turbinado sugar.

9. Place a sheet of foil on the bottom rack of the oven to catch any drips from the pie. Place the pie on the center rack and bake for 20 minutes. Reduce the heat to 375°F and bake for 35 to 40 minutes, covering the pie with a pie shield or a sheet of foil with a hole cut out in the center about halfway through. The crust should be golden brown and the filling juices bubbling.

10. Let the pie cool for at least 2 hours before slicing. Serve slices with the vanilla ice cream (if using).

Pro Tips & Tricks

- For the best-tasting pie, use ripe peaches. The skins will be easier to peel, and ripe peaches will release their natural pectin while they bake, resulting in a thick and saucy pie filling.

- You can make this recipe with peeled or unpeeled peaches. (I have found some store-bought peach skins just don't budge, even with blanching). Also, taste your peaches. If they are tart, use ¾ cup sugar. If they are supersweet, you can decrease the sugar to ½ cup.

Cranberry-Apple-Almond Crisp

We make apple crisps on repeat through fall and winter—namely because it's Vadim's favorite dessert but also because it would be a shame to not take advantage of all the fresh apples and cozy fall flavors. I mean, how dreamy is the aroma of a freshly baked apple anything wafting through the kitchen?! Serve this with a scoop of vanilla ice cream; it's such a treat when it melts slightly over the warm crisp.

SERVES 10 TO 12

FOR THE CRUMB TOPPING

1 cup (2 sticks) unsalted butter, diced, room temperature, plus more for greasing

1¾ cups all-purpose flour (see How to Measure Flour Properly on page 20)

1 cup rolled, old-fashioned, or quick-cooking oats

½ cup (packed) light brown sugar

¼ cup granulated sugar

½ teaspoon ground cinnamon

¼ teaspoon fine sea salt

½ cup sliced or slivered almonds

FOR THE APPLE CRISP FILLING

11 to 12 medium Granny Smith apples (about 4 pounds)

1 cup cranberries, fresh or frozen (no need to thaw), or ½ cup dried cranberries

2 tablespoons freshly squeezed lemon juice

1 cup granulated sugar, or to taste (see Pro Tips & Tricks)

3 tablespoons all-purpose flour (see How to Measure Flour Properly on page 20)

1½ teaspoons ground cinnamon

1. Preheat the oven to 375°F. Generously grease a 9 × 13-inch casserole dish with butter. Set aside.

2. MAKE THE TOPPING: In a large bowl, use your hands to combine the flour, oats, brown sugar, granulated sugar, cinnamon, and salt. Add the butter and work it into the mixture with your hands until pea-size crumbs form throughout. Mix in the almonds and set aside.

3. MAKE THE FILLING: Peel, core, and cut the apples into ¼-inch-thick slices. You should have 12 cups of sliced apples. In a large bowl, add the apples and cranberries. Sprinkle the lemon juice over the fruit and toss to coat.

4. In a medium bowl, stir together the sugar, flour, and cinnamon. Sprinkle the mixture over the apples and cranberries and toss to combine. Transfer the filling to the prepared dish and spread the crumb topping evenly over the filling.

5. Bake for 45 to 50 minutes, until the topping is golden and crisp and the apples are bubbling at the edges. An instant-read thermometer inserted in the center should register above 175°F.

Pro Tips & Tricks

- We love apple desserts so much that we invested in an apple slicer and corer. It's the best tool ever because you can peel, slice, and core each apple in 5 seconds (literally!). It cuts the prep work for any apple dessert by at least 90 percent.

- If you're using a different crisp apple that is sweeter than Granny Smith, you'll want to decrease the granulated sugar in the filling to ¾ cup.

Mom's Famous Rogaliki
(Rugelach)

My mother taught me how to make rugelach, or as she calls them, *rogaliki*. They are her standby sweet treat for Sunday lunches at her house, as well as for potlucks, and everyone looks forward to enjoying them week after week. They are a blend between a pastry and a cookie, crisp and buttery on the outside with a soft and flaky jam-filled center. This recipe is also quick to make, doesn't require any ingredient to soften or come to room temperature, and makes a big batch—because these disappear *fast*.

MAKES 60 RUGELACH

4 cups all-purpose flour, plus more as needed (see How to Measure Flour Properly on page 20)

2 teaspoons rapid rise or instant yeast

½ teaspoon fine sea salt

1 cup (2 sticks) unsalted butter, melted and cooled to 110°F

1 cup whole milk, warmed to 110°F

2½ tablespoons granulated sugar, divided

1 cup berry jam or blended preserves (see Pro Tips & Tricks)

1 cup confectioners' sugar, for finishing

1. In a medium bowl, whisk together the flour, yeast, and salt. Set aside.

2. In the bowl of a stand mixer fitted with the paddle attachment or in a large bowl with a hand mixer, combine the butter and milk. With the mixer on medium-low speed (or speed level 2 if your mixer has this setting), add the flour mixture 1 cup at a time, letting it incorporate with each addition and scraping down the bowl as needed. Once all the flour is incorporated, continue mixing the dough for another 3 to 5 minutes. It should be very soft and won't stick to your hands or the sides of the mixing bowl. If the dough is still sticking to your fingertips, add up to 2 tablespoons more flour, 1 tablespoon at a time. Cover the dough with plastic wrap and let the dough rest at room temperature for 30 minutes.

3. Line two rimmed baking sheets with parchment paper and set aside.

4. Divide the dough into five equal pieces and loosely cover them with plastic wrap. On a clean, smooth surface, use a rolling pin to roll one piece of the dough into a 10-inch circle, less than ⅛ inch thick.

5. Sprinkle ½ tablespoon of the granulated sugar over the entire surface of the dough. Using a pizza cutter, cut the dough into 12 even triangle slices (as you would cut a pizza). Add a marble-size portion of the jam over the wider part of each dough triangle, then start rolling up the dough from the jam side, keeping a fairly tight roll as you go. Place the rolled rugelach tail side down on the prepared baking sheet, about 1 inch apart. Repeat with the remaining dough.

RECIPE CONTINUES

6. Let the rugelach proof in a warm place (like a 100°F oven) for 30 to 45 minutes, until they have visibly puffed. You can also do this at room temperature, but it will take twice as long.

7. If you proofed the rugelach in the oven, remove them. Place the oven racks in the top and bottom thirds of the oven and preheat the oven to 350°F.

8. Bake the rugelach for 25 to 30 minutes, or until the tops are just starting to turn lightly golden, rotating the baking sheets halfway through. Let the rugelach rest for 10 minutes on the baking sheets.

9. Add the confectioners' sugar to a medium bowl. Roll the warm rugelach in the confectioners' sugar and transfer them to a large serving tray. (It's OK to stack the finished rugelach.) Don't be tempted to skip the confectioners' sugar step; the rugelach aren't overly sweet, and it helps round out their flavor.

Pro Tips & Tricks

- When choosing a jam or preserves to fill these with, the thicker, the better. More watery mixtures will get too runny when the rogaliki bake.

Raspberry Cake Roll

What I love so much about this recipe is that it looks *way* more difficult to make than it really is. I promise! When you roll up the moist, tender sponge cake fresh from the oven, it "teaches" the cake to curl, making it a lot easier to roll up when the cake is assembled. Also, incorporating fresh raspberries is like guaranteeing that your cake will have that perfect pop of flavor against the creamy mascarpone filling. And if I still haven't convinced you that you should make this gorgeous cake, consider that you can make it a day ahead—which takes a lot of pressure off!

SERVES 12 TO 14

FOR THE SPONGE CAKE

⅓ cup confectioners' sugar

¾ cup all-purpose flour (see How to Measure Flour Properly on page 20)

½ teaspoon aluminum-free baking powder

¼ teaspoon fine sea salt

5 large eggs, room temperature

¾ cup granulated sugar

1 teaspoon pure vanilla extract

FOR THE SYRUP

½ cup raspberry preserves

2 tablespoons water, or as needed

FOR THE RASPBERRY FILLING

1 cup heavy cream, chilled

½ cup granulated sugar

8 ounces mascarpone, chilled

2 teaspoons pure vanilla extract

12 ounces fresh raspberries, divided

Confectioners' sugar, for dusting

1. MAKE THE SPONGE CAKE: Preheat the oven to 375°F. Line a 13 × 18-inch rimmed baking sheet with parchment paper and set aside. Do not grease the baking sheet or the cake won't rise properly. Lay a clean linen or tea towel on a work surface and dust generously with the confectioners' sugar.

2. In a medium bowl, whisk together the flour, baking powder, and salt. Set aside.

3. In the bowl of a stand mixer fitted with the whisk attachment or in a large bowl with a hand mixer, combine the eggs and granulated sugar and beat on high speed for 7 to 8 minutes, until ribbons form on the surface when you lift the whisk. The mixture should at least double in volume and turn pale yellow in color.

4. Use a silicone spatula to fold in the flour mixture a third at a time, making sure each addition is just incorporated before folding in the next. Fold until no streaks of flour remain, making sure to scrape the bottom of the bowl to catch any pockets of flour. Add the vanilla and fold until just incorporated. Spread the batter evenly in the prepared baking sheet, all the way to the edges of the pan.

5. Bake for 10 to 12 minutes, until the cake is golden and doesn't indent when you gently press the top. When the cake is done, immediately run a knife around the edges of the pan and carefully transfer the cake with the parchment paper by sliding it onto a cooling rack. Then, use the parchment paper to help you flip the cake top side down onto the sugar-dusted towel. Gently peel back and discard the parchment. While the cake is still hot, start with the short end to roll the cake with the towel into a tight log. Set the rolled cake on a cooling rack to cool to room temperature.

6. MAKE THE SYRUP: In a small bowl, stir together the preserves with the water. You want the mixture to be syrupy so it will easily spread over the cake. Add more water, if needed. Set aside.

RECIPE CONTINUES

Raspberry Cake Roll *continued*

7. MAKE THE RASPBERRY FILLING: In the bowl of a stand mixer fitted with the whisk attachment or in a large bowl with a hand mixer, beat together the cream and granulated sugar on medium-high speed for 3 to 4 minutes, until stiff peaks form. Set aside.

8. In a medium bowl, stir together the mascarpone and vanilla. Use a spoon or spatula to fold the whipped cream into the mascarpone a third at a time, mixing until incorporated after each addition. Set aside.

9. In a small bowl, use a fork to coarsely mash half of the raspberries, then fold them into the filling until just dispersed. Do not overmix.

10. ASSEMBLE THE CAKE: Once the cake is cooled to room temperature, carefully unroll it. Some small cracks are expected and normal! Drizzle the syrup over the surface of the cake and spread it evenly with the back of a spoon. Dollop the filling all over the cake and use a spatula to spread it evenly all the way to the edges. Carefully roll your cake back up, keeping a fairly tight roll.

11. Cut off the ends of the roll, if desired, for a neater look, then transfer the cake to a serving platter. Cover the cake with plastic wrap and refrigerate for 1 to 2 hours or up to overnight. (Chilling it will help set the filling and make the cake easier to slice.) Just before serving, dust the cake with confectioners' sugar and scatter the remaining raspberries over and around the cake.

Tres Leches Cupcakes

Vadim and I are both obsessed with tres leches cake and have been for years. I mean, what's not to love about a sponge cake that's been saturated until fluffy and moist with three different kinds of milk?! To make it even more exciting and festive, I've taken the traditional pan-baked version and turned it into cupcakes.

MAKES 24 CUPCAKES

FOR THE CUPCAKES

1 cup all-purpose flour (see How to Measure Flour Properly on page 20)

1½ teaspoons aluminum-free baking powder

¼ teaspoon fine sea salt

5 large eggs, whites and yolks separated

1 cup sugar, divided

⅓ cup whole milk

1 teaspoon pure vanilla extract

FOR THE SYRUP

8 ounces evaporated milk

6 ounces sweetened condensed milk

¼ cup heavy cream

FOR THE FROSTING

2 cups heavy cream

2 tablespoons sugar

1 cup fresh berries, for garnish

1. MAKE THE CUPCAKES: Place an oven rack in the center of the oven and preheat the oven to 350°F. Line a 24-count cupcake tin with cupcake liners (preferably aluminum or parchment) and set aside.

2. In a large bowl, whisk together the flour, baking powder, and salt. Set aside.

3. In a medium bowl, combine the egg yolks with ¾ cup of the sugar. Vigorously beat with a whisk for 2 minutes, until the mixture is pale yellow. Whisk in the milk and vanilla to combine. Set aside.

4. In the bowl of a stand mixer fitted with the whisk attachment or in a large bowl with a hand mixer, beat the egg whites on high speed for about 1 minute, until foamy. With the mixer running, pour in the remaining ¼ cup of sugar and continue to beat on high speed for 1 minute, until the egg whites are stiff but not dry. Set aside.

5. Pour the egg-yolk mixture into the flour mixture and use a spatula to blend together until combined. Gently fold in the egg-white mixture, scraping from the bottom of the bowl, until just incorporated—do not overmix!

6. Use an ice cream scoop to divide the batter evenly between the 24 cupcake liners, filling each about three-quarters full. Bake for 15 to 20 minutes, until golden brown on top and a toothpick inserted into the center comes out clean. Let the cupcakes cool in the pan for 10 minutes before transferring them to a cooling rack to cool completely.

7. MEANWHILE, MAKE THE SYRUP: In a medium bowl, stir together the evaporated milk, sweetened condensed milk, and cream.

8. When the cupcakes have cooled, transfer them to a rimmed baking sheet to catch any drips. Use a small paring knife or skewer to poke seven or eight holes into the top of each cupcake, about halfway through. Spoon about 1 tablespoon of the syrup onto each cupcake. It will pool at the top before soaking in. Once it's absorbed, add more syrup, about ½ tablespoon at a time, until all of the syrup has been used. Set aside while you make the frosting.

9. MAKE THE FROSTING: In the bowl of a stand mixer fitted with the whisk attachment or in a large bowl with a hand mixer, beat together the cream and sugar on high speed for 1½ to 2 minutes, until thick, whipped, and spreadable.

10. Transfer the frosting to a piping bag with a large open-star tip or your desired piping tip. You could also use a plastic zip-top bag with the corner snipped. Pipe the frosting around the tops of the cupcakes. Garnish with the berries and serve.

Pro Tips & Tricks

- **Make ahead:** You can store the frosted cupcakes in the refrigerator for up to 24 hours. Garnish with the berries before serving.

Red, White, and Blue Berry Tiramisu

I think that all cooking and baking during the summertime should be easy and breezy—and this dessert is no exception. The melt-in-your-mouth, syrup-soaked ladyfingers with the whipped mascarpone-cream topping and fresh berries is just the thing for warm weather entertaining. Plus, it easily feeds a crowd, which makes it perfect for the ultimate summer celebration: Fourth of July, which also happens to be Vadim's birthday. It's such a showstopper with its patriotic decoration, and the serving dish is always so easy to clean . . . because there's usually none left at the end of the evening!

SERVES 14 TO 16

FOR THE GRAND MARNIER SYRUP

1¼ cups warm water

½ cup sugar

2 teaspoons lemon zest

3 tablespoons Grand Marnier

FOR THE WHIPPED MASCARPONE-CREAM TOPPING

16 ounces mascarpone, chilled

2 tablespoons Grand Marnier

1½ cups heavy cream, chilled

½ cup sugar

1 teaspoon pure vanilla extract

FOR ASSEMBLY

38 to 40 ladyfingers (about 14 ounces)

1½ pounds berries (see Pro Tips & Tricks)

1. MAKE THE SYRUP: In a small shallow bowl, stir together the water, sugar, lemon zest, and Grand Marnier until the sugar has dissolved. Set aside.

2. MAKE THE TOPPING: Add the mascarpone to a medium bowl and fold in the Grand Marnier until well blended. Set aside.

3. In the bowl of a stand mixer fitted with the whisk attachment or in a large bowl with a hand mixer, whip the cream, sugar, and vanilla on medium-high speed for about 3 minutes, until medium-stiff peaks form. Use a spatula to gently fold the whipped cream into the mascarpone in thirds, mixing until just incorporated between each addition.

4. ASSEMBLE: Dip the ladyfingers, one or two at a time, into the syrup. You'll want to dip quickly on both sides without over-soaking them, or they'll get too soft. Arrange the dipped ladyfingers in a single layer in a 9 × 13-inch casserole dish.

5. Spread half of the topping over the first layer of ladyfingers and sprinkle on a third of the berries. If some of your berries are larger, gently push them down into the topping to create an even surface for the next layer of ladyfingers.

6. Dip and arrange the remaining ladyfingers over the fruit and evenly spread the remaining topping on top, making sure to spread it to the edges of the dish. Cover with plastic wrap and refrigerate for 8 hours or overnight.

7. To serve, arrange the remaining berries over the top, either evenly scattering the berries or creating a patriotic star or flag pattern. Serve chilled.

Pro Tips & Tricks

- Grand Marnier is an orange liqueur that tastes very mild, and no one comments that the cake tastes "boozy," but if you prefer to substitute, try orange juice or lemon juice to taste.

- I prefer using whole berries that don't need to be sliced for the center of the cake, such as blueberries and raspberries, because sliced fruit tends to soften and discolor more quickly. Sliced fruit can be used to decorate the top of the cake just before serving.

Blueberry Galette
(aka The Lazy Pie)

This recipe came together when Vadim and I were craving pie but didn't want to put in all the effort that a from-scratch double crust requires. As a solution, I took an incredibly simple flaky pastry dough and heaped it with a fresh blueberry filling. Traditionally it's called a galette, but I like to think of it as my lazy pie because it's so easy and quick to assemble. I love serving it warm and à la mode with a scoop of vanilla ice cream, which melts into the blueberries.

SERVES 4 TO 6

FOR THE CRUST

1⅓ cups all-purpose flour (see How to Measure Flour Properly on page 20), plus more for dusting

1 tablespoon granulated sugar

½ teaspoon fine sea salt

½ cup (1 stick) unsalted butter, cut into ½-inch cubes and chilled

5 to 6 tablespoons ice water, plus more as needed

FOR THE BLUEBERRY FILLING

4 cups fresh blueberries, rinsed and well-drained

⅓ cup granulated sugar (see Pro Tips & Tricks)

2 tablespoons all-purpose flour

1 teaspoon lemon zest (from 1 lemon)

1 tablespoon freshly squeezed lemon juice

1. MAKE THE CRUST: In a food processor fitted with the blade attachment, combine the flour, sugar, and salt. Pulse until well mixed. Add the butter and pulse eight to ten times, until the butter is pea sized. Add the ice water 1 tablespoon at a time, pulsing between each addition. Your dough is ready when it just begins to clump and holds together when pinched with your fingertips. If needed, add more water, 1 tablespoon at a time.

2. Turn out the dough onto a clean work surface and form it into a disk. Don't overwork it; just pat it into a disk shape. Cover with plastic wrap and refrigerate for at least 1 hour or up to 3 days.

3. When ready to assemble, preheat the oven to 425°F. On a floured sheet of parchment paper, use a rolling pin to roll out the dough to a 12-inch circle. Dust with more flour if needed to keep the dough from sticking to your rolling pin. Transfer the dough on the parchment paper to a rimmed baking sheet and refrigerate while you make the filling.

4. MAKE THE FILLING: In a medium bowl, toss the blueberries with the sugar, flour, lemon zest, and lemon juice. Stir until the flour is incorporated and starts to look a little syrupy.

5. Spread the filling over the center of the prepared crust, leaving a 2-inch border. Fold the edges of the galette up and over the filling, pinching together the overlapping edges to form a nice seal. Try to patch up any cracks in the dough.

6. ASSEMBLE: In a small bowl, use a fork to beat together the egg and water. Brush the crust with the egg wash and sprinkle with the turbinado sugar. Dot the top of the blueberries with the butter and bake for 25 to 28 minutes, until the crust is golden brown and the berry juices are bubbling. It's OK if some of the blueberry juices leak from the crust; that's what the parchment paper is for!

7. Let the galette cool for 10 to 15 minutes before serving. Serve with the vanilla ice cream (if using).

FOR ASSEMBLY

1 large egg

1 tablespoon water

1 tablespoon coarse turbinado sugar

1 teaspoon unsalted butter, diced

Vanilla ice cream, to serve (optional)

Pro Tips & Tricks

- If your blueberries are very sweet, you may want to use a bit less sugar, closer to ¼ cup.

- If you don't have a food processor, you can use a pastry blender and a wooden spoon to form the dough.

- Do not skip refrigerating the dough. Chilling hardens the butter inside the dough so that it maintains its structure as it bakes. This way, the butter won't ooze out, turning it into a sad, flat crust.

All of these recipes can easily be scaled up or down, and I've included guidelines for estimating about how much food to have per person in each recipe, though I always count on having a little extra. And while I've suggested a whole bunch of different toppings, sauces, and garnishes for each spread, don't feel as though you need to include every single one. Go with as many as you feel fits the occasion, size of the group, and guests' preferences.

10

EASY ENTERTAINING

When you live within ten minutes of your parents, four sisters, their spouses, and ten nieces and nephews—and you all love to eat!—you learn a thing or two about how to feed a crowd. After I got married and first started cooking, I'd get in way over my head with wanting to make everything feel fancy. I made every rookie mistake in the book: choosing a brand-new recipe to try out on my guests, attempting to prepare dishes that needed to be served right out of the oven, and thinking my menu needed to rival a restaurant's with multiple courses. If anyone innocently wandered into the kitchen while I was trying to get everything ready—*watch out*. Hosting used to stress me out.

Over the years, though, I've learned how to work smarter, not harder. Now I reach for simple, tried-and-true recipes that I know work every time, can be prepped ahead, and can be customized to each of my guests (also known as putting my guests to work making their own plate—pretty genius!). And yet, with some thought given to the presentation (pretty bowls and cutting boards go a long way!) and strategic homemade touches, people are always impressed. But the best part is that I'm way more relaxed, which means that my guests feel more at home, and we all have a better time.

The recipes in this section are dedicated to you being able to embrace what entertaining should be all about—making sure everyone has what they need to feel comfortable and satisfied while also being able to kick back and enjoy yourself, too. This chapter is packed with easy, adaptable meals that you can make your own, with all of my best tips, so that you can do what parties are meant for: have fun!

Crepe Board

Whenever I want to serve a breakfast or brunch that feels polished but still needs to feed a lot of people, I always go for this spread. I use the crepe recipe from my no-fail Sweet Cheese Crepes with Raspberry Sauce (page 31) as a base (without the cheese filling), then offer a variety of topping options so guests can have fun creating their own. The overall effect is nothing short of sophisticated. I love this for baby showers, bridal showers, birthdays, or Mother's Day—or even for dessert.

WHAT YOU'LL NEED

Crepes (page 31; made without the cheese filling or sauce), estimate 3 per guest

Raspberry sauce (page 31; optional)

OTHER SAUCE SUGGESTIONS

Jam or fruit preserves

Sour cream or Greek yogurt

Lemon curd

Nutella

Honey

Mascarpone

Whipped cream

FRUIT SUGGESTIONS

Berries, such as strawberries, blueberries, blackberries, or raspberries

Sliced stone fruit, such as apricots, nectarines, peaches, or plums

Sliced citrus, such as clementines, oranges, or grapefruit

Sliced bananas

Sliced kiwi

Sliced pear

Grapes

Pomegranate seeds

HOW TO SET IT UP

1. Prepare the crepes and allow them to cool to room temperature. Prepare the raspberry sauce (if using). Meanwhile, slice any fruit you plan to use.

2. Fold the crepes into triangles by first folding them in half, then in half once again. (They're easier to grab off a tray this way and look prettier, too.) At this point, you could put the folded crepes on a plate, cover with plastic wrap, and refrigerate overnight. The same goes for prepped raspberry sauce.

3. To build the crepe board, arrange the folded crepes in a big zigzag pattern down the center of a large cutting board or serving tray. Spoon your desired sauces into small bowls or ramekins and situate them on the board. Next, fill any spaces with the fruit. Add tongs or other serving utensils and serve.

Pro Tips & Tricks

- You can make both the crepes and raspberry sauce ahead, as well as slice your fruit, and store it all in the fridge (except for banana).

- When choosing fruit to serve, the most flavorful and cost-effective option will always be what is in season. A great out-of-season option for berries is using thawed frozen sliced strawberries in sugar (a product that you can find in most grocery stores in the frozen section that's nice and saucy), or sprinkle thawed frozen berries with a little sugar.

Fully Loaded Bagel Bar

It doesn't get more classic for brunch or lunch than a bagel spread with all the fixings. Luckily, it's also one of the easiest ways to put out an impressive-looking meal. I love including all the traditional toppings—sliced veggies, capers, dill—plus a homemade Smoked Salmon Spread (page 262) or Herb Cream Cheese Spread (page 262). But if you'd rather keep things simple and go with plain or store-bought flavored cream cheese, just put it in a pretty dish and no one will think twice about it!

WHAT YOU'LL NEED

A variety of bagels, preferably pre-sliced at the bagel shop. If the bagel bar is the entire meal, count on 1 whole bagel per person. If it's part of a larger spread, plan on half. Throw in a couple extra, just in case! If serving fresh bagels, have a toaster available for anyone who prefers theirs toasted.

TOPPING SUGGESTIONS

Smoked Salmon Spread (ingredients on page 262)

Herb Cream Cheese Spread (ingredients on page 262)

Thinly sliced smoked salmon (I like cold-smoked salmon, which is moist, tender, and sold in thin slices; estimate 2 ounces per person)

Plain cream cheese

Capers (drained if packed in brine)

Thinly sliced red onion

Sliced tomatoes or whole cherry tomatoes (they're pretty when left on the vine)

Sliced cucumbers

Sliced avocado (I like to sprinkle mine with everything-but-the-bagel seasoning)

Fresh dill sprigs

INGREDIENTS CONTINUE

1. MAKE THE SMOKED SALMON SPREAD: In a food processor, combine the cream cheese, sour cream, lemon juice, Tabasco (if using), and salt. Blend until smooth. Add the salmon and chives and pulse until just combined. Season with more salt and pepper, if needed. Refrigerate in an airtight container until ready to serve, up to 3 days.

2. MAKE THE HERB CREAM CHEESE SPREAD: In a small bowl, combine the cream cheese, chives, dill, and garlic. Use a fork to mash the herbs into the cream cheese until well incorporated. Refrigerate in an airtight container until ready to serve, up to 3 days.

HOW TO SET IT UP

3. Separate the slices of salmon and lay them in ribbons in one section of the board.

4. Add your cream cheese, capers, and onions to small bowls or ramekins and arrange them around the board. Fill in the spaces with the tomatoes and cucumbers. At this point, you could cover the board with plastic wrap and refrigerate for 1 to 2 hours until serving. Otherwise, continue by creating a fan with the avocado slices and sprinkling them with the everything-but-the-bagel seasoning, if desired. (It looks so fancy with barely any effort!) Scatter sprigs of fresh dill to fill any spaces. Add serving utensils to the spreads and small serving tongs or forks for lifting items from the board.

5. If your board is large enough, add the sliced bagels, or arrange them separately in a basket or on a platter.

RECIPE CONTINUES

FOR THE SMOKED SALMON SPREAD

8 ounces plain cream cheese, room temperature

½ cup sour cream

1½ teaspoons freshly squeezed lemon juice

½ teaspoon Tabasco hot sauce, plus more to taste (optional)

¼ teaspoon fine sea salt, plus more to taste

4 ounces smoked salmon, chopped (about 1 cup; lox or hot-smoked salmon flakes will work here)

1 tablespoon chopped fresh chives, plus more for garnish

Freshly ground black pepper to taste

FOR THE HERB CREAM CHEESE SPREAD

8 ounces plain cream cheese, room temperature

¼ cup finely chopped chives or green onions (green parts only)

2 tablespoons finely chopped fresh dill

1 garlic clove, pressed or grated

Pro Tips & Tricks

- Fresh bagels will make all the difference in the quality of your bagel bar. If you can't get bagels the day you're serving them, you can buy the bagels whenever it is convenient and freeze them while still fresh. Slice your bagels, place the two halves back together, wrap each individual bagel in plastic wrap, and store them in a freezer-safe bag. Once they are thawed or toasted, they taste just like fresh bagels.

- Store the bagels in a plastic bag at room temperature (not in the fridge, or they'll dry out!), and add them to the board last to keep them from drying out.

- To make this spread in advance, store your spreads and capers in individual dishes that can be covered with plastic wrap, and refrigerate until serving (2 to 3 days in advance). You could also assemble the entire board with your salmon, spreads, and sliced veggie toppings (excluding avocado, which will turn brown), cover with plastic wrap, and store in the refrigerator for 2 to 3 hours before serving.

Famous Fish Tacos

My brother-in-law Slavik taught me how to make these tacos, and it has been an entertaining menu staple for my sisters and me for years. It came as no surprise, then, that when I shared this recipe with the internet, people couldn't get enough of it. Maybe it's the boldly flavored yet supersimple fish preparation or maybe it's the sriracha-lime crema, but no matter what, it's such a fun and easy way to feed a lot of people. I don't think I'll ever stop loving these tacos.

WHAT YOU'LL NEED

Fish Tacos (ingredients below)

Sriracha-Lime Crema
  (ingredients on page 265)

TOPPING SUGGESTIONS

Shredded purple cabbage

Sliced avocado

Diced tomatoes

Diced red onion

Chopped fresh cilantro

Grated cotija cheese

Lime wedges

FOR THE FISH TACOS

1 teaspoon fine sea salt

½ teaspoon ground cumin

½ teaspoon ground cayenne
  pepper

¼ teaspoon freshly ground
  black pepper

1½ pounds tilapia fillets

1 tablespoon extra-light
  olive oil

1 tablespoon unsalted butter

24 small white corn tortillas

1. MAKE THE FISH: Preheat the oven to 375°F. Line a rimmed baking sheet with parchment paper or a silicone baking mat and set aside.

2. In a small bowl, combine the salt, cumin, cayenne, and black pepper and mix well. Evenly sprinkle the seasonings over both sides of each piece of tilapia and then place the fillets on the prepared baking sheet. Lightly drizzle them with the oil and dot each piece with the butter. Bake for 20 to 25 minutes, until cooked through and golden. To brown the edges of the fish, turn the oven to broil and cook for 3 to 5 minutes.

3. WHILE THE FISH BAKES, MAKE THE CREMA: In a medium bowl, whisk together the sour cream, mayo, lime juice, garlic powder, and sriracha (if using). Refrigerate until ready to serve, up to 3 days.

4. Next, toast the tortillas. You can do this a couple of ways:

On a griddle: This is our favorite way to make a bunch of tortillas at once. Preheat a griddle to medium-high heat. Add the tortillas in a single layer and toast for 15 to 30 seconds, until golden brown in some spots, on each side.

On a skillet (preferably cast iron): Heat a large skillet over medium-high heat. Add the tortillas in a single layer (a very large pan can accommodate up to 3 at a time) and toast for 15 to 30 seconds, until golden and hot, on each side.

5. Transfer the toasted tortillas to a large plate and keep them covered with a clean kitchen towel as you finish toasting the remaining tortillas.

INGREDIENTS CONTINUE

RECIPE CONTINUES

Famous Fish Tacos *continued*

½ cup sour cream

⅓ cup mayonnaise

2 tablespoons freshly squeezed lime juice

1 teaspoon garlic powder

1 teaspoon sriracha sauce (optional; see Pro Tips & Tricks)

HOW TO SET IT UP

6. Transfer the fish to a serving platter and use forks to gently break it up into large flakes. Add your toppings to serving bowls and plates, along with serving utensils. Leave the tortillas under the towel to keep them warm as people serve themselves. Put out the crema with a spoon, or for a nice touch, transfer it to a squeeze bottle. It makes it feel like you're dining out, and it's less messy for a crowd.

Pro Tips & Tricks

- This recipe is already party size (it makes 24 tacos), but it can easily be scaled up or down.

- Don't feel like you need the fish to be piping hot out of the oven. It's delicious served at room temperature and can be made up to 2 hours in advance.

- The crema is really what makes the tacos special, so I highly recommend not skipping it. You can omit the sriracha if you want a milder sauce.

- You can use flour tortillas if that's your preference. But I love the flavor and texture of corn tortillas. They're also naturally gluten-free, which is always appreciated by those with food sensitivities.

- This recipe works well with shrimp, too. For every pound of shrimp (thawed, if frozen) use half of the spice measures called for in the original recipe.

Chili Bar

Building a chili bar is one of my favorite ways to entertain because it's so homey and rustic, and yet such a crowd-pleaser—especially for game days or weekend dinners with friends. Don't be intimidated by the ingredient list; it's mostly pantry staples, and the recipe comes together quickly with minimal effort. You can even make the chili an entire day ahead, and warm it up before serving, which, if I'm being honest, is the best way to serve chili anyway because the flavors have had time to meld.

WHAT YOU'LL NEED

Chili (ingredients below)

TOPPINGS AND SIDES SUGGESTIONS

Shredded Mexican cheese or your favorite shredded cheese

Sliced fresh or jarred jalapeños

Sour cream

Chopped fresh cilantro

Thinly sliced green onion (white and green parts)

Lime wedges

Diced avocado

Tortilla chips

FOR THE CHILI

1 tablespoon extra-light olive oil

1⅓ to 1½ pounds lean (85/15) ground beef

1 large yellow onion, diced

1½ teaspoons fine sea salt, plus more to taste

1 teaspoon ground cumin

1 teaspoon chili powder (see Pro Tips & Tricks)

1 teaspoon garlic powder

½ teaspoon dried oregano leaves

½ teaspoon sugar

1. MAKE THE CHILI: In a 5½-quart Dutch oven or large pot over medium-high heat, heat the oil. Add the beef and sauté, breaking it up with a spatula as it cooks, for about 5 minutes, until cooked through. Reserve at least 2 tablespoons of oil in the pot and discard any excess. (You could also leave it all in; I think it makes a better chili!)

2. Return the pot to medium-high heat and add the onion, salt, cumin, chili powder, garlic powder, oregano, sugar, and pepper. Cook, stirring frequently, for 5 minutes, until the onions are softened. Stir in the tomatoes, tomato sauce, black beans, kidney beans, and broth. Bring the mixture to a boil, then reduce to a simmer. Partially cover the pot and cook for 30 minutes, stirring occasionally. Just before the 30-minute mark, season with more salt and pepper, if needed, and thin the consistency with more broth, if desired.

HOW TO SET IT UP

3. Transfer the chili to a slow cooker and set to the Keep Warm setting, or place the pot of chili on the table on a trivet. Be sure to include a ladle or large spoon. Arrange the toppings and any accompaniments in serving bowls and on plates and add serving utensils.

Pro Tips & Tricks

- This recipe serves 5, but you can easily scale it up to serve an even bigger crowd. Just be mindful that you'll most likely need a larger pot and slightly longer cook times for each step.

- To rinse the beans, it's most efficient to empty both cans of beans into a colander, then rinse under cold water until it runs clear.

- This chili is fairly mild, but if you prefer even less spice, use ½ teaspoon or less of the chili powder. Or if you prefer more spice, use more to taste!

- This recipe makes a thick and hearty chili. If you like a thinner consistency, you can add more broth to thin it out.

¼ teaspoon freshly ground black pepper, plus more to taste

1 (28-ounce) can diced tomatoes, with their juice

1 (15-ounce) can plain tomato sauce

1 (15-ounce) can black beans, rinsed and drained (see Pro Tips & Tricks)

1 (15-ounce) can kidney or pinto beans, rinsed and drained (see Pro Tips & Tricks)

½ cup Homemade Chicken Bone Broth (page 126) or store-bought low-sodium chicken or beef broth or stock, plus more for thinning

Supreme Baked-Potato Bar

If you thought baked potatoes were the world's best and easiest weeknight meal, then wait until you've tried an entire baked-potato bar for a casual party. The only prep required is popping the potatoes into the oven. (My method yields an irresistibly good baked potato with crisp, salty skin and a fluffy, light center.) Then the trick is all in how you customize this spread to work for you—go with no-cook garnishes for superquick and easy, or add a homemade touch with a batch of my chili (page 266), Alfredo sauce (page 152), or beef taco filling (page 270). Baked potatoes are best served right out of the oven with a crispy skin, but they can also be made ahead (see Note).

WHAT YOU'LL NEED

Medium russet potatoes
   (1 per person)

Extra-virgin olive oil

Kosher salt

Unsalted butter (1 tablespoon
   per potato)

TOPPING SUGGESTIONS

Cheese (we love shredded
   Mexican cheese or cheddar
   cheese)

Sour cream

Chili (page 266)

Alfredo sauce (page 152)

Beef taco filling (page 270)

Steamed broccoli bits

Bacon bits or cooked and
   chopped bacon

Sliced or diced jalapeño

Sliced chives or green onion

Note: If not serving the baked potatoes right away, carefully wrap them in foil and keep them in the oven or an instant pot or slow cooker on the lowest heat or Keep Warm setting.

1. Preheat the oven to 450°F. Line a rimmed baking sheet with parchment paper. If you have a wire cooling rack, set it over the baking sheet for even cooking around the potatoes.

2. Scrub the potatoes clean under running water and dry with a towel. Use a fork to poke holes all over the potatoes to prevent them from exploding, about five to six pokes per potato.

3. Rub the potato skins with the oil, about ¼ teaspoon per potato. Sprinkle each potato with a generous pinch of the salt, then flip the potatoes over and generously season the other side as well.

4. Set the potatoes on the prepared baking sheet, keeping the potatoes at least 1 inch apart so heat can circulate. Bake for 45 to 60 minutes, depending on the size of your potatoes, until they are fork-tender and an in-oven or instant-read thermometer inserted in the center registers 210°F.

5. If not serving the potatoes right away, wrap them with foil and hold them in the oven at 200°F, or the residual heat from having baked the potatoes, until ready to serve. When ready to serve, slice the potatoes longways through the center until they fold open like a book. (Try to avoid cutting them all the way through.) Add 1 tablespoon of the butter to each potato and serve.

HOW TO SET IT UP

6. Arrange the potatoes on a platter or tray. Add the desired toppings to small bowls, plates, or ramekins. If serving chili or taco filling, I like transferring these to my slow cooker, which I can put right on the table and use to keep them warm. Otherwise, you can transfer them to a serving bowl. Be sure to include serving utensils for all the toppings.

Ultimate Beef Taco Bar
with Homemade Crispy Taco Shells

If you're looking for a meal that will not only feed a larger group but also satisfy *everyone* in attendance (the kids will eat it, too!), this is it. It's no exaggeration to say that these are the best beef tacos I've ever had, in restaurants or otherwise. I think the secret is twofold: the meat is saucy and rich thanks to the RO*TEL, while the homemade taco shells are so much more flavorful than anything that comes out of a box. Plus, who doesn't love loading up their own tacos with all the toppings?

WHAT YOU'LL NEED

Beef Taco Filling (ingredients below)

Crispy Taco Shells (ingredients on the opposite page) or store-bought

TOPPING SUGGESTIONS

Shredded cheddar cheese

Shredded iceberg lettuce

Diced tomatoes

Chunky Guacamole (page 61) or store-bought

Sour cream

Assorted salsas

Assorted hot sauces

Lime wedges

Chopped fresh cilantro

FOR THE BEEF TACO FILLING

2 pounds (80/20 or 85/15) ground beef chuck

2 (10-ounce) cans RO*TEL Diced Tomatoes & Green Chilies, with their juice

2 teaspoons chili powder

1 teaspoon ground cumin

1 teaspoon fine sea salt, plus more to taste

½ teaspoon garlic powder

½ teaspoon onion powder

1. MAKE THE FILLING: Heat a large skillet over medium-high heat. Add the beef and cook, stirring occasionally and breaking up the beef with your spoon or spatula, for about 5 minutes, until cooked through. Carefully tilt the pan and use a spoon to skim off and discard all but 2 tablespoons of excess fat.

2. Add the RO*TEL, chili powder, cumin, salt, garlic powder, and onion powder. Reduce the heat to medium and cook, continuing to break up the meat and tomatoes, for 8 to 10 minutes, until most of the tomato liquid has evaporated. Season with more salt, if needed, and remove the pan from the heat. Cover to keep warm while you make the shells.

3. MAKE THE TACO SHELLS: Line a rimmed baking sheet with paper towels and have your salt nearby.

4. In a medium or large skillet over medium heat, add ¼ inch of the oil. When the oil shimmers or registers 350°F on an instant-read thermometer, carefully slide the first tortilla into the pan and fry for 12 to 15 seconds, until golden and bubbly on the first side. Use tongs to flip the tortilla and immediately fold it in half. Fry for another 10 to 12 seconds per side, until golden brown. Transfer the shell to the prepared baking sheet and immediately lightly sprinkle with the salt.

5. If you don't have a taco shell mold, use your fingers to gently open the taco shell by 1 to 2 inches, then set it upside down to cool and drain. This will make them easier to fill. Repeat with the remaining tortillas.

Next-Level Cheese Board

We can't talk about parties without talking about cheese boards. Specifically, the best and only cheese board recipe that you'll ever need. Sometimes referred to as a charcuterie board—which is just a fancy way of saying, "a mix of meats and cheeses arranged on a tray"—think of this as the first and last word on grazing. It feels abundant and inviting, you can completely customize it to your personal preferences or those of your guests, and it's easily dressed up or down, which makes it perfect for any occasion (and budget). When you have a few simple tricks up your sleeve (which I'll give you, of course), you'll be able to create an endless variety of expertly beautiful boards.

WHAT YOU'LL NEED

Cheeses: Select a variety of cheeses—ideally one from each category for a good range of flavors and textures—and add them to your board.

Spreadable creamy cheeses, such as a triple cream cheese like Saint-André or Délice de Bourgogne or Herb Cream Cheese Spread (page 262)

Soft cheeses, such as goat cheese, brie, or marinated mozzarella balls

Hard cheeses, such as cheddar or Manchego

Meats: Go for a selection of different flavors and textures.

Salamis

Prosciutto

Dry coppa

Summer sausages

Pickled items: Salty, briny items balance the rich meats and cheeses. Try:

Olives, such as pitted Castelvetranos or Kalamatas

Gherkins or baby dill pickles, for a less expensive option

HOW TO SET IT UP

1. Start by pre-slicing some of your cheeses, which encourages your guests to dig in and help themselves. I like cutting harder cheeses into thin slices or cubes and slicing a "starter wedge" out of a wheel of brie. If you're serving a cheese in a marinade or oil, place it in a ramekin to keep things neater. Roughly arrange your cheeses evenly around your board. Don't worry, you'll be filling in all that empty space!

2. Next, fold round slices of meats into halves or triangles (halve them, then fold in half again) and separate thinly sliced meats into ribbons. Arrange the meats around the cheeses.

3. Add any condiments, spreads, drizzles, pickles, and olives to small bowls or ramekins and nestle them in the remaining empty spaces. For the sweeter condiments, try to pair those with the cheeses they work well with, such as brie and goat cheese.

4. Layer the fruit and nuts between the other items—this is when working on a rimmed tray or platter comes in handy, since you can really load it up!

5. If you still have room, add the crackers. Otherwise, put out a platter for just those items.

6. Make sure to include serving utensils for each of the individual items.

Condiments and Spreads:
People are always surprised by how much they love a drizzle or dollop of something sweet with cheeses, but they can be served with sweet, savory, or a mix of both! Try:

Honey

Jam or fruit preserves

Hummus

Fresh fruits and nuts: These pair well with cheese and also offer a fresh counterbalance for munching. Try:

Grapes (precut the vines into smaller portions)

Apples (to make a pretty heart shape, cut the apple in half and scoop out the seeds; place each half cut side down on a cutting board and thinly slice; then gently push the middle slices down)

Berries (rinse but thoroughly pat dry so they don't get mushy; leave them whole)

Rich-tasting nuts, such as roasted walnuts, pecans, or cashews

Carby things: What everything gets piled onto! Offer a selection of:

Crackers: I like including a couple different types, like water crackers or artisan crackers, plus a gluten-free option for any guests with sensitivities

Pita chips: These have great crunch and flavor and are sturdy enough for dipping

Crostini: Slice a baguette into rounds, brush both sides of each round with olive oil, and toast in a 400°F oven for 6 minutes, or until lightly golden.

Pro Tips & Tricks

- A great cheese board is built on three pillars: taste, texture, and variety—meaning you include items that are sweet, savory, salty, crunchy, pickled, and carby. I've used these categories when making suggestions for what to include.

- You do not need to break the bank for your board. Less expensive cheeses, such as cheddar, goat cheese, or an herb cream cheese (like the one on page 262), are just as tasty as pricier Saint-André or Manchego. I love buying a mixed pack of cured meats at Costco, which saves more money and time than buying them all separately. Or you could swap out more expensive cured meats for sliced summer sausages.

- Your serving board can be anything from a specialty rimmed cutting board to a round or rectangular cutting board to a platter or a rimmed baking sheet (it totally works—by the time you load it up with your offerings, you can barely tell that it's just a baking sheet!). You can also put multiple boards together, if making a larger spread. Some people do this directly on their counter if they're going supersize and don't need to refrigerate anything in advance.

- You'll want a collection of ramekins and small bowls for holding sauces, dips, jams, spreads, honey, and any wet ingredients, like pickles or olives. They do not need to match! I like using a variety of them that I've collected over the years.

- You don't need to invest in fancy cheese knives unless you really want to. Small forks, spoons, butter knives, and tongs will work just fine.

Entertaining Menus

Part of the stress of inviting people over is trying to figure out what to cook and which dishes go well together. In addition to the delicious, works-every-time party platters and boards in this section, I also wanted to include some of my favorite menus using dishes in this book. They are all perfect for impressing whoever is coming over for dinner and for celebrating all of life's milestones, big and small.

Birthday Party Menu

Baked Mac and Cheese (page 154)

Cheeseburger Sliders (page 178)

California BLT Chopped Salad with Creamy Ranch Dressing (page 98)

Diana's Chocolate Birthday Cake with 6-Minute Chocolate Buttercream (page 229)

Fourth of July

Cowboy Caviar Salsa (page 66)

Cowboy Burgers (page 192)

Cucumber, Tomato, and Avocado Salad (page 80)

Red, White, and Blue Berry Tiramisu (page 252)

Pool Party

Grilled Salmon Sandwiches with Lemon Aioli (page 190)

Cabbage Avocado Salad (page 96)

That Yummy Fruit Salad (page 231)

For the kids (and kids at heart): Strawberry-Coconut Ice Pops (page 233)

Pizza Night

Tuscan Pizza with White Sauce (page 139); toppings in individual bowls for people to dress their own pizzas

Salade Maison (Our House Salad) (page 86)

Best-Ever Brownies (page 223)

Pasta Night

David's Fettuccine Alfredo (page 152)

Thank-You-Mom Chicken Schnitzel (page 164)

Green Beans Almondine (page 206)

Strawberry Panna Cotta (page 218)

Holiday Brunch

Sweet Potato and Bacon Hash (page 27)

Maple-Bacon Oatmeal (page 28)

Sweet Cheese Crepes with Raspberry Sauce (page 31)

Cinnamon Rolls with Cream Cheese Frosting (page 33)

Ukrainian Night

Classic Ukrainian Borscht (page 122)

Smoked Salmon Crostini (page 58)

Potato Pierogi (Vareniki) (page 145)

Baba's Cucumber Spears (page 213)

Cinnamon Apple Cake (page 224)

Mexican-Inspired Night

Chicken Tortilla Soup (page 124)

Shrimp Avocado Tostadas (page 180)

Mexican Street Corn Salad (page 102)

Tres Leches Cupcakes (page 250)

Weekend Dinner or Dinner for Company

Perfect Grilled Steak with Mustard-Pepper Sauce (page 189)

Crispy Roasted Potatoes with Garlic and Rosemary (page 205)

Spring Greens Salad with Goat Cheese, Cranberries, and Balsamic Vinaigrette (page 101)

Blueberry Galette (aka The Lazy Pie) (page 254)

Weekend Dinner or Dinner for Company

The Most Amazing Lasagna (page 136)

Heirloom Tomato and Burrata Salad (page 92)

Baba's Cucumber Spears (page 213)

Mom's Famous Rogaliki (Rugelach) (page 245)

Weekend Dinner or Dinner for Company

Baked Salmon with Garlic and Dijon (page 171)

Perfect Parmesan Asparagus (page 202)

Whipped Mashed Potatoes (page 201)

Fresh Peach Pie (page 239)

Weekend Dinner or Dinner for Company

Roasted Chicken and Gravy (page 168)

Whipped Mashed Potatoes (page 201)

Milk Bread Rolls (page 198)

Cabbage Avocado Salad (page 96)

Cranberry-Apple-Almond Crisp (page 243)

Weekend Dinner or Dinner for Company

Spice-Rubbed Pork Tenderloin (page 167)

Creamy Pesto Pasta (page 132)

Classic Greek Salad (page 89)

Best-Ever Brownies (page 223)

Movie Night or Game Day

Chunky Guacamole (page 61)

Crispy Bacon Jalapeño Poppers (page 73)

Baked Spinach-Artichoke Dip (page 62)

Cinnamon-Sugar Donuts (page 234)

Soup and Salad Night

Caprese Bruschetta (page 74)

Zuppa Toscana (page 110)

Mediterranean Grilled Chicken Salad (page 82)

Berry Cheesecake Bars (page 226)

Valentine's Day

Country Club French Onion Soup (page 120)

Chicken in Mushroom Wine Sauce (page 194)

Whipped Mashed Potatoes (page 201)

Apple-Pomegranate Kale Salad (page 95)

Raspberry Cake Roll (page 247)

Acknowledgments

It takes a village to write a great cookbook, and I am truly blessed and grateful for everyone who came alongside me to turn my dream into a reality—and make it better than I could have asked or imagined.

Thank you to my agent and biggest advocate, Janis Donnaud. I'm so glad I have you in my corner. You may not remember this, but many years ago when my blog was tiny, you gave me the time of day to listen to my pitch for a cookbook. I will always remember that; thank you for believing in me even then!

Thank you, Rachel Holtzman, for capturing my voice and my stories, and for making sure my recipes are as clear as possible. You've made this process a joy and freed me up to focus on the fun stuff—cooking! Thanks for keeping me on track and organized.

Thank you to the wonderful team at Clarkson Potter: Susan Roxborough, my editor, for your meticulous attention to detail and your expertise and advice for making this the best book that it can be. Marysarah Quinn, my book designer—I was thrilled to bits to find out you were working on my book, knowing all the famous cookbooks you've made so special. You have a keen eye for style and design, and this beautiful book is proof. To everyone who helped bring my book into existence and share it with the world, especially production editor Bridget Sweet, production manager Heather Williamson, copyeditor Michelle Gale, proofreader Karen Ninnis, publicist Kristin Casemore, and marketer Stephanie Davis, thank you!

Thank you to our photography team: Charity Burggraaf, you were such a joy to work with. Thanks for traveling to Idaho and capturing the sweetest moments with my family. You are so kind, generous, and hardworking; you are a gem! Thank you, Nathan Carrabba, for your expertise in food styling. You are an artist and made every dish look inviting and picture-perfect. To all of the styling assistants—Tyler Hill, Julie Bishop, Michelle Weller, and Devan Dror—I appreciate your dedication and hard work. Watching a team of skilled cooks make all of my recipes was such a treat for me!

To my own team at Natasha's Kitchen—Vadim Kravchuk, Svetlana Khochay, Kathleen Joyce, Alla Kachur, Fran Conder, and David Kravchuk—thank you for keeping the blog running smoothly, and for making this cookbook possible without me losing my marbles, because I was determined to dribble both balls (the blog and the cookbook) at the same time. Thank you for your hard work and dedication over the years and for being part of the Natasha's Kitchen family. I know it sounds funny, but when I think about you, I think of you as like Aaron and Hur, who helped Moses when his arms got tired and the battle was won. Having you as a part of my cookbook creation village not only meant the world to me, but it will also help our audience feel even more loved, heard, and connected.

Thank you to my sisters, who have always been my most faithful friends. I know that no matter what, I can trust that you won't tell anyone about my embarrassing old sock habits . . . I love that you and your kids will be in the book—and that you were all such honest taste testers. You keep my bar for quality very high!

Thank you to my mom and mother-in-law, who were always so generous in sharing recipes and cooking knowledge, and who answered my questions without hesitation. Your generosity inspires me to pay it forward and teach others to cook as well.

Thank you to my husband and business partner, Vadim, for all the extra things. You never hesitated to support me during this process, whether it was stepping in to make breakfast, spending meaningful time with the kids, or washing the mountain of dishes when I felt overwhelmed. And while people think I'm being nice or modest when I tell them that you're the better cook, I really do think so! Thank you for believing in me from the start. You have made me a better human, and I love you.

Thank you to my kids, David and Diana, who taste tested all of my recipes, even when there was an ingredient you didn't love. (We discovered some new favorite foods along the way, didn't we?!) I appreciate your adventurous spirit, but most of all, I appreciate your enthusiasm and you reminding me why I do what I do. Thanks to your support, many other families will have new, delicious meals to try!

A very heartfelt thank-you to all my followers, fans, subscribers, and home cooks who make and share our recipes and cheer us on. I think of you when I develop my recipes, and it is always with the hope that they will inspire you to cook and make your lives better, easier, healthier, and filled with lifelong moments of togetherness and love. This cookbook is for you!

Last, but certainly not least, a big thank-you to my community of recipe testers. Thanks to your feedback, I can rest assured that the recipes in this book are as easy to follow and as delicious as they can possibly be.

Cyndi Van Aalst
Ellada Abramov
Bonnie Adachi
Damilola Afolabi
Lauren Alexander
Sara Al-Farhan
Janet Altman
Gloria Alvarez
Jamie Anderson
Janet Anderson
Julie Anderson
Abigail Applegate
Shawn Avard
Amber Bailey
Elizabeth Baker
Joy Baker
Teresa Banda
Lynne Barbosa
Bette Barkley
Janice Barnes
Dave Barnett
Inés de la Barrera
Danielle Beard
Kimberly Becerra
Terry Becker
Gary Beckner
Lisa Bedson
Sarah Bender
Liz Berry
Angela Bettencourt-
    Hernandez
Lisa Billing
Amber Bingham
Connie Bishop
Donna Blake
Sierra Blue
Emily Boesmiller-Hoch
Lynne Bohman

Nancy Borne
Louise Boudreau
Rena Boutin
Donna Bowers
Erin Bridges
Henrietta Buckley
Margie Buckley
Alina Burich
Bonnie Campos
Deborah Case
Jody Catencamp
Krystal Chamaillard
Natasha Chevalier
Brenda Chobanik
Alecia Christensen
Sophia Chumak
Laurie Ciolkosz
Rebecca Clark
Kim Coburn
Tracey Cogar
Olena Commons
Wendy Concha
Judy Coomer
Connie Corbett
Renee Coughlin
Jessica Crites
Neha D'Souza
Lynnea Dahlgren
Michelle Dame
Georgia Damoulakis
Ani Danielyan
Laci DaSilva
Olga Datskiy
Joanna Davidson
Kathy DeCock
Julia Derksen
Jack Dexter
Luzmaria Diaz

Sarineh Didarloo
Cheri Di Dio
Tammy Domingo
Julie Dominguez
Joanne Dove
Lindsay Downs
Beth Doyle
Danielle Drake
Kathy Duden
Laura Edwards
Debra Eilers
Ana Elcik
Janeen Eldredge
Maya Saliba Elkhoury
Wendy Engelmann
Marietta Evans
Traci Evans
Michele Eversoll
Susan Fay
Renea Featherstone
Emilie Fedorov
Stephanie Fekete
Nicole Ferraccio
Zhana Filip
Jane Finch
Biana Finkel
Melinda M. Flohr
Erin Fontenot
Kathy Fox
Trish Franzen
Monica Frey
Sally Galanek
Jeanette Van Galder
Sandra Christina Gauder
Andrea Geraghty
Merrill Getto
Nora Glaspy
Sharon Glovick

James Goetz
Elvira Gorash
Barb Gotski
Kellie Gough
Olga Govorushko
Carole Graff
Diane Gray
Amanda Green
Vicki Greenman
Lauren Griffin
Millie Griswold
Katherine Gritton
Dawn Gronner
Margaret Grundeen
Kathy van Grunsven
Hilda Guzman
Barry Hadford
Carol Hajduk
Sylvia Harder
Lisa Harris
Will Harris and Emily
    Harris
Megan Henderson
Gina and Sarah Vanden
    Heuvel
Korin Hinch
Sarah Hinson
Doris Hogan
Danielle Holliday
Dawn Howard
Kelly Humko
Roxy Hunter
Melanie Ikerman
Amanda Jacobs
John Jacobson
Keisha Jakes
Arlene Jennings
Cynthia John

Tiffany Joliat
Anne Kasperek
Angelina Kazmirovskaya
Lara Keever
DeeAnn Kelly
Lisa Kemp
Barbara Kerslake
Jeanette Kislanka
Christina Koch
Daniela Koepke
Michelle Krakora
Jennifer Krause
Maryna Kravchuk
Amy Kretsch-Ward
Jody Kropidlowski
Andrea Langan
Nancie Lannon
Jodi Lebrun
Diana Lee
Imelda Lim
Kim Loner
Anne Lopez
Haley Love
Takisha Lucas
Laurie Luscombe
Cathy Lyons
Lisa MacNeil
Marcia Makarenko
Sarah Marcinko
Riham Marei
Paula Margonie
Laurie Martin
Ria Mathew
Marie Mayer
Christine McCarthy
Debra McCarty
Peggy McDaniel
Meghan McGee
Rene' McGill
Mikelle Medley
Dara Mehta

Eunice Mercado
Diana Mesaros
Elena Mihaila
Lori Miles
Eliana Millan
Joan Monaghan
Melanie Morgan
Lauren Morrell
Amanda Muirhead
Gita Natovich
Laura Nickel
Paula Nigrelli
Marie Normandin
Katie Norton
Becky Nutbrown
Kim Oliver
Jeff Orren
Lisa Pantoja
Dava Parr
Jennie Pattison
Lisa Pennington
Joanne Perella
Jodi Perrigo
Yvonne Phillips
Kelley Pickens
Bridget Piekarczyk
Melissa Pierce
Maria Pogwist
Maggie Prater
Patricia Quintas
Deb Raduns
Dana Rafidi
Rene Ramsay
Shari Redfern
Lorrie Reed
Haroula Reitz
Paula Rice
Jamie Ridley
Jennifer Roberts
Kristen Robinson
Doris Robledo

Holly Roby
Sarah Runion
Nancy Russell
Natasha Ryder
Deb Saia
Kristia Salisbury
Kim Sampson
Kate Sánchez
Deidre Scarzone
Sherry Scates
Cari Schauer
Rebecca Schumann
Patricia Schuppert
Erica Scime
Vedrana Sehovic
Christy Semenoff
Yolanda Sever
Natalie Shakhnovsky
Zhanna Sheykhet
Wendy Shindler
Kathy Singer
Nadia Skudera
Mary Smaw
Nelia Smit
Amanda Smith
Gerda Smith
Irene Smith
Maria Smith
Nataliya Solodkiy
Rebekah Spielman
Tanya Spurlock
Kim Steeber
Elaine Steffani
Liliana Stern
Yvonne Stewart
Leslie Strickland
Anna Sullivan
Megan Swarts
Stephanie Sztanski
Sanaz Talebi
Joanne Tatham

Verna Tessier
Karin Thack
Katie Thomas
Michelle Cragel Thomas
Leah Thompson
Cynthia Timko
Luann Tirelli
Lupe Torres
Stefanie Trenda
Renata Tripp
Teri Trujillo
Angela Turturro
Vicky Ustimenko
Lisa Valentine
Claudine Valot
Myra Vance
Olena Veryha
Debbie Virgin
Scott Ward
Kate Weaver
Andrea Weber
Janet Weber
Paula Weil
Karen Wheelock
Inna White
Cathy Williams
Linda Williams
Ivy Wilson
Jean Wisinski
Eloise Witham
Delia Howling Wolf
Tina Woodburn
Elizabeth Woodfork
Maria Guerriero Worbetz
Paula Worsley
Victoria Yarmushko
Luba Yesipenko
Shawna Zayonc
Yuhuan (Eva) Zeng

Index